The Financial Media's Comments

"Dan Pederson's knowledge of savings bonds is amazing. No matter how picky the questions, he knows the answer and, better yet, can explain them clearly.
—Ronaleen R. Roha, *Kiplinger's Personal Finance Magazine*

"A good guide through the savings bond maze. . . ."
—Janet Bodnar, Author of *Dr. Tightwad's Money Smart Kids*

". . . a valuable tool for savings bond investors, who often find themselves at the mercy of uninformed bank employees. The book could pay for itself in extra interest earnings for investors who use it to determine the best time to redeem their bonds."
—Helen Huntley, *St. Petersburg Times*

". . . [Pederson's book] addresses an investment issue that touches millions of people. . . . I will bet that your shelf of money books has nothing on this subject, even though you and your family own bonds. Buy one for your accountant, lawyer, and know-it-all uncle."
—Patricia J. Wagner, *The Bloomsbury Review*

"As an independent journalist, I have a file drawer of these [savings bond] questions from readers, and the place I've relied on for accurate answers has been Dan Pederson's company, The Savings Bond Informer, Inc."
—Robert K. Heady, founding publisher of *Bank Rate Monitor*
Co-author of *The Complete Idiot's Guide to Managing Your Money*

"If balance sheets and maturity dates give you a headache, Dan Pederson is a numbers cruncher you should get to know. The southwest Detroiter's new consumer handbook . . . tells readers the pratfalls of bond ownership in sometimes blunt but always easy-to-understand language."
—Hawke Fracassa, *The Detroit News*

". . . I recommend Pederson's book, well worth the . . . price. . . . "
—Humberto Cruz, *Chicago Tribune*

"Pederson, who runs a Detroit-based service that provides bond owners with written analyses of their holdings, has explained all in this book."
—Linda Stern, *The Washington Post*

"A plain-language guide . . . it offers tips on the best times to redeem your bonds, details on swapping EE bonds for HH bonds, tax aspects, . . . and other goodies."
—Neil Downing, *The Providence Journal-Bulletin*

D0521680

Bond Owners' Comments

"Started reading and couldn't put the book down! Thought I was fairly knowledgeable of the bond program, but learned something new in each chapter. . . ."
—B.P., Michigan

"Finally a book on something that desperately needed to be clarified. Thanks."
—Mr. & Mrs. R. E., Illinois

"You should get a copy of your book in every library in America. . . ."
—David T., New Jersey

". . . well organized. You should write books for others on complex matters. . . ."
—Demerle A., New York

"What a great book! Easy to read and understand. I found parts humorous and nostalgic. Very educational. . . ."
—Emily, Michigan

"You are the only source of 'real world' information on bonds. Thanks so much."
—Harold M., Minnesota

"Your book has given me a lot to think and plan on."
—Seymour B., California

"I was surprised to find out from you that 7.5% bonds that had matured [reached face value] in 1996 were only to have an interest rate of 4%."
—Margaret C., New York

"One of the guys [at work] had a question about which bonds to cash in for his son's college fund. Well, with the information I got from the book, I was able to save him hundreds of dollars in interest. (He was going to cash at the wrong time.) Rest assured that no one at the bank would have told him that nor would the U.S. government."
—Roland M., New York

"My search for a way to evaluate my . . . savings bonds after my wife passed away in August 1997 ended in futility. . . . I finally found a copy of [your book] in the public library. . . . I called and ordered a copy for myself. . . . My estate planner immediately ordered two copies. . . . My tax/trust attorney ordered two copies. . . . My credit union, which cashed all of my low interest bonds, ordered copies. . . . They even called me to answer questions some of their customers had asked about bonds. I was able to help them."
—William V., Florida

"All banks and libraries should carry your book."
—Jean K., Indiana

SAVINGS BONDS

4th
EDITION
EXPANDED
AND
UPDATED

SAVINGS
BONDS

When to Hold, When to Fold
and Everything In-Between

FOREWORD BY ELLEN STARK, *MONEY* MAGAZINE
DANIEL J. PEDERSON

Sage Creek Press

Traverse City, Michigan

To Mom & Pop Abrams
Your work ethic and love for God have had a great influence on my life.
Thank you for praying for me every day.
I hope to run the race as well as you have.

For where your treasure is, there your heart will be also.
Matthew 6:21

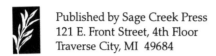
Published by Sage Creek Press
121 E. Front Street, 4th Floor
Traverse City, MI 49684

Publisher's Cataloging-in Publication
(Provided by Quality Books, Inc.)

Pederson, Daniel J.
    Savings bonds : when to hold, when to fold, and everything in-between / Daniel J. Pederson — 4th ed.
    p. cm
    Includes bibliographic references and index.
    Previously published as part of U.S. savings bonds: a comprehensive guide for bond owners and finance professionals.
    ISBN 1-890394-29-7

    1. Savings bonds—United States. 2. Government securities—United States. I. Title

HG4936.P43 1998   332.63'232
                        QB198-1260

Editor: Christina Bych

Printed in the United States of America
10 9 8 7 6 5 4 3

Disclaimer: While the author and publisher have made every effort to provide information which, at the time of publication, is as accurate and complete as possible in regard to the subject matter covered, it is acknowledged that mistakes, both in content and typography could exist. Current investment information should be obtained from the Department of Treasury, Bureau of the Public Debt, before making any decisions to buy, sell, reissue, or exchange any U.S. Savings Bonds. This publication is sold with the understanding that neither the author nor the publisher are engaged in rendering legal, tax, accounting, and like services. If legal advice, tax advice, or other expert assistance is required, the services of a professional in that field should be sought.

For purchasing information, including quantity discounts, contact:
The Savings Bond Informer, Inc. (800) 927-1901.

Contents

List of Tables and Figures

Tables

Figures

Foreword

Two and a half years ago, I faced a dilemma familiar to millions of Americans: What should I do with the savings bond that had been gathering dust in my nightstand drawer? Sixteen years earlier, an aunt and uncle had given me this $50 U.S. Series EE savings bond as a high school graduation gift. What was the bond worth? Had it reached maturity? Was it still earning interest? If so, how much? As the banking writer for a major personal finance publication, *Money* magazine, I felt a bit embarrassed that I was so in the dark. But my experiences over the following weeks—when I set out to answer what I thought were simple questions about a single savings bond—proved to me that my ignorance wasn't all that surprising. For all its popularity, the savings bond can be a baffling investment.

Finding out how much my bond was worth proved relatively easy. A teller at my bank quickly checked Treasury Department tables, similar to the ones I could order in the mail or download from the Internet. The bond my aunt and uncle had bought for $25 in 1980 had reached its $50 face value eleven years later and was now worth $84.66.

Determining what interest rate my bond was paying was far trickier. Bank tellers, the U.S. government's 800 number and glossy pamphlets, and even the Internet were little help. I was more fortunate than most savers trying to answer the same questions would have been. As a journalist, I could pick up the phone and reach officials at the Treasury Department or, better yet, Dan Pederson, the preeminent source on savings bonds. Dan patiently explained, as he does in this book, how the government calculates interest rates on old savings bonds—a Byzantine system if ever there was one, especially because the rules change so often. My bond was earning 6%, and would for another five years, but the real lesson I learned is that while buying and cashing in savings bonds is pretty easy, managing them as investments is tough, especially when you're on your own.

I decided to cash in my savings bond, even though that triggered a minor tax bill. (I had missed my opportunity to use the bond for education and avoid federal taxes all together.) But in the end I still managed to get a pretty good education out of my bond. Good luck learning about yours.

Ellen Stark
Associate Editor
Money Magazine

Preface

Although most of this edition was in written in late summer 1998, the research unknowingly began May 1986. I had been in the position of the Supervisor of the Savings Bond Division of the Federal Reserve Bank of Chicago-Detroit Branch for a grand total of five weeks.

The area that I managed received 200 to 500 calls each day from the general public and financial institutions. The majority of these calls were channeled to the telephone answering unit, the customer service area of the division. At the time, one person handled the calls, with the overflow randomly dispersed throughout the division.

The man responsible for taking these calls left for a one-week vacation and, as the rookie supervisor, I had to determine who would "cover the phones." Since the number of calls that a person handled was not one of the significant activities tracked and measured, respect and enthusiasm for this job was low. Rather than pull someone from one of the "more important" activities of processing volumes of transactions, I, being naive, decided to cover the phones myself. At the designated moment on Monday morning, the weekend recording was turned off and the fun began. That was the longest, most difficult week of my career at the Federal Reserve Bank. Call after call, the questions came: Tell me. Help me. How do I . . . ? When does this happen? How does that work? Does it matter if I . . . ? Which form should I use to . . . ? This new supervisor came away with a profound sense of how much he did not know. But more important, the phone time allowed me to assess the knowledge base of my division, the resources that were available to answer questions, and the demands and expectations of the consumer.

Perceiving a need, in 1990 I left the Federal Reserve Bank to start The Savings Bond Informer, Inc., a company that provides bond statements and analysis on United States Savings Bonds. Having worked closely with thousands of bond owners and financial professionals for twelve years, this work is a result of listening, learning, researching, and helping.

I never thought there would be a need for a fourth edition of this book, but major changes in savings bond rules over the last two years have made the need for clearly defined answers even more critical.

With each new writing, I reflect on the most prominent themes that have emerged from conversations with thousands of bond owners. One of the biggest reasons for this edition is the new I bond—the first new savings bond product in eighteen years. But even more important are the bond owners' repeated questions, "Should I hold or should I fold? How do bonds compare with other investments?" These questions, along with thousands of cases where bond owners have lost money that could have been theirs, convince me of the critical role of a non-government perspective.

In stronger terms than ever before you will see me point at the $5.3 billion in bonds that have stopped earning interest. This is money that belongs to individual Americans. It was not "gifted" to the government. Yet, not only is the bond program inactive in any form of returning the money, they are restricting access to legitimate bond holders through a series of anti-bond holder rules. The government saves over $250 million annually by using this money interest-free—money that could be used to set up a plan to assure that the rightful owners (many older Americans who faithfully supported the government through their purchases) and/or their heirs receive what is due to them.

The following pages will address the major areas of information that bond owners need to know. It is not an attempt to answer the question, "Are U.S. Savings Bonds the right investment for me?" That question can only be answered by assessing all the options available to each individual investor. This book will provide bond owners the tools necessary to maximize their bond holdings, enabling them to begin any comparison process that they desire.

While this book is not a government publication, materials published by the Treasury Department and the Internal Revenue Service have been incorporated. In addition, the tax chapter (Chapter 10) was extensively researched by Brent Dawes, CPA, manager at American Express Tax and Business Services. The perspective of a CPA resulted in numerous "Tax Tips" and "Tax Traps." All documents used or referred to have been listed in the Bibliography. The Glossary explains unfamiliar terms.

If I am not mistaken, this is not the kind of book that you will stay up until 3:00 a.m. reading because the story line is unrelenting. I am confident, though, that it will meet your expectations as the most thorough guide available on the topic of U.S. Savings Bonds.

Acknowledgments

For the development of this book and The Savings Bond Informer, Inc., I am deeply grateful to:

—David Pederson, my brother, who urged me to write this book.

—My associates at the FRB of Chicago-Detroit Branch. Especially my friends Robert Jones, Willie Mae Hall, and Larry Pasden: They provided invaluable counsel during my tenure at the FRB.

—My outstanding associates at The Savings Bond Informer: Lydia, Maria, and Raquel Garcia, Paul and Sara Meriweather, Terreance Coleman, Marlene Rodriguez, and Steve. Thank you for your dedication and commitment. The way you handle our clients with dignity and great service results in the numerous letters of "thanks."

—My Seed Family, for investing, critiquing, and counsel that provided an important role in shaping the direction of our company. (Hill House rules in golf.)

—To many friends for support, ideas, and encouragement. Greg Schupra's challenges have sharpened and pushed me. He, Ray Frederick, and Jack and Theo Robinson have always believed. Dan Johanon provided countless pieces of practical advice in addition to offering his technical skills. Randy Bonser made significant contributions that remain foundational to this edition.

—Brent Dawes. I'll never understand a language that includes "elections" that have nothing to do with voting, "nominees" that are not running for office, and a "cash basis" which is not how much change I have left after springing for pizza. Did a former politician create the tax language? Or did a tax man create the political process? His contributions to this book are tremendous.

—Christina Bych, an exceptional editor and consultant. Thanks again for your tremendous insight and ideas and skill at taking what I thought was a perfect page and graciously showing us how to make it ten times better. Once again, Wow!

—Last and most important, my family, especially Anna Marie, my wife, best friend, business partner, and greatest supporter. I am grateful for her advice, encouragement, and skill. Without her, this book and our business would never have happened. (She also had a hand in the cover.) Ron and Anne Von Gunten for always being willing to help in whatever capacity was needed. Grandma & Grandpa Pederson for encouragement, and for blessing our children by watching them while we worked "overtime." Esther Marlow, for helping lay the foundation of our operation. Dan Marlow, for hours of consulting and marketing ideas. Anna Anderson: Nike must have studied her life before they coined the phrase, "just do it." Whatever it took, she stood ready and "just did it."

Chapter 1

WHY A BOOK ON
U.S. SAVINGS BONDS?

► *The Importance of a Non-Government Perspective*
► *Two Primary Misconceptions about U.S. Savings Bonds*
► *Lack of Information Leads to Costly Mistakes*
► *What You Can Expect from this Book*
► *What You Cannot Expect from this Book*
► *How to Use this Book*

More than 55 million Americans collectively hold approximately $180 billion in U.S. Savings Bonds, making savings bonds one of the world's most widely held securities. Yet, until the publication of this first edition in 1994, bond owners had no consumer-friendly guide to aid in making the crucial decisions that can ultimately result in maximizing their investments.

Since that first edition, the government has enacted three major rule changes that have made savings bonds even more complex—and the information presented in this book even more important. This fourth edition, *Savings Bonds: When to Hold, When to Fold and Everything In-Between* has been thoroughly updated and revised. It is filled with tables, examples, and strategies and has three new chapters, including one which thoroughly analyzes the new I bond.

The information presented is *not* an attempt to convince the reader to buy more bonds or to sell the bonds already owned; rather the focus is on educating

1

bond owners so that they may better handle the investments they already have. And it could mean a difference in the thousands of dollars.

The Importance of a Non-Government Perspective

If you were buying stock, you would not rely entirely upon what a company said about its product. The seller is going to present his product in the most favorable light possible, because jobs, careers, and reputations hinge on its success or failure. Savings bonds are no different. The government maintains a staff whose sole job is to promote the sale of its product—savings bonds. Thus, there is a danger in relying only on government information. For example, you will not be informed of the pitfalls of various transactions; the numerous cases where bond owners have made costly mistakes; or the advantages of selective redemption.

Since the author has no vested interest in whether you "hold" or "fold" your bonds, you will always get "both sides of the coin." In addition, twelve years of experience serving savings bond investors both within the Savings Bond Program—as a supervisor of the Savings Bond Division of the Federal Reserve Bank—and through his company, The Saving Bond Informer, Inc., has provided a close look at what investors need and want.

Two Primary Misconceptions about U.S. Savings Bonds

U.S. Savings Bonds have been familiar to us for some time. Americans started purchasing Series E bonds in the 1940s. Fondly remembered as "War Bonds," people bought them to support our country during World War II. Understanding them has always seemed a simple matter: Everybody knows about U.S. Savings Bonds, right? The typical pattern has been to collect bonds over the years and then to redeem them whenever it is time to make that big purchase. Unfortunately, this "simple" approach has often led to costly mistakes.

Misconception #1: *U.S. Savings Bonds Are a Simple Investment*

The concept of savings bonds as a simple investment is derived from the fact that they are easy to purchase. They can be bought at thousands of banks across the country or through a Payroll Savings Plan at work. However, on closer inspection it is discovered that they are not as simple as we have chosen to believe.

Each bond carries a unique set of information specific to that bond alone. This includes interest rates (two of them for most bonds), timing issues, maturity dates, values, and accrued interest. Knowing the unique information that applies to each one of your bonds can make a significant difference in the return on your investment. Not knowing can mean forfeiting hundreds or, in some cases, thousands of dollars.

Misconception #2: *Everyone Knows How Savings Bonds Work*

The author has conducted hundreds of savings bond seminars for bankers, attorneys, accountants, financial planners, brokers, and bond owners. One of the first questions posed to the participants is the most basic and common question about bonds: How long does it take a bond that was purchased in 1994 to reach face value at the guaranteed interest rate? At every seminar, there are at least three or four different answers offered, often as many as six or seven.

In a 1994 survey of 400 bank personnel, only 38% could answer the question correctly. Indeed, a bank in Florida reported that bonds reach face value in two years, which would mean that the bonds would have to pay interest at a rate of 36%. Another bank indicated that it takes thirty years for a bond to reach face value and, as a result, the interest rate would have to be under 2.5%. The confusion surrounding this most basic question indicates that there is a great amount of misunderstanding on the more detailed and technical matters.

The reason for such an expanse of misinformation is that savings bonds operate according to different rules depending on their type (series) and when they were purchased. For example, two Series E bonds with the same face value, but purchased at different times, can come under different rules (which, in turn, lead to different rates of interest and strategic timing considerations). Yet, many people treat bonds as though they are all the same.

Some of the most significant changes in the bond program have occurred in the 1990s. The government eliminated the guaranteed rate on new purchases in May 1995; they converted to a monthly increase pattern in May 1997; and they introduced the I bond in September 1998.

Savings bonds are certainly not a "simple investment." Furthermore, the perception that everyone knows how they work has led to a mindset that has often prevented bond owners from seeking the critical information they need in order to be knowledgeable about their bonds.

Lack of Information Leads to Costly Mistakes

After every seminar the author gives, a line quickly forms of people ready to tell "their savings bond story." Often the tale involves a financial mistake brought on by the advice of a misinformed person:

- A man redeemed all of his bonds right before retirement, during the year when he was in the highest income bracket of his lifetime. He did not realize that all the interest income from the redeemed bonds would be reported in that calendar year.

- A woman read a publication that advocated cashing in bonds that had reached face value to purchase new bonds under the new rules. At the time, many of her bonds were earning rates of 7.5% under the old rules, while the new rules' rate would have netted her substantially less.

- A woman recently widowed was advised to cash all of her bonds; she later learned that her bonds would have continued to earn interest for an additional eight years.

- A father purchased an EE bond for its educational feature only to discover that he may not meet the criteria to qualify for the tax-free status.

- A couple needed money for a down payment on a new home and so randomly cashed 50 of their 100 bonds. If they had applied the principles of selective redemption, they would have had an additional $1,000 to $2,000 to use toward the purchase.

- A financial planner learned that over $50,000 of his client's $240,000 bond holdings had stopped earning interest over five years ago.

- When advising a customer on how to remove the first-named living owner from a bond, a banker did not counsel the new recipient on tax issues. Subsequently, the new owner declared bond interest that had already been declared at the time of reissue: the result—double taxation.

- An accountant did not know that bonds do not automatically receive a "stepped-up" basis (see Glossary).

It is our desire that by sharing these stories and by providing the much needed information that these bond owners lacked, you will not be left with your own tale of woe. Instead, whether you choose to fold, exchange, or hold your bonds, your choice will be based on facts.

What You Can Expect from this Book

U.S. Savings Bonds are a do-it-yourself proposition. Have you ever received a statement containing the precise details for each of your bonds? Statements are sent for savings accounts, checking accounts, and mutual fund accounts. There was no such instrument available for U.S. Savings Bonds until the author created one in 1990. Once you invest in savings bonds, it is up to you to ask the right questions and find the right source for answers. After reading this book, or the chapters that apply to your situation, you will have a better idea of what questions you need to ask. In most cases, the answers have been provided; on the rare occasion that they are not, an appropriate resource has been supplied.

More specifically, this book will enable you to maximize your investment in U.S. Savings Bonds in two ways. The first is by building your understanding of how savings bonds work. Second, step-by-step instructions are provided on how to track your investment and how to organize and keep important records on your bonds. Tables and figures, usually found at the end of the chapter, illustrate key concepts and provide examples of what to do.

Several areas are especially noteworthy, such as:

- four ways savings bonds are double taxed
- an introduction to the concept of selective redemption
- the results of a survey regarding the savings bond information banks provide to the public
- a comparison of savings bonds to other conservative investments
- retirement strategies
- leaving bonds as an inheritance

As previously mentioned this edition also contains three new chapters: Chapter 8, "Making the Decision to Hold or Fold"; Chapter 17, "Especially for Grandparents and Other Gift Givers"; and Chapter 18, "The New I Bond."

What You Cannot Expect from this Book

This is not a book about municipal bonds, corporate bonds, bond mutual funds, Treasury bills, Treasury notes, or Treasury bonds. There are plenty of comprehensive publications available on these topics. This book will only deal with issues directly related to U.S. Savings Bonds: Series E, EE, H, HH, I, and Savings Notes/Freedom Shares.

This book is not a government publication. However, several government publications have been used as reference and are noted in the Bibliography.

Finally, you will not find advice on whether or not to invest in savings bonds or what to do with your interest earnings upon redemption of your bonds. Although you will be given the tools needed to evaluate and compare your investment with other options, this book will not make investment decisions for you. While the pros and cons of making certain decisions are often given for your consideration, this job is best left to you or someone, such as a financial professional, who is familiar with your overall financial picture.

How to Use this Book

This book can be used as a guide or as a reference. As a guide, it explains some of the most technical information in an easy-to-understand manner. When called for, it will take you step-by-step through various processes. As a reference manual, it has been organized to provide quick and easy access to information. The Contents provides not only chapter titles, but also the subheadings that describe the main points of each chapter. These subheadings are repeated at the beginning of each chapter; a quick browse will direct you to the proper section within a given chapter. To ease your search when the text refers you to Chapter 3, for example, we have included the chapter number with the chapter title in the running head atop each right-hand page. We have also frequently included "Quick Tips" to highlight the essential points in each chapter. The Glossary provides definitions of bond-related terms and phrases. (Check here first when you come across something unfamiliar.) The Index lists savings bond activities and terms alphabetically so that the page number can be quickly located. Appendix B provides a brief summary of the contents of this book in a helpful question-and-answer format.

In an attempt to make the information easy to follow, you will find that some areas are repetitious. Often a piece of data will apply to several different issues. Rather than refer you to other chapters, which creates time-consuming page turning, the material is summarized for immediate use, followed by directions to more detailed information on the topic.

There is a wealth of information in Chapter 19, "U.S. Savings Bond Resources." It covers both government and non-government agencies that provide a variety of savings bond services. It also lists the various forms needed to complete savings bond transactions and where to obtain them. The directory of phone numbers and addresses will lead you to any additional help you may need.

Millions of Americans have relied on U.S. Savings Bonds as a way to save and invest. The following pages will provide you with the opportunity to understand, evaluate, and track your savings bond investment.

Chapter 2

BANKS AND BONDS
The Untold Story

▶ *U.S. Savings Bonds Are Not a Bank Product*
▶ *The Changing Relationship between Banks and Bonds*
▶ *Merger Mania Doesn't Help*
▶ *Evaluation of Bank Services:*
  The Good, The Bad, and The Ugly
▶ *How to Determine the Level of Service Your Bank Provides*
▶ *Quick Tips on Accepting Savings Bond Information*
  from Banks

Few other industries have been asked by the government to take actions adverse to their own interests in the way the banks have been exhorted to sell U.S. Savings Bonds through the years.
                    —Paul S. Nadler, "Uncle Sam Out of Line,"
                    Banker's Monthly (November 1992), p. 8

If you own U.S. Saving Bonds, you may have bought them at your local bank or through a Payroll Savings Plan. Because banks handle a variety of financial products and services, bond owners often assume that the bank is knowledgeable about bonds. As you will see, this assumption could prove to be very costly.

U.S. Savings Bonds Are Not a Bank Product

U.S. Savings Bonds are a product of the federal government. They are not, nor have they ever been, a product created and fully supported by the banks. Because bonds are not a bank product, financial institutions rely on information from the government when informing the public about them.

Banks receive small fees for handling the bond purchase application and for redeeming bonds. They do not receive money for advising individuals on their bond holdings. Banks would not describe bonds as a moneymaker. They handle bonds as a courtesy, to prevent customers from moving to another bank (and taking their money with them). As a result, most banks do not put a high priority on training their personnel in answering questions on U.S. Savings Bond timing and interest rate issues. Training dollars are typically spent on bank products more likely to generate substantial revenue.

The Changing Relationship between Banks and Bonds

Before you get angry at your bank, consider this: How would you feel if you were selling a product that not only competed with your own product line, but was twice as good as your product, and, on top of that, left you with no profit? That was the unenviable position in which banks found themselves during 1992: Bonds had a guaranteed rate of 6% while savings accounts, along with some certificates of deposit (CDs), were struggling to reach 3%. Needless to say, the smart bankers were not excited to see an all-time high of $17.6 billion in savings bond sales. Why? Many buyers were shifting their money from CDs into savings bonds; that is, they were taking money out of bank products and investing it in a government product—and the banks had to help them do this.

In the last five years, The Savings Bond Informer, Inc. (TSBI) has received an increasing number of calls from people saying, "My bank no longer deals with savings bonds." This is particularly true of clients on the West Coast and, most recently, clients in the Northeast. Given that savings bonds compete for the dollars of bank customers, it is not surprising that some banks are decreasing their level of service related to bonds. (Savings bond transactions can be conducted via the mail through a Federal Reserve Bank. See Chapter 19, "U.S. Savings Bond Resources," for the phone number and address of the FRB that services your state. Call for instructions before proceeding with a transaction.)

When dealing with your bank on savings bond issues, there are two questions to be concerned with:

✓ What level of service do they provide?
✓ Will they put their answers in writing?

Merger Mania Doesn't Help

If you have followed the papers, or watched the signs in front of your local banks, you know that "merger mania" is sweeping the banking industry. While this may benefit the stockholders, it does not necessarily help savings bond owners, as the following comments illustrate:

> *"It used to be that my bank knew about savings bonds, the tellers had been there a long time. Now that my bank has changed [merged] I have new tellers and they know very little about savings bonds."*

> *"Thank goodness for your book. I had to educate my bank on the entire exchange process. Not only did the tellers not know what to do, but the managers didn't know either."*

A merger intensifies the need for changes in many operations. The emphasis is placed on getting the two merger partners to begin to operate as one. Systems are replaced, personnel changes made, new rules implemented, and some old practices eliminated. How much attention do you think is given to training people in savings bond analysis so they can assist you with your investment? If you think little to none, you are right.

Evaluation of Bank Services:
The Good, The Bad, and The Ugly

The Good

Many banks act as a point of sale for the purchase of bonds and a point of redemption for the cashing of bonds. For the most part, banks do a good job identifying what a bond is worth. They have standardized tables that provide redemption values. In fact, in a recent survey, many bank tellers would give the value of a bond in response to questions about interest rates or timing issues. However, as with any money matter, it makes good sense to double-check the calculations yourself whenever possible. A financial planner recently called with the following story.

> *I was working on a case for an estate settlement. The law firm needed bonds evaluated, so I used your service to provide a report for them. Today they called to tell me they had cashed some of the bonds. There was one problem, though: they received $1,000 less than they thought they should have. After checking your report, they called the bank and asked them to recheck their figures. Sure enough, the bank amount was wrong. The bank apologized several times for their error. The bottom line is that had we not had the report, we would not have known we were being shorted.*

Because he was an informed consumer, the client got the money due the same day. (In over a dozen cases last year, bond owners were able to identify errors when redeeming bonds because they had an independent source to verify the amount they should receive; the adjustments were made on the spot or very soon thereafter.)

Watch out, though. If a bank overpays you, an unpleasant surprise may be forthcoming. Another financial planner reported that the bank had contacted a client several months after redeeming some bonds. The bank claimed they had overpaid the client and requested that the money be returned.

Note: The government does check bond payment amounts through a system called E-Z Clear. However, it can take up to eight weeks for an adjustment on a pricing error to be made, and only differences over $25 are automatically adjusted (lesser amounts can be adjusted upon request from the financial institution). However, the adjustment is not made directly with the bond owner. The government adjusts the difference with the financial institution; it is the responsibility of the financial institution to refund or seek payment from a bond owner in the event of an over- or underpayment. It is very important for bond owners to independently verify the amount they should receive upon redemption. **Suggestion:** For alternatives to confirming your bonds' worth, see Chapter 7, "Tracking Your Investment," and Chapter 19, "U.S. Savings Bond Resources."

The Bad

As a bond owner, you must have accurate information. The reason inaccurate information exists is that bank tellers, who are not analysts, often act as consultants on bonds. Note the following example.

> *In 1991 a man went into a bank in Michigan with E bonds he had purchased in the 1970s. He asked the teller what he should do. After consulting her charts, she informed him that the bonds were no longer earning interest and that he should redeem them all. He followed her advice and liquidated all of his bonds from the 70s that he had purchased through payroll deduction.*

Why was this a disaster? First, his bonds had not stopped earning interest: The teller had given him incorrect information. His bonds would have continued to earn interest until after the year 2000. Second, when he redeemed the bonds, he had to declare *all* the interest income that year. The tragedy was that this man was two years from retirement and so was in *the highest income bracket of his lifetime*. Third, many of his bonds had been earning attractive rates of 7.5%. Understandably enraged by his experience, this man had no recourse. He, unfortunately, did not get any of the teller's information in writing.

Never trust verbal information about interest rates and timing issues. If you choose to rely upon your bank, ask that all the information they give you be put into writing, including the name of the person with whom you spoke. Also record the date and location of your inquiry.

The Ugly

Assume you ask a bank teller a question about the interest rates your bonds are earning. What is the likelihood that you asked someone knowledgeable, someone who can produce the correct answer? Our research indicates that fewer than one out of ten bank personnel can accurately answer bond questions. Yet, approximately nine out of ten bank representatives will either confidently give inaccurate answers or admit they "don't know." Going to the next level of management does not ensure accuracy, either; those in upper management deal with savings bonds even less frequently.

The author recently had an interesting experience at a bank in California. As is his custom when traveling around the country, he entered a bank to ask savings bond questions. He showed the teller his bond and asked, "What rate of interest is this bond earning and is there a particular date that it will increase in value?" After ten minutes the teller returned with the bond and said, "sign here to cash the bond. "There was no attempt to answer the questions or even express ignorance by saying, "I don't know." The objective was to cash the bond regardless.

In another humorous, yet sad, state-of-affairs, three tellers gathered to discuss the author's question on interest rates. Within ear- and eyeshot, they took a vote to determine the "right" answer. Then one of them returned and confidently reported the result of the vote as if it were fact. (**Note:** The "winning" response was incorrect.)

So, what does this mean to Jane Q. Public, bond owner? She walks away believing what she has been told. Someday Jane will act on the information she was given and will probably never realize that she did not receive the maximum potential return on her bond investment.

How to Determine the Level of Service
Your Bank Provides

Repeated complaints from bond owners led The Savings Bond Informer to design and conduct surveys of banks regarding the savings bond information they provide to the public. A 1998 phone survey of 100 banks nationwide revealed that less than 8% of the banks could accurately answer a question about interest rates and the dates a specific bond accrues interest. Of those questioned, 22% referred the caller to the "government"; 15% offered a wrong answer; and 22% simply responded, "I don't know." Of those responding, 33% said to call 1-800-USBONDS for help. Of those who suggested the 800 number, all were asked, "Does that number have a person who will assist me?" Over 75% said, "yes." While changed in August 1998, for the ten years previous that number was a recorded line, which, among other things, referred bond owners back to their banks for information about interest rates. It is no surprise that investors are often frustrated and angry at the lack of help they have received. They have been the proverbial dog chasing the tail. A few other responses were especially noteworthy.

> *"Let me check this newspaper article I saved, because a lot of people come in here with bonds."*

> *"The interest rate on your bonds varies, it doesn't stay the same and no one can tell you."*

> *"Sometimes they change monthly, sometimes they don't, there doesn't seem to be any method to the madness that I can see."*

The latest findings support the results of TSBI's 1994 400-bank survey. In that survey (documented in the third edition of *U.S. Savings Bonds: A Comprehensive Guide for Bond Owners and Financial Professionals*), 23% of the answers from banks were accurate. Of the 400 banks surveyed, only four answered all five questions—those that any bond owner would ask about his or her bonds—accurately (a 1% chance of having bond questions accurately addressed).

Two questions focused on interest rates and timing issues for older bonds. Only 8% of the answers to these questions were correct; over 90% of the banks surveyed did not or could not give accurate information. To their credit, 48% of the banks admitted they did not know. However, 44% of the banks answered boldly and inaccurately.

Some of the more dramatic, and woefully wrong, answers were so frightening that they deserve to be printed. Here are the top six losing responses.

Question: *Is the interest on a bond purchased in January of 1963 compounded? If yes, is it daily, monthly, quarterly, semi-annually, or annually?*

1. "Monthly" (most common response)

2. "Kinda like quarterly, yet it's not"

3. "Calculated monthly, paid quarterly"

4. "Doesn't matter. Very complicated, based on when you bought it, how much you paid, and a lot of other factors"

Correct answer: *Compounded semi-annually.*

Two additional responses were noteworthy:

1. One person said that a bond purchased in January 1963 is currently earning 18% interest. (This certainly beats the savings account rate that bank is offering.)

2. Another person said this same bond would never stop earning interest. What a deal!

By now you get the point.

The conscientious bank employees said, "I don't know." This does not help you, the bond owner, but neither does it hurt you. The damaging answers were from those people who *confidently* gave wrong information.

The problem is not bond valuation, although independent verification is always advisable; rather, it is untrained bank personnel trying to answer questions concerning interest rates and increase dates. By now you see the pattern.

A Test For Your Bank Teller

Questions

1. Is interest compounded for bonds purchased in the 1970s or 1980s? If so, is it daily, monthly, quarterly, semi-annually, or annually?

2. What is the current guaranteed interest rate for a bond purchased in January 1978? How long is that rate in effect?

3. Is there a specific month or months that would be best to cash a bond dated November 1973?

Answers

1. The interest on these bonds accrues and is compounded semi-annually. Why is this important? If you cash your bond even one day before a semi-annual increase, you will forfeit up to six months of interest.

2. This bond has a current guaranteed rate of 6%, which will be in effect until January 2003. Why is this important? Knowing specific interest rates, and how long those rates are active, will help you make hold or sell decisions.

3. Yes. For a bond purchased in November 1973, the months of increase are September and March. Why is this important? See answer #1 above.

If your teller says it does not matter when you cash your bond, he or she obviously does not understand how bonds work.

Four Additional Mistakes to be Aware Of

1. Clients of The Savings Bond Informer, Inc. have reported being told that their bond statements, which show E bonds from December 1965 and after as thirty-year bonds, are wrong. (These tellers incorrectly assume that all E bonds earn interest for forty years.) Consult Table 4.2, "Guide to Extended and Final Maturity Periods," on page 49.

2. With millions of bond owners affected by low guaranteed rates in the mid-1990s, bank personnel often tell owners that their bonds are earning the market rate. That is particularly damaging to those who bought bonds during January through October 1986 and who are led to believe that they are earning more than they really are. See Chapter 3, "Understanding Interest Rates," starting on page 17 for a complete explanation of guaranteed and market-based rates. It also describes what really happens to those bonds that used to earn 7.5%.

3. Many bank redemption tables now have a column that indicates the "average annual yield" since purchase. This is NOT the interest rate that these bonds are currently earning. Yet many bank tellers assume, because it is the only rate on their chart, that this is what the bond owner is getting. Several banks have told the author that a particular bond was currently paying over 7%, when in reality it was paying only 4%.

4. When you cash a bond, a 1099-INT form is generated by the bank. Copies are sent to the IRS and to the bond owner. A broker had a client who cashed more than $100,000 of savings bonds. The bank issued a 1099-INT for over $80,000. A bond statement from The Savings Bond Informer, Inc. revealed that the 1099-INT should have been less than $60,000. Because the bond owner was able to identify the error, the bank was forced to admit and correct their mistake. Without independent verification, this investor would have paid over $6,000 in taxes that they were not liable for. The government does not independently verify that a 1099-INT is correct when issued by a bank.

Remember, free information is not a bargain unless it is correct.

Quick Tips on Accepting Savings Bond Information from Banks

- Because banks receive no payment for handling bonds, training dollars are often spent elsewhere. As a result, banks provide inaccurate or insufficient information on savings bond interest rates and timing issues much of the time.

- While banks are good at valuing your bonds, always recheck transactions and consider using an independent source for verification.

- A 1994 phone survey of 400 banks nationwide and a 1998 follow-up survey of 100 banks revealed that less than 8% could accurately answer questions about interest rates and dates a bond accrues interest (timing issues).

- You might want to conduct a simple test to determine your bank's level of savings bond competence.

- Always ask that the information you receive be put in writing. Don't forget to document the date and who gave you the information, including the person's name, the bank, and location.

Chapter 3

UNDERSTANDING INTEREST RATES

▶ *Why Interest Rates Are Important*
▶ *What Rates Are Your Bonds Earning?*
▶ *The Confusion Over Interest Rates*
▶ *Common Misconceptions*
▶ *Interest Rate Rules and How They Work*
▶ *October 1986: An Illustration
   of How the Interest Rates Work*
▶ *When Do Interest Rates Change?*
▶ *Quick Tips on Interest Rates*

No doubt Galileo and Einstein would have been intrigued with the savings bond program if they were alive today. Piecing together the data that has affected the interest rates on your bonds is a challenge. And while knowing how to piece together the data may not lead to a scientific breakthrough, it can result in better decisions that lead to more money.

This chapter begins by illustrating why interest rates are important in determining when to hold and when to fold. Next, it looks at the interest rates that apply to your bonds (at the time of writing) and when those bonds will stop earning interest. The chapter concludes with a brief discussion of the confusion that surrounds interest rates, the misconceptions this confusion has led to, and how the interest rates work. A special section details the October 1986 bond. This bond is the most popular bond ever purchased, and it also serves as a great illustration of the way interest rates are applied to a bond.

Why Interest Rates Are Important

The current interest rate that a bond is earning and the length of time that this rate will be in effect provides a measurement for the bond's future value. It is essential to understand this when comparing bonds. As with a marketable Treasury Security (a Treasury note or bond), a high interest rate (or coupon rate) gives one savings bond a greater future value than another bond with a lower interest rate (assuming both bonds have equal redemption value at present). On a practical level, if a couple wants to cash half of their bonds, they will be best served if they can differentiate between the worst-performing and the best-performing bonds. Consider the following example:

> *Robert and Rita own 150 savings bonds. The total value of their portfolio is $100,000—$30,000 of which is deferred interest. They want $50,000, but don't know which bonds to cash. One co-worker suggests cashing the oldest bonds first, while others insist that they should take the newest bonds. Robert and Rita decide they need information in writing, so they order a detailed bond statement customized to their holdings. The statement reveals that half of their bonds are earning 4% and the other half are earning 6%. They identify the 4% bonds and cash them first. The remaining bonds continue to grow at 6%. They will realize an additional $1,000 a year in interest by having identified the best and worst performing bonds. Over the next five years they will have earned over $5,000 that, had they haphazardly cashed some bonds, might have gone unrealized.*

Age should not be the sole determining factor when deciding which bonds to cash; yield plays a significant role and needs to be considered. Current yields (for a six-month period) can be found in the government publication "United States Savings Bonds/Notes Earnings Report" (see page 226 to order). This government yield, along with a short-term (two-year) and long-term (five-year) rating of future performance, is offered in The Savings Bond Informer Bond Statement. (See page 79 for more information.)

What Rates Are Your Bonds Earning?

Bonds do not all receive the same rate of interest. Current interest rates range from 4% to 6.1%, depending on series and date of issue (with the one exception following).

Series H and HH bonds: Interest rates vary from 4% to 6%, depending on the issue date of the bond. Any Series H bond over 30 years old is paying 0%. Any Series HH bond over 20 years old is paying 0%. (The first HH bonds, issued in 1980, will stop earning interest in the year 2000.)

Savings Notes/Freedom Shares: Those that still earn interest are receiving between 4% and 5%. All savings notes over 30 years old receive 0%. All savings notes will have stopped earning interest by October 2000.

Series E bonds and Series EE bonds over five years old: Interest rates range from 4% to 6.1%, depending on the issue date. No bond earns over 6.1%. Any E bond issued November 1965 or before, and that is over 40 years old, is earning 0%. Any E bond issued December 1965 and after, and that is over 30 years old, is earning 0%.

Series EE bonds less than five years old: Generally, these bonds range from 4% to 5.5%. However, bonds issued from March 1993 to April 1995 have a retroactive "catch-up" which is added to the value of the bond on the five-year anniversary. Thus, these bonds can yield over 10% in that fifth year. Bonds issued from March 1993 to April 1995, and that are not yet five years old, will be the best performers in the bond program over the next one to two years. After they turn five years old, they will yield between 4.5% and 5.5% if interest rates remain relatively flat.

Series I Bonds: The first I bond was issued September 1, 1998. The earnings rate for I bonds issued in September and October 1998 is 4.66%. This is a combination of a fixed rate of 3.4% and a CPI-U (Consumer Price Index-Urban Consumers) based rate of 1.26% (when annualized). The rates on outstanding I bonds will fluctuate every six months dependent on changes in the CPI-U. The rates on new-purchase I bonds are reset every six months, in May and November. See Chapter 18 for more information on the I bond.

The Confusion Over Interest Rates

Savings bonds operate according to their type (series) and the rules in effect at the time of purchase. For example, two Series E bonds with the same face value purchased at different times may come under different rules. Or, two bonds purchased at the same time, but of different series (such as the Series E and EE bond), may operate according to different rules. Over the last sixteen years, the bond program has undergone four major rule changes. This has meant six changes in the guaranteed rates and more than forty-four changes in the market rates. These changes have lead to confusion in three areas: the way in which the rates are defined; the way in which the rates are calculated; and which rates apply at which time.

Three Different Types of Interest Rates

Until 1982 there was only one type of interest rate—the guaranteed rate. The guaranteed rate assigned to a bond depended on the date of purchase and the specific maturity period a bond was in. In 1982 the government introduced the market rate. Designed to make bonds more attractive, this rate provided an upside potential: A bond can earn an interest rate above the guaranteed interest rate if it is held for five years or longer. Thus, the government began calculating two values for each Series E, EE, or Savings Note/Freedom Share (SN/FS).

Changes made in May 1995 and May 1997 both simplified and complicated the interest rate structures. The government's "new rules" simplified the issue by allowing only one interest rate to apply at any given point in time to Series EE bonds issued on or after May 1, 1995. The complication is that most bond owners hold bonds governed by the "old rules." The result is that there are three unique types of interest rates that apply to U.S. Savings Bonds: the guaranteed/fixed rate, the market rate (with four subcategories), and the CPI-U indexed rate. Every bond has either one or two of these rates that affect it's performance.

Table 3.1 indicates which rate applies to each series of bond. While H and HH bonds have been included in this table, and are briefly mentioned at the end of the chapter, an in-depth discussion of these bonds appears in Chapter 12. The I bond is covered in detail in Chapter 18.

Table 3.1 Types of Interest Rates that Apply to Each Series

Series	Type of Rate
I—September 1998 and after	CPI-U Indexed Rate and Fixed Rate
HH	Guaranteed Rate
H	Guaranteed Rate
EE—May 1997 and after	Market Rate
EE—May 1995 to April 1997	Market Rate
EE—Pre-May 1995	Average Market Rate and Guaranteed Rate
SN/FS	Average Market Rate and Guaranteed Rate
E	Average Market Rate and Guaranteed Rate

That the combined changes resulted in three different types of interest rates would be confusing enough. To add insult to injury, however, the way in which these rates have been defined and applied also has become complicated.

The Guaranteed Rate: Defined and Applied

The guaranteed interest rate is the minimum rate that a bond will yield in the current maturity period (in some cases the bond may have to be held at least five years to receive this guarantee). For an expanded explanation of how this rate works, see pages 26 and 27.

The guaranteed rate is sometimes referred to as a "fixed" rate. However, while the guaranteed rate is just that, guaranteed, the fixed rate, as in the case of the new I bond, may not be guaranteed (in the way we think of guaranteed; i.e., I perceive guaranteed to mean "I will definitely get this amount," however, you may get less than your fixed rate on the I bond in periods of deflation). The following is a synopsis of how the guaranteed rate is applied to bonds purchased at various times throughout the history of the program.

I Bonds purchased September 1998 and after: A fixed rate is assigned to the bond at the time of purchase. An inflation-adjusted rate is added to the fixed rate every six months to determine the actual earnings rate for each six-month period.

EE Bonds purchased May 1995 and after: There is no guaranteed rate.

E and EE bonds and SN/FS purchased prior to May 1995: A guaranteed rate is assigned to a bond at the time of issue. *This rate is only good for the original maturity period and can change each time a bond enters an extended maturity period.* (See Chapter 4, "Timing Issues and Maturity Periods," for an explanation of maturity periods.)

The Market Rate: Defined and Applied

The term "market rate" can mean many things: an average of many market rates, 85% of a six month T-bill average; 85% of the five-year Treasury yield average; or 90% of the five-year Treasury yield average. It may help to understand that there are two benchmarks against which the market rate is determined: the six-month Treasury bill (T-bill) yields and the five-year Treasury yields. (See page 27 for in-depth explanation of how the market rate works.) The following is a summary of how the market rate is applied starting with the most recent changes.

EE Bonds purchased May 1997 and after: The market rate is 90% of the average of five-year Treasury yields. This rate is published every May and November. See Table 3.2.

EE Bonds purchased May 1995 to April 1997: The market rate is 85% of the six-month T-bill yield for the first five years and then 85% of the average of five-year Treasury yields after the bond is five years old. These rates are published every May and November. See Table 3.3.

E Bonds, Savings Notes, and EE bonds purchased prior to May 1995: The market rate is 85% of the five-year Treasury yields. However, this individual rate is combined with other individual market rates to form the average market rate for bonds. And, the average market rate may or may not be what a particular bond is earning.

Note: Throughout the remainder of this chapter you will see reference to the following four rule changes:

- *September 1998 I Bond Rules*
  These rules apply only to Series I Bonds Purchased September 1, 1998 and after.

- *May 1997 EE Bond Rules*
  These rules apply only to Series EE bonds purchased May 1, 1997 and after.

- *May 1995 to April 1997 Gatt-cha Rules*
  These rules apply only to Series EE bonds purchased between May 1, 1995, and April 30, 1997, and are a result of the GATT agreement. (See page 25 for more information.)

- *Pre-May 1995 Rules*
  These rules apply to Series E, EE, or SN purchased prior to May 1, 1995.

Common Misconceptions

Here are the four most common misconceptions.

Misconception #1: *All bonds earn the same rate of interest.*

Pre-May 1995 Rules for E, EE, and SN/FS
No. Each bond can have a unique guaranteed and average market-based interest rate. The rate for any given bond is determined by its issue date and series.

May 1995 to April 1997 Gatt-cha Rules for EE
No. Each bond receives a market rate (based on 85% of the six-month T-bill yield) every six months for the first five years. After five years the bond receives a new market rate every six months. This market rate is based on 85% of the five-year Treasury yield.

May 1997 Rules for EE
No. Each bond receives a new market rate every six months. This market rate is based on 90% of the five-year Treasury yields.

Misconception #2: *The interest rate that is quoted when you buy a bond is good for the life of the bond.*

Pre-May 1995 Rules for E, EE, and SN/FS
No. The guaranteed rate that was in effect when the bond was purchased is the minimum rate during the original maturity period. A bond will continue to earn interest well after the original maturity period, but the guaranteed rate can change each time the bond enters an extended maturity period.

May 1995 to April 1997 Gatt-cha Rules for EE
No. The rate published at the time of purchase has no bearing on future rates for these bonds. The market rate initially assigned to a bond applies for the first six months only (based on 85% of six-month T-bill yields). A new market rate is published every six months. This pattern continues until the bond is five years old, when the market rate is based on 85% of the five-year Treasury yields.

May 1997 Rules for EE
No. Each bond receives a new market rate every six months. This market rate is based on 90% of the five-year Treasury yields.

Misconception #3: *Older bonds have lower interest rates than newer bonds or newer bonds have lower interest rates than older bonds.*

Pre-May 1995 Rules for E, EE, and SN/FS
No and **no.** Older bonds can carry guaranteed rates as high as 6%. Many newer bonds earn only 4% to 5.5%. The interest rate varies from bond to bond. In some cases, older bonds may be earning only 4%, while a newer bond could be 100 to 200 basis points higher. (See Glossary for the definition of "basis points.")

May 1995 to April 1997 Gatt-cha Rules for EE
Each bond in this time period receives a new interest rate every six months. The rates will generally not vary by more than 50 basis points from bond to bond. Often the spread is less than 25 basis points.

May 1997 Rules for EE
Each bond receives a new interest rate every six months. Historically, the rates have not varied by more than 60 basis points from bond to bond.

Note: The spread between these bonds and the Gatt-cha bonds has been 59 to 105 basis points, always in favor of the bonds governed by the May 1997 rules.

Misconception #4: *The market rate that is published every May and November is the interest rate for all bonds.*

Pre-May 1995 Rules for E, EE, and SN/FS
No. The individual market rate published each May and November has no significance by itself. This is not the rate these bonds are earning. (For further explanation see "Interest Rate Rules and How They Work.")

May 1995 to April 1997 Gatt-cha Rules for EE
The market rate in effect at the time of purchase will influence the bond for the first six months only. A new market rate will be assigned every following six months. This pattern continues until the bond is five years old, at which time a long-term market rate will effect the bond every six months. The first rate published under these rules has no effect on the bond's future rates.

May 1997 Rules for EE
If purchased May 1, 1997, or after, Series EE bonds receive a new market rate every six months. This market rate is based on 90% of the five-year Treasury yields.

Interest Rate Rules and How They Work

The most recent rule changes are the easiest to understand. This section starts with these recent changes and works back to the rules for older bonds.

May 1997 EE Bond Rules

Under these rules, bonds increase in value monthly and the interest is compounded semi-annually. They have no guaranteed rate, but are governed by a new market rate that is published every six months—May 1 and November 1. This rate is based on 90% of the average of the five-year Treasury yields for the preceding six-month period. Thus, the rate published in the government's most recent announcement (May 1998) will govern a bond for the first six months. For instance, if a bond was purchased June 10, 1998, the rate published May 1, 1998—the first rate assigned to all bonds purchased from May 1, 1998 to October 30, 1998—is applied to this bond for the first six months. On December 1, 1998, this bond will be six months old and the rate published November 1, 1998 will be in effect for the next six months. (For a history of recent rates, see Table 3.2).

Note: Investors who cash these bonds before they are five years old suffer a penalty: They forfeit three months of interest. These are the first bonds in the history of the program to operate under this condition. For more complete information on the pros and cons of purchasing Series EE bonds, see Chapter 14.

Table 3.2 Interest Rates for EE Bonds Purchased May 1997 and After

Date Rate was Published	Interest Rate
May 1, 1997	5.68%
November 1, 1997	5.59%
May 1, 1998	5.06%

May 1995 to April 1997 Gatt-cha Rules

These rules were enacted as a result of GATT (the General Agreement on Trades and Tariffs). Although touted as better for investors, the rules have proven much worse for the owner who holds his or her bonds for at least five years. (Thus, the term "Gatt-cha.") Because the public did not respond favorably, the Treasury changed the program May 1, 1997.

Under these rules bonds increase in value semi-annually. They have no guaranteed rate, but earn interest at a market rate that is adjusted every six months. For the first five years, the market rate is based on 85% of the six-month T-bill yields. This rate is determined by measuring the three-month period prior to May and November. After the bond is held for five years, a market rate based on 85% of the five-year Treasury yields for the six-month period prior to each May and November is assigned. Thus far, only rates based on T-bill yields have applied. The following table displays the rates published so far.

Table 3.3 Rates Published for EE Bonds Issued May 1995 to April 1997

Date Rate was Published	Interest Rate
May 1, 1995	5.25%
November 1, 1995	4.75%
May 1, 1996	4.36%
November 1, 1996	4.56%
May 1, 1997	4.63%
November 1, 1997	4.53%
May 1, 1998	4.47%

Here's how it works: A bond purchased in December 1995 would have been assigned the rate of 4.75% for the first six months. On June 1, 1996 (six months later), that bond was assigned a new rate of 4.36%. This rate was in effect until December 1, 1996, when a new rate of 4.56% was assigned. Every six months the bond is assigned a new interest rate that is tied to the performance of the six-month T-bills in the first five years of the bond's life.

Pre-May 1995 Rules

This group probably represents the majority of bonds you hold. Before examining the complex nature of these rules, special attention must be focused on EE bonds issued between March 1993 and April 1995. Although these bonds are governed by the Pre-May 1995 Rules, they are given special attention here because of a unique occurrence.

EE bonds issued between March 1993 and April 1995

These bonds will be the best performers of any bonds in the program over the next one to two years. Why? Because they receive a fixed rate of 4% until they turn five years old. Then, at the five-year mark, they receive the average of the market rates retroactive to the date-of-purchase. This can be a double-digit yield for the year in which that retroactive increase is added. After the five-year mark, these bonds will earn close to the individual market rate (based on 85% of five-year Treasury yields) that is assigned every six months (currently between 4.5% and 5.5%). One more important note: These bonds increase in value monthly until they turn five years old. After that, they increase in value semi-annually.

Now let's examine the rest of the bonds governed by the pre-May 1995 rules. A primary source of confusion is that few people understand that the government has established two independent methods for calculating the value of each bond. One based on the guaranteed interest rates published during the life of the bond. The second method, totally independent from the first, is based on the average of the market-based rates published for a bond.

The Guaranteed Rate

As stated earlier, the guaranteed interest rate, which was assigned at purchase, is the minimum rate the bond will yield until the end of its *original maturity period,* that is, until it reaches face value. (**Note**: In some cases a bond must be held for at least five years to receive this guarantee.) The guaranteed rate is not in effect for the life of the bond. This is a particular surprise and disappointment to bond holders who bought in the mid-1980s at 7.5%. They thought that rate would be good for as long as the bond was held. In reality, those investors were guaranteed 7.5% for the original maturity period only (ten years, in this case).

For Series E and EE bonds, original maturity periods vary from five to eighteen years, depending on the issue date. After that time, the bond enters an *extension* of ten years and is assigned a new guaranteed rate, the rate that will be in effect for that ten-year period. The original maturity period for SN/FS is four years, six months. A table of the original maturity period for each bond can be found on page 37.

For example, assume in the following illustration that the bond will be held to *final maturity* (when it will stops earning interest); in this case, that will be thirty years from the date-of-purchase. A Series EE bond purchased in July 1984 had a guaranteed rate of 7.5% and an original maturity period of ten years. In July 1994, the bond entered its first ten-year extended maturity period. The guaranteed rate for that bond during this first *extended maturity period* dropped to 4%. Why? Bonds are assigned the guaranteed rate that is in effect on the date they enter a new extension period. As of July 1994, the guaranteed rate was 4%, so this bond will have a guaranteed rate of 4% until July 2004. In July 2004, the bond will enter its last extension of ten years. The guaranteed rate for the last ten years will be whatever the guaranteed rate is as of July 2004. That final guaranteed rate is assigned to the bond until its final maturity in July 2014.

The Average of the Market-Based Rates

> The market-based interest rate is set at 85 percent of the average yield, during the time the bonds are held, of marketable Treasury securities with five years remaining to maturity.
>
> —"U.S. Department of the Treasury, Bureau of the Public Debt, U.S. Savings Bond Division, Savings Bond Buyer's Guide: 1993-1994," Pubn. SBD-2085

As stated, the market rates published every May and November are calculated on the previous six months' data for marketable Treasury securities with five years remaining to maturity. For instance; the rate published on May 1, 1994, was 4.7%. This was the first semi-annual rate for bonds purchased from May 1, 1994, to October 31, 1994. However, this is not the rate these bonds *currently* earn.

The key here is the difference between the *individual* market-based rate and the *average* of the market-based rates. A recent caller named Joan asked, "I bought bonds in the 1980s at 11+%. I know they are still earning that interest, but for how long?" How did Joan arrive at the inaccurate conclusion that her bonds were earning over 11%? Because the first *individual* rate published for her bonds was 11.09%. However, she never earned 11.09% because that number became part of an average once her bonds were held five years. Examine

Table 3.4, page 36, for a comparison of individual market-based rates and the average of the market-based rates for a given time period.

The market-based variable rate generated enthusiasm when the 11.09% rate was announced with the program's introduction in November 1982. Joan, thought they were buying bonds that paid 11.09%. But they were not. First, Joan would have to hold her bond for at least five years from the date of purchase to be eligible for the market-based rate program. If she held the bond for fewer than five years, the market rate has absolutely no effect. Second, all the rates published during the holding period of a bond (five years or longer) are averaged. This average is then rounded to the nearest quarter or hundredth (depending on issue date and/or the date the bond may have entered an extension). This rounded average is used to calculate a value for the bond based on the average of the market rates.

As you can see, Joan never received over 11% on her bond. In fact, the current value of her bond is about equal under both interest rate structures and her guaranteed rates actually produce a greater redemption value. Why? In this case, the value based on the guaranteed rate of 7.5% over the first ten years and 6% in the bond's current extension (average of 6.97%) is greater than the value using the average of the market rates of 6.87% (as of May 1998) over the life of the bond.

What is the bottom line? The significant number in the market-based rate program is the *average of the market rates for the specific bonds you hold.* One thing you can determine from the *individual* market rate published every May and November is this: If the individual rate published is higher than the average, it will push the average up; if the individual rate published is lower than the average, it will pull the average down.

During a 1994 TV interview, the author mentioned that the guaranteed rate for bonds purchased that day was 4%, even if they were held for only one, two, or three years. Following the broadcast, an angry bond owner called in: "Bonds are paying 4.7% right now, the new rate was just announced this week!" This person did not understand that he was not getting "4.7% right now."

To qualify for the average of the market rates, bonds must be held for at least five years. All of the individual market rates published during this time will be averaged. If this average of the market rates produces a bond value greater than the value produced from the guaranteed rate (4%), then the investor would receive the average of the market rates.

Bonds purchased with a guaranteed rate of 4% (March 1, 1993 to April 30, 1995) will see a significant jump in value once they have been held five years. Why? Up to the four-year, eleven-month mark, the bond value is based on a guaranteed rate of 4%. Once held five years, the average of the market rates published over the life of the bond will be taken back to the date of purchase and compounded forward (if the average is greater than 4%). A bond purchased on March 1, 1993 had ten published rates over the first five years; the average of those rates is 5.19%. When the bond turned five years old (March 1998) this average rate of 5.19% was credited retroactive to the date of purchase. The result was a one-time double digit yield for the fifth year.

As you can see from Table 3.4 (page 36), only four times out of twenty-two (twenty-two because only bonds at least five years old were counted) was the average market rate higher than the first published market rate. This is an historic view, and one that has been affected by falling interest rates in the 1990s.

An economy that produces rising interest rates over a long period of time could easily create an average market rate that is higher than the first published market rate. For example, a bond purchased November 1993 was assigned a first market rate of 4.25%. The second market rate assigned to this bond was 4.7%. The third rate was 5.92%. The fourth rate was 6.31%. The fifth rate was 5.16%. The sixth rate was 4.85%. The seventh was 5.53%. The eighth was 5.36%. The ninth was 5.28% and the tenth, 4.77%. This bond must be held five years to be eligible for the average of the market rates. These ten rates average 5.21%. As of November 1, 1998, that rate will be credited retroactive to the date of purchase. As you can see, the average rate of 5.21% is almost 100 basis points higher than the initial rate of 4.25%.

So next May or November, when all the newspapers publish the government's press releases promoting the market rates, you will be able to anticipate the forecast. When some writer inaccurately says, "This is the new rate for all bonds held today," you will know better. Only the market rate based on 85% of five-year Treasury yields will apply to bonds purchased prior to May 1, 1995, and that rate becomes part of an average that may or may not affect your bonds.

October 1986: An Illustration of How the Interest Rates Work

During the last several years, one question has been posed to the author more than any other: "I bought bonds in October 1986 with a guaranteed rate of 7.5%. What interest rate are those bonds earning now?" Before we explore the answer to this question, let's examine why the question is critical and how the responses received from various sources illustrate the gross amount of misinformation that is disseminated about savings bonds.

October 1986 was the last month that bond owners could purchase bonds and lock in the guaranteed rate of 7.5%. And buy they did. Three days before the end of the month, the government announced that it would lower the guaranteed rate from 7.5% to 6% on November 1, 1986. That gave people three days to buy 7.5% bonds.

At the time of the rate change, the author was supervising the savings bond division of the Federal Reserve Bank of Chicago-Detroit Branch. His area typically averaged 50 bond purchase applications a day. During the last three days of October 1986, his area received over 10,000 applications. Other Federal Reserve Banks also recorded record volume. This represented the largest three-day purchase period in the history of the bond program since World War II.

More recently, The Savings Bond Informer, Inc. has received calls from hundreds of bond owners who have been given incorrect or misleading information about the interest rates these bonds now earn. The source of much of this misinformation is the bank teller, as demonstrated in Chapter 2. In personal inquiries to over a dozen banks, the author was told that these bonds now pay more than 7%. This error is the result of bank personnel not understanding the data they have.

The author also received calls from people who reported that Federal Reserve Banks had told them that they were earning a market-based rate (4.85% for the period in question). In fact, even those who are part of the savings bond program sometimes have a tough time explaining how the interest rates on these older bonds work. In an article that appeared in the *Providence-Journal Bulletin* (October 8, 1996), a savings bond representative said this about the October 1986 bonds, "Technically your bonds are eligible to earn interest at a rate of about 4.85% over the next six months." We are all "eligible" for a lot of wonderful things, but experience shows us that we often don't get all that we are "eligible" for.

First, the market rate of 4.85% is irrelevant by itself. At the time of writing, not one bond out there is earning 4.85%. That rate, as described earlier in this chapter, is averaged together with other market rates published during the life of a bond. Thus, it is important only in relationship to the other market rates in effect for that bond.

Few understand the relationship between the guaranteed and the average market-based interest rates, and fewer still can explain it. Based on these two sets of rates, the government is calculating two unique redemption values. The bond owner receives whichever value is higher, based on whichever set of rates produces the greatest redemption value. The highest individual rate at any given point in time is *not* automatically received. This is important to understand as we look at the effect of the guaranteed rate and then at the effect of the average market-based rate.

The guaranteed rate was higher the first ten years (7.5%); after year ten, the individual market rate is higher than the new guaranteed rate (4%). Therefore many people assume that they are automatically receiving the higher market rate. A bond owner does not receive the guaranteed rate for the first ten years and then convert to the market rate added onto the guaranteed rate from year eleven on.

A Value Based on the Guaranteed Rate

The October 1986 bonds had a guaranteed rate of 7.5% for the first ten years, its original maturity period. At the end of the original maturity period, the bonds entered an "extended maturity period." This first extension is ten years; a second ten-year extension will begin when the bond is twenty years old. When a bond enters an extension, it picks up the guaranteed rate that is in effect on that date. Subsequently, these bonds picked up a new guaranteed rate of 4% because that was the guaranteed rate on October 1996. This 4% becomes the floor for the next ten-year period. And, as the author tells clients of The Savings Bond Informer, Inc., 4% is the best representation of what you will actually earn for at least the first seven to nine years of this ten-year extension. Table 3.6 (page 38) demonstrates this. The value of a $1,000 bond based on the guaranteed rate is shown (redemption value may vary from the government redemption tables by a few pennies due to rounding).

Take note that the average market-based rate has no place in column "C" where the value based on the guaranteed rate is calculated. You do not get the guaranteed rate for the first ten years and then automatically start earning the market-based rate. The guaranteed rate for the first ten years is followed by the guaranteed rate for the second ten-year period (4%). Nowhere does the average market-based rate affect values created by using the guaranteed rates.

The reason for emphatically stating that the market-based rates do not affect the values created by the guaranteed rates is because that is the biggest misconception being perpetuated. People think, "I got the 7.5% for ten years and now I automatically get the market rate which I know is 85% of five-year Treasury yields and certainly more than 4%." Sorry to be the bearer of bad news, but that view is wrong.

A Value Based on the Average of the Market-Based Rates

As you learned earlier in this chapter, what is now called the market rate (known as the "variable market rate" before the May 1995 rule changes) is published every six months. However, this rate has no significance by itself. Do not look at the rate by itself and assume, "Oh, this bond must be earning xyz% because that is what the government published as a market rate."

Once the October 1986 bond had been held for five years from the date of purchase, it became eligible for the average of the market rates, retroactive to the date of purchase. Over the five years, ten rates had been published—one every six months. At the five-year mark, the average of those ten rates was 6.93% (see Table 3.4, page 36, last column). A redemption value based on that average would obviously create a lower value than that created by the guaranteed rate of 7.5%. So even though this type of bond was eligible for market based rates, they had no effect at the five-year mark.

At the ten-year mark, a similar situation exists. Twenty market rates have been published for the October 1986 bond. The average of those rates is down to 6.2% as seen in Table 3.4, page 36, last column (the low rates in years six through ten pulled the average down). Now it is even more obvious that 6.2% retroactive to the date of purchase will produce a lower redemption value than the guaranteed rate of 7.5% since date of purchase. The side-by-side charts in Table 3.6 (page 38) demonstrate this fact.

Significant Head Scratching Begins Here

Most bond owners assume now that the 7.5% rate has expired they will receive the 6.11% average market rate (the average of the twenty-two rates) or, at the very worst, the individual market rate of 5.53%. Um, sorry. Let's examine Table 3.6 (page 38) to see what actually happens.

The October 1986 bond is now over ten years old. What happened in year eleven and what will happen in the years beyond? In year eleven, as always, two values were created for this bond. One value was based on the guaranteed rates; the second, on the average of the market-based rates. For the guaranteed rate table, an interest rate of 4% (the current guaranteed rate in the extended maturity period) is used for year eleven. You now have ten years at 7.5% and one year at 4%. This produces the redemption value of $1,086.26 (see Table 3.6, the row labeled "23-eleven years").

For a value based on the variable rate at the end of eleven years, there are twenty-two market rates to consider. The average of those twenty-two rates is 6.11%. That average is taken retroactively to the date of purchase and then compounded forward to arrive at the redemption value of $969.37. This is much lower than the redemption value using the guaranteed rates ($1,086.26). At the end of eleven years, then, the market rate was still having no impact on the bond.

What is the best representation of what the bond actually earned in the eleventh year? The 4% guaranteed rate. (**Note:** the actual yield may be slightly lower or higher—3.97% to 4.07%—due to rounding.)

So, anyone who says that the bond earned the market-based rate in year eleven is among the uninformed. The proof, by the way, is in the pudding, and in this case the pudding is the redemption table (Figure 3.1). As of October 1996, the redemption value for a $50 October 1986 bond, was $52.22. The redemption value as of April 1997 was $53.28. The amount of increase is 2.03% or an annual rate of 4.06%. The author rests his case.

Figure 3.1 Redemption Values for an October 1986 Bond

"As of" Date	Value of $50 Bond
October 1996	$52.22
April 1997	$53.28

Adapted from Form PD 3600, Tables of Redemption Values, Dept. of the Treasury, Bureau of the Public Debt.

From the date the October 1986 bond entered the extension, how long will it be before the owner receives more than 4%? The answer is seven years, if the long-term rate averages 6.11% over the next six years—a generous assumption. If the market rate averages 5.2% over the first extended maturity period (October 1996 to October 2006), this bond will earn 4% during the entire ten-year extension. The actual annual yield will be between 3.97% and 4.07% due to rounding. Examine Table 3.6 (page 38) to see where the values based on the market rate begin to exceed the values based on the guaranteed rates in row numbers 35 and 38.

Many investors are very frustrated with a 4% return on a long-term investment product. This rate is lower than the three-month T-bill rate at the time of writing.

In the early 1990s, as interest rates fell dramatically, the Treasury was stuck paying what they had promised in 1986—7.5%. That is, they were locked into paying a premium—more than market conditions would have paid—on the October 1986 bond. The investor had made a good choice and was actually beating the system. Now, however, the tables have turned. According to the rules governing savings bonds, bond owners are asked to swallow a guaranteed rate of 4% for as long as ten years if they want to hold onto their October 1986 bonds. The patriotic investor may feel that it all evens out in the end. However, if one looks at bonds as an investment, without the patriotic obligation, these bonds should be recognized as the worst performers of any savings bonds held.

When Do Interest Rates Change?

Series H and HH bonds: The interest rate assigned to the bond at issue is good for the first ten years. Every ten years the bond will receive a new rate. The rate for any bond entering an extension since March 1993 has been 4%. This 4% rate is set at the Treasury's discretion and there is no schedule for rate adjustment.

Savings Notes/Freedom Shares: These bonds will earn between 4% and 5.25% through final maturity (thirty years). All savings notes will have stopped earning interest by October 2000.

Series E bonds and Series EE bonds over five years old: These bonds can be affected by either the guaranteed rate or the market-based rate. A new market rate is published each May and November. The guaranteed rate, which was 4% at the time of writing (October 1998), last changed March 1, 1993. There is no scheduled change in the guaranteed rate.

Series EE bonds purchased May 1995 and after: New market rates are published every May and November.

Series I bonds: The fixed rate for these bonds will be announced each November and May, but do not expect frequent changes. Since it is not tied to any index or security, the rate will probably remain relatively constant from one announcement to the next. The CPI-U (consumers price index-urban consumers) will change every six months. This will be announced each May and November. For a complete explanation of the I bond, see Chapter 18.

Quick Tips on Interest Rates

- An important measurement for the future value of a savings bond is the current interest rate a bond is earning and the length of time that rate will continue.

- The age of a bond should not be the only data used in determining which bonds to cash, the interest rate must be considered.

- Your bonds are currently earning between 4% and 6.1% if they are over five years old and have not reached final maturity.

- Savings bonds are governed by the rules in effect at the time of purchase and by their type (series). All accrual bonds fall under one of the following sets of rules: September 1998 I Bond Rules; May 1997 EE Bond Rules; May 1995 to April 1997 Gatt-cha Rules; or the Pre-May 1995 Rules.

- There are three types of interest rates: the guaranteed or fixed rate, the market rate (with four subcategories), and the new CPI-U indexed rate.

- Being aware of the common interest rate misconceptions will enable you to avoid costly mistakes.

- Interest rates can change when bonds enter extensions.

- EE bonds purchased between March 1993 and April 1995 will earn a double-digit yield for the year in which their retroactive increase is added.

- Many people have questions about October 1986 bonds. These bonds are no longer earning 7.5%.

Table 3.4 Historic View of the Market-Based Interest Rate on U.S. Savings Bonds Purchased Prior to May 1995

Issue Date	Bond's Lifetime Avg. Market Rate	First Long-Term Market Rate	Average Market Rates for an October 1986 Series EE Bond
thru 4/30/83	6.80	11.09	
5/83 to 10/83	6.66	8.64	
11/83 to 4/84	6.60	9.38	
5/84 to 10/84	6.50	9.95	
11/84 to 4/85	6.38	10.94	
5/85 to 10/85	6.21	9.49	
11/85 to 4/86	6.08	8.36	
5/86 to 10/86	5.99	7.02	
11/86 to 4/87	5.95	6.06	
5/87 to 10/87	5.94	5.84	
11/87 to 4/88	5.95	7.17	For an October 1986 bond, the average of the first ten rates was 6.93%
5/88 to 10/88	5.89	6.90	
11/88 to 4/89	5.84	7.35	
5/89 to 10/89	5.76	7.81	
11/89 to 4/90	5.65	6.98	
5/90 to 10/90	5.57	7.01	
11/90 to 4/91	5.48	7.19	
5/91 to 10/91	5.37	6.57	
11/91 to 4/92	5.28	6.38	For an October 1986 bond, the average of the first twenty rates was 6.2%
5/92 to 10/92	5.19	5.58	
11/92 to 4/93	5.16	5.04	
5/93 to 10/93	5.17	4.78	
11/93 to 4/94	5.21	4.25	
5/94 to 10/94	5.32	4.70	
11/94 to 4/95	5.40	5.92	
5/95 to 10/95	N/A	6.31*	
11/95 to 4/96	N/A	5.16*	
5/96 to 10/96	N/A	4.85*	
11/96 to 4/97	N/A	5.53*	
5/97 to 10/97	N/A	5.36*	
11/97 to 4/98	N/A	5.28*	
5/98 to 10/98	N/A	4.77*	

*This market rate does not affect bonds purchased after 4/30/95.

Table 3.5 Guaranteed Minimum Rates and Original Maturity Periods
For Series EE, E, and Savings Notes
(This table is for the month of September 1998)

Issue Date	Original Maturity Period	Guaranteed Through Current Maturity Period	Life of Bond (years)
SERIES EE			
May 1995 to present	17 yrs.	no guaranteed rate	30
March 1993 to April 1995	18 yrs.	4.0	30
November 1986 to February 1993	12 yrs.	6.0	30
March 1983 to October 1986	10 yrs.	4.0	30
November 1982 to February 1983	10 yrs.	6.0	30
May 1981 to October 1982	8 yrs.	6.0	30
November 1980 to April 1981 ·	9 yrs.	6.0	30
January 1980 to October 1980	11 yrs.	6.0	30
SERIES E			
March 1978 to June 1980	5 yrs.	4.0	30
December 1973 to February 1978	5 yrs.	6.0	30
December 1972 to November 1973	5 yrs. 10 mos.	6.0	30
June 1969 to November 1972	5 yrs. 10 mos.	4.0	30
October 1968 to May 1969	7 yrs.	4.0	30
December 1965 to September 1968		no longer earning	30
June 1965 to November 1965	7 yrs. 9 mos.	4.0	40
January 1961 to May 1965	7 yrs. 9 mos.	6.0	40
June 1959 to December 1960	7 yrs. 9 mos.	4.0	40
October 1958 to May 1959	8 yrs. 11 mos.	4.0	40
May 1941 to September 1958		no longer earning	40
SAVING NOTES			
October 1968 to October 1970	4 yrs. 6 mos.	4.0	30
May 1967 to September 1968		no longer earning	30

Adapted from "Guaranteed Minimum Rates," Bureau of the Public Debt, U.S. Savings Bond Marketing

Table 3.6 Example of October 1986 Series EE Bond

A Row Number	B Date of increase after initial purchase of October 1986	C Value based on 7.5% for first ten years, 4% for second ten	D Value based on 6.11% average market rate over twenty years	E Value based on 5.9% average market rate over twenty years
1		500.00	500.00	500.00
2	Apr/87	518.75	515.28	514.75
3	Oct/87	538.20	531.02	529.94
4	Apr/88	558.39	547.24	545.57
5	Oct/88	579.33	563.96	561.66
6	Apr/89	601.05	581.19	578.23
7	Oct/89	623.59	598.94	595.29
8	Apr/90	646.97	617.24	612.85
9	Oct/90	671.24	636.10	630.93
10	Apr/91	696.41	655.53	649.54
11	Oct/91	722.52	675.55	668.70
12	Apr/92	749.62	696.19	688.43
13	Oct/92	777.73	717.46	708.74
14	Apr/93	806.89	739.38	729.65
15	Oct/93	837.15	761.97	751.17
16	Apr/94	868.54	785.25	773.33
17	Oct/94	901.11	809.24	796.14
18	Apr/95	934.91	833.96	819.63
19	Oct/95	969.96	859.44	843.81
20	Apr/96	1,006.34	885.69	868.70
21-ten years	**Oct/96**	**1,044.08**	**912.75**	894.33
22	Apr/97	1,064.96	940.63	920.71
23-eleven years	**Oct/97**	**1,086.26**	**969.37**	947.87
24	Apr/98	1,107.98	998.98	975.83
25	Oct/98	1,130.14	1,029.50	1,004.62
26	Apr/99	1,152.74	1,060.95	1,034.26
27	Oct/99	1,175.80	1,093.37	1,064.77
28	Apr/2000	1,199.32	1,126.77	1,096.18
29	Oct/2000	1,223.30	1,161.19	1,128.52
30	Apr/2001	1,247.77	1,196.67	1,161.81
31	Oct/2001	1,272.72	1,233.22	1,196.08
32	Apr/2002	1,298.18	1,270.90	1,231.37
33	Oct/2002	1,324.14	1,309.73	1,267.69
34	Apr/2003	1,350.62	1,349.74	1,305.09
35-seventeen yrs	**Oct/2003**	**1,377.64**	**1,390.97**	1,343.59
36	Apr/2004	1,405.19	1,433.47	1,383.22
37-eighteen yrs	Oct/2004	1,433.29	1,477.26	1,424.03
38	**Apr/2005**	**1,461.96**	1,522.39	**1,466.04**
39-nineteen yrs	Oct/2005	1,491.20	1,568.90	1,509.29
40	Apr/2006	1,521.02	1,616.83	1,553.81
41-twenty yrs	Oct/2006	1,551.44	1,666.22	1,599.65

Chapter 4

TIMING ISSUES AND MATURITY PERIODS

▶ *Common Misconceptions*
▶ *Timing Issues at Redemption*
▶ *Timing Issues at Exchange*
▶ *Timing Issues at Final Maturity*
▶ *Timing Issues at Purchase*
▶ *What Does "Maturity" Mean?*
▶ *Quick Tips on Timing and Maturities*

Have you ever passed by a store and seen a sign that made you wonder? A couple of my favorites are "Beer and Worms" (hopefully not in the same container) and "Crafts and Ice Cream" (in kindergarten we learn what things should and should not be grouped together). While timing issues and maturity periods may, at first, seem like an odd pair to group together, they are interrelated because maturity periods can affect a savings bond's interest rate. When interest rates are affected, it leads to the all-important decision of when (timing) to "hold" or "fold." Therefore, this chapter will begin with an element basic to all financial instruments—timing issues—and end with an explanation of what is meant by the term "maturity" and how that, in turn, affects timing issues.

Common Misconceptions

One of the greatest hindrances that bond owners encounter are the misconceptions that they themselves hold about timing issues.

Misconception #1: *It does not matter when you cash a bond.*

Yes, it does. If you ignore timing issues, you can say good-bye to a maximum of up to six months of interest on most bonds.

Misconception #2: *All bonds increase in value at the same time.*

No, this is a dangerous assumption. Each bond has a unique increase date. Most bonds increase semi-annually; however, Series EE bonds purchased between March 1, 1993, and April 30, 1995, increase monthly up to the fifth year. Series EE bonds purchased May 1997 and after increase monthly. And Series I bonds increase monthly.

Many people mistakenly think that the increase occurs every May and November because that is when the market-based rates are published. Others think that the increase occurs every March and September because that is when the redemption tables are published. Those events have no connection to the actual date a particular bond will increase in value.

Misconception #3: *All bonds increase in value on the issue date and six months later.*

No. This misconception is particularly damaging to owners who hold older Series E bonds. Over 60% of the Series E bonds that are still earning interest increase in value at a time other than the issue date (and again six months later). Nothing on the bond tells you when the increase will occur. See Tables 7.5 and 7.6, pages 84 and 85.

Misconception #4: *Timing is not important when exchanging for HH bonds.*

Yes, it is. Many bond owners exchange their Series E, EE, or Savings Notes (SN) for HH bonds so that they can receive current income. The same timing issues that apply to the redemption of bonds also apply to an exchange. Choosing when to exchange can make a significant difference in your overall financial picture. See "Timing Issues At Exchange" on page 43 for more information.

Timing Issues at Redemption

Deciding when to cash a bond rests solely with the bond owner. The bank's role is to supply the bond owner with the correct amount of money on the day that the bond is redeemed. You—not the bank—are responsible for making certain that the time you picked to redeem is in your best interest. Unfortunately, many people do not realize the importance of properly timing redemption, as is illustrated in the following example.

A recently retired high school counselor owned U.S. Savings Bonds. He had previously cashed several $1,000 bonds purchased in the 1950s which had not yet reached final maturity. He thought that bonds increased in value every month and that it did not matter when they were cashed. Each of his bonds was valued at over $5,000.

The result was that this man forfeited up to $175 on each bond he cashed. If he cashed ten bonds in this manner, it would mean a loss of $1,000 to $2,000 in interest. (For options on obtaining a report which provides specific information on timing issues, see Chapter 7, "Tracking Your Investment.")

A difference of even *one day* can mean the loss of hundreds or thousands of dollars. This is because cashing a bond one day before an interest increase results in missing out on six months' interest for most bonds. Seldom is the best time "accidentally" selected.

How do I know when my bonds increase?

Each bond has a unique increase date pattern. Many older bonds increase at intervals that do not coincide with the issue date and six months later. See Tables 7.5 and 7.6 (pages 84 and 85) for the increase dates.

Exceptions: Any Series EE bond purchased between March 1, 1993, and April 30, 1995, will increase in value monthly for the first five years (thereafter they will increase in value semi-annually). This change in the bond program accompanied the drop in the guaranteed interest rate from 6% to 4%. Also, any Series EE bond purchased May 1997 and after will increase in value monthly.

Once the correct month is identified, on which day should I cash my bonds?

The increase will always occur on the first business day of the month. It will hold that value until the next scheduled increase, either the next month (for bonds that increase monthly) or six months later (for bonds that increase semi-annually). You will receive the same amount of money whether you redeem a bond on the first business day of the month or the last. **Note:** The date stamped on a bond does not alter this principle. This is illustrated in the bond on the next page.

Although the date stamped on this bond is March 28, 1990, the bond will still increase the first day of the month for each month that an increase is due, which in this case is March 1 and September 1.

Figure 4.1 Series EE Bond dated September 1986

Timing the Redemption of H and HH Bonds

H and HH bonds pay interest every six months. If you cash prior to final maturity, you will want to plan your redemption for immediately following an interest payment. Cash in too soon and you will forfeit up to six months of interest. For instance, an HH bond dated February 1987 pays interest every February 1st and August 1st. The best time to redeem this bond would be on or shortly after February 1st and August 1st.

On the back of the new HH bonds there is a statement that reads:

Redemption may be deferred up to one month if the bond is received in the month immediately preceding an interest due date with a written request to defer redemption until such date.

Technically, this means you can send your H or HH bonds to a Federal Reserve Bank (FRB) up to a month prior to the time you want to cash and tell them to hold the bond until the first of the next month so that you will receive your interest payment. The author advises not to do this. Just wait and send in your bond the first day of the month, on the date you received your interest payment. Here's why:

A client of TSBI submitted a request for redemption to a FRB along with a letter requesting that the bonds be held until the next interest payment (less than one month away from the date of his letter). Unfortunately, the bonds were cashed immediately and the interest payment (several thousand dollars) was not sent. This investor was never notified that his request (to hold the bonds) would not be honored. Consequently, he petitioned the Bureau of the Public Debt for payment of the interest that was due him and was advised of the steps he needed to take, one of which included NOT cashing the check for the redemption proceeds.

Two or three months down the road, the bond owner received both the redemption proceeds and the check for the interest. But he lost two things: Since he was unable to cash the redemption proceeds check for almost three months (the check was over $50,000), he was unable to invest the money for that period of time. Even at 5% that was a loss of over $600. Second, he lost a considerable amount of time, supplying all the necessary paperwork, making phone calls, etc.

Wait until you have received your interest. You may lose a couple of days if your redemption check doesn't arrive until the 5th or 6th of the month, but you may have saved yourself a much bigger headache and an even bigger loss.

Timing Issues at Exchange

An exchange occurs when you take the value of a Series E or EE bond or SN at the time of redemption and roll it over into a HH bond rather than accept the redemption value in cash. (This is often done to continue the tax deferral on the interest income of older bonds and also to receive a semi-annual interest payment from the new HH bonds.)

Suppose you have $50,000 in E bonds that you want to exchange for HH bonds because you want that semi-annual interest payment and the 4% interest rate. (The author is not suggesting that this is the best alternative. See Chapter 12, "Exchanging for HH Bonds," for more considerations.) Assume the average guaranteed interest rate on your E bonds is 6% and that you are giving no thought to the timing of the exchange. In a typical case, you would forfeit $750 to $1,500 by not investigating the best time to exchange. This is money that could have purchased an additional HH bond. If the forfeiture is $1,000, you not only missed the extra principal of an additional HH bond, but if you had held it for ten years, that HH bond would have netted an additional $400 in interest ($40 a year for ten years). Your loss now approaches $1,500.

Again, refer to Chapter 12, "Exchanging for HH Bonds," for exchange strategies and the selective redemption alternative.

Timing Issues at Final Maturity

When a Series E or EE bond or SN reaches final maturity (the point at which the bond stops earning interest), it will receive the last increase on the first day of the month in which the bond stops earning interest. For instance, a bond purchased July 1963 will receive its last increase July 1, 2003. No additional value will be added to the bond after that date.

Sometimes the final increase will be for a period less than six months. You may recall that bonds purchased prior to December 1965 used to have an odd number of years and months to final maturity. Final maturity on these bonds has since been changed to an even forty years. For instance, a July 1963 bond originally had a final maturity date of thirty-seven years and nine months from the date of purchase. Now this same bond will reach final maturity in forty years—July 2003. This bond's semi-annual increase occurs every April and October. So, it will receive an increase in April 2003 and again in July 2003—only three months later. The *final* increase is the only time when an E bond increase will not occur semi-annually.

A Series E bond issued in 1964 will earn interest longer than a Series E bond issued in 1966. Why?

A puzzled bond holder wrote in reference to the bond statement she had ordered from The Savings Bond Informer:

> *My bonds are Series E, purchased from 1965 to 1979. The statement gives the date that interest earnings would stop as 30 years from the date-of-purchase. I was under the impression that the bonds would earn interest for 40 years. Please explain if there is an error in the statement.*

The report that this bond owner received was 100% correct. Bonds that she thought would earn interest for forty years (those purchased December 1965 and after) are only going to earn interest for thirty years. Another bond owner stated:

> *It really surprised me that thirty-three of my 200 bonds had stopped earning interest. My bank didn't tell me anything about this. I didn't realize the "30-year, 40-year thing."*

Many bond owners don't realize the "30-year, 40-year thing."

Note: Any E bond forty years old or older has stopped earning interest. At the end of 1995, thirty-year-old E bonds (issued December 1965 and after) began to reach final maturity, thirty years from their issue date. This means that at the time of writing, all bonds issued in 1966 and 1967 have stopped earning interest, while those issued in 1962 and 1963 are still earning interest.

Which Bonds Have Stopped Earning Interest?

As of December 1998, the following bonds are no longer earning and/or paying interest:

•Series E bonds issued from 1941 to December 1958.
•Series E bonds issued from December 1965 to December 1968.
•Series H bonds issued from 1952 to December 1968.
•Savings Notes/Freedom Shares issued from May 1967 to December 1968.

Table 4.1 Final Maturity

Series & Issue Date	Final Maturity (Total number of years bond will earn interest)
Series EE	
1/80 to present	30 years
Series E	
12/65 to 6/80	30 years
5/41 to 11/65	40 years
Savings Notes	
5/67 to 10/70	30 years
Series H	
2/57 to 12/79	30 years
Series HH	
1/80 to present	20 years

Adapted from Final Maturity Schedule, Bureau of the Public Debt, U.S. Savings Bond Marketing Office

Exchanging for HH Bonds at Final Maturity

Do not wait too long. Once a bond stops earning interest, you have a one-year grace period within which to exchange it for an HH bond. However, you will earn no interest from the date of final maturity until the exchange. If you hold the bond for more than one year beyond final maturity, your only option is to redeem it. See Chapter 12 for information on exchanging for HH bonds.

Timing Issues at Purchase

A bond's issue date is the first day of the month in which it was purchased (assuming that the funds used to purchase the bond were available to the bank the month in which it was bought). Therefore, purchasing bonds late in the month is best because they will begin to earn interest from the first day of the month in which they were purchased.

What Does "Maturity" Mean?

Bond owners have sometimes been counseled to redeem bonds when they reach "maturity."Maturity has often been incorrectly defined as"reaching face value." Consequently, owners redeem bonds that would have continued to earn interest for another ten or twenty years. Investors also have to declare the full amount of interest in the year of redemption. It really hurts when this happens to people who are only a few years from retirement: They declare the interest income when they are most likely in the highest tax bracket of their lives.

Rules for Bonds Issued prior to May 1995

Bonds carry three different maturities: original maturity, extended maturity, and final maturity.

Original Maturity is the maximum amount of time it will take a bond to reach face value at the guaranteed interest rate. This date is set at purchase, regardless of when the bond actually reaches face value.

For example, an EE bond purchased in 1994 has an original maturity period of eighteen years. The guaranteed interest rate is 4%. If this bond ends up with an average market-based interest rate of 5%, it will reach face value in about fourteen years. However, the original maturity period will still be eighteen years. This means that the guaranteed rate of 4% will not change until the bond enters an extended maturity at the end of the eighteenth year.

Extended Maturity periods are always ten years long, except for the last one, which can be less. An extended maturity period begins when your bond reaches the end of the original maturity period. Bonds issued prior to May 1, 1995, will take on a new guaranteed rate as they enter their extended maturity period. A bond may have more than one extended maturity period. See Table 4.2 (page 49) for clarification.

Final Maturity is the date after which the bond will no longer earn interest. At final maturity you have two options: You may exchange your bonds for HH bonds (up to one year past final maturity) or redeem them. The value of your bond remains "frozen" once the bond reaches final maturity. In addition, IRS rules state that you are to report the interest earned in the year the bond reaches final maturity whether you cash it or not (unless you exchange for HH bonds).

Review an example of how the term "maturity," as described in three different forms above, would work on an EE bond purchased in November 1986. See Table 4.2 (page 49), the third line under Series EE.

A bond purchased in November 1986 will earn interest for thirty years. At the guaranteed rate of 6%, the bond will reach face value in twelve years. (**Note:**

If this bond earns more than 6%, it will reach face value in less than twelve years. The original maturity period, however, is still twelve years.) At the end of twelve years, the bond will enter a ten-year extended maturity period. At the end of this extended maturity period, the bond will be twenty-two years old. Since a bond purchased in November 1986 earns interest for thirty years, the last extended maturity period will only be eight years. The bond reaches final maturity thirty years from purchase, in November 2016.

Table 4.2 provides the original maturity and extension periods for Series E and EE bonds and SNs.

Why All Bonds are Not Created Equal

The original maturity period of a bond can range anywhere from fifty-four months to eighteen years. The variance is a result of different interest rates and purchase prices at the time of issue. As previously stated, some bonds earn interest for thirty years and others for forty years. In Table 4.2, note that a bond with an original maturity period of eight years, eleven months (purchased May 1959) will have a maturity schedule of three ten-year extensions and a final extension of one year, one month.

Each time a bond enters an extended maturity period, the guaranteed interest rate for that bond becomes whatever the current guaranteed rate is at the time. A bond purchased in January 1986 had an original maturity period of ten years and a guaranteed rate of 7.5%. Since the guaranteed rate was 4% on January 1, 1996, this bond now has a guaranteed rate of 4% for the next ten years.

Remember: The average of the market rates can be a factor on any bond five years or older. See Chapter 3, "Understanding Interest Rates."

Maturity Periods for EE Bonds Issued after April 1995

All EE bonds issued after April 1995 have an interesting twist. These bonds will receive a one-time catch-up—an increase in value to face value—if the bond has not yet reached face value by year seventeen. In essence that guarantees a minimum rate of about 4.12% if the bond is held for seventeen years.

The original maturity period for bonds issued under these rules is seventeen years. These bonds will continue to earn interest for a full thirty years from the issue date: an original maturity of seventeen years, an extended maturity period of ten years, and a second extended maturity period of three years.

What rate of interest will be earned after original maturity? The Treasury Department has not committed itself to a specific interest rate structure or pattern beyond seventeen years at the time of writing. While none of the bonds issued under the new rules will reach the seventeen-year mark until 2012, this will be an important issue for bond owners to watch.

Author's Note: The original maturity period for bonds under the new rules is significant in the unlikely event that the seventeen-year catch-up is necessary. It is also significant because the Treasury could assign different interest rates and/or interest rate structures to your bonds as they enter extended maturity periods. It would make sense for a bond to earn interest at 90% of the five-year Treasury yield for each six-month period as it enters an extended maturity period, but that is not a sure thing. The final maturity period is important as always, because the bond will not earn any more interest after that date.

Take time to learn about your savings bond investment. The number of people who relate stories of misinformation and financial mishap to The Savings Bond Informer, Inc. are evidence enough: Knowing each stage your bonds will go through is critical in avoiding costly mistakes.

Quick Tips on Timing and Maturities

- You can forfeit hundreds (in some cases, thousands) of dollars by cashing or exchanging bonds even *one day* before the interest accrual date.

- Most bonds have a unique increase accrual pattern that may or may not coincide with the issue date and subsequent six-month anniversary date.

- Series EE bonds purchased between March 1, 1993 and April 30, 1995 increase in value *monthly* for the first five years, semi-annually thereafter.

- You will receive the same amount whether you cash on the first day of the month that interest is credited to your bond or the last. Therefore, it is better to cash sooner in the month rather than later.

- You only have a one-year grace period to make an exchange after a bond stops earning interest.

- The best strategy when purchasing bonds is to buy late in the month since interest accrues from the first day of the month.

- Most bonds carry three maturities: original, extended, and final. When your bonds have reached final maturity—the point at which they are no longer earning interest—you need to cash or exchange them.

- Savings bonds stop earning interest after either thirty or forty years (depending on the rules they fall under), except HH bonds, which stop at twenty years.

Table 4.2 Guide to Extended and Final Maturity Periods

Issue Date	Original Maturity Period	First Extended Maturity Period	Additional Extended Period	Additional Extended Period	Additional Extended Period	Final Maturity (total # of years bond will earn interest)
SERIES EE BONDS						
5/95 to present	17 yrs	10 yrs	3 yrs			30 yrs
3/93 to 4/95	18 yrs	10 yrs	2 yrs			30 yrs
11/86 to 2/93	12 yrs	10 yrs	8 yrs			30 yrs
11/82 to 10/86	10 yrs	10 yrs	10 yrs			30 yrs
5/81 to 10/82	8 yrs	10 yrs	10 yrs	2 yrs		30 yrs
11/80 to 4/81	9 yrs	10 yrs	10 yrs	1 yrs		30 yrs
1/80 to 10/80	11 yrs	10 yrs	9 yrs			30 yrs
SERIES E BONDS						
12/73 to 6/80	5 yrs	10 yrs	10 yrs	5 yrs		30 yrs
6/69 to 11/73	5 yrs 10 mos	10 yrs	10 yrs	4 yrs 2 mos		30 yrs
12/65 to 5/69	7 yrs	10 yrs	10 yrs	3 yrs		30 yrs
All Series E bonds purchased after November 1965 will earn interest for 30 years.						
6/59 to 11/65	7 yrs 9 mos	10 yrs	10 yrs	10 yrs	2 yrs 3 mos	40 yrs
2/57 to 5/59	8 yrs 11 mos	10 yrs	10 yrs	10 yrs	1 yr 1 mo	40 yrs
All Series E bonds over 40 years old have stopped earning interest.						
SAVINGS NOTES						
5/67 to 10/70	4 yrs 6 mos	10 yrs	10 yrs	5 yrs 6 mos		30 yrs

Chapter 5

ORGANIZING YOUR BONDS

▶ *The Importance of Organizing Your Bonds*
▶ *What Information Is Needed for Record Keeping?*
▶ *Where Should Bonds Be Kept?*
▶ *How Should Bonds Be Organized?*
▶ *Where Should Your Bond Record Be Kept?*
▶ *Inventory Checks Are Critical*
▶ *"To Do" List*

You may be a very organized person. The books on your shelves may be in alphabetical order by the author's last name; all your spices may be lined up by name, container size, and country of origin. On the other hand, there are those of us who have trouble matching our socks each morning. As for organization—please!

Whatever your personal style, remember that bonds are the "do-it-yourself" investment. Record keeping is your responsibility.

The Importance of Organizing Your Bonds

When it comes to U.S. Savings Bonds, organization is a good idea. Why? Americans are currently holding more than $5.3 billion in savings bonds that have stopped earning interest. Many of these bonds are tucked into dresser drawers, stuffed into shoe boxes, or locked in safe-deposit boxes. In addition, many bonds remain unclaimed because the now-deceased bond owners kept no records for their heirs.

Most people treat their assets with considerable attention and scrutiny. Your savings bond investment should be no different. If a salesman tried to sell you a financial investment with the closing pitch, "Don't pay any attention to this for the next twenty to thirty years," you would probably tell him to get lost. Yet this is how many people handle their savings bonds.

The ability to provide detailed information to the Bureau of the Public Debt (BPD)—should the bonds ever become lost, stolen, or ruined—is a great reason to keep good records. True, the BPD does keep a master file of all bonds issued, but the more information you can provide, the quicker they can research and replace the bonds for legitimate claims.

What Information Is Needed for Record Keeping?

The following information should be recorded for each bond that you own:

- Social Security Number
- Serial Number
- Series
- Registration (names on bond, address)
- Issue Date (month and year)
- Face Value (or denomination)

Here is an example of where to find this information on the front of your bonds.

Figure 5.1 Series EE Bond dated September 1986

The Social Security Number. This number is found about one-third of the way down from the top of the bond, just above the bond owner's name. There is no social security number on most bonds issued prior to January 1974.

Serial Number. The serial number can be found in the lower right-hand corner. It ends with the series if your bonds are E, EE, H, or HH.

Series. The series identification will be in one of the four corners and usually at the end of the serial number.

Issue Date. This can be found in the top right-hand corner of the bond. (Ignore the issue stamp, which includes a specific day of the month. The issue date is above the stamp date.)

Face Value. The face value of the bond is the amount printed in the upper corner. The face value is *not* the purchase price (except in the case of Series I bonds).

(The bond pictured on page 52 is a Series EE with an issue date of September 1986 and a face value of $75. The social security number is 444-66-2222 and the serial number is K55555555EE).

Figure 5.2 (page 56) can be used to record this information; however, if you decide to track your investment, you may prefer to use the Do-It-Yourself Worksheet, Table 7.1, page 80. Review both alternatives before beginning.

Photocopies as Backup Records

If you do not feel like writing down all that information, make photocopies of your bonds. The front has all of the important information, so you don't need to copy the back. According to the bond consultants at the BPD, photocopying and faxing copies of bonds is legal. Photocopies can in no way be negotiated nor do they have any monetary value. But they can serve as a valuable resource to reconstruct bond holdings that have perished or that have been lost or stolen.

Where Should Bonds Be Kept?

While U.S. Savings Bonds do not need ultra-expensive housing, do not be careless. You might want to do better than one bond owner who returned fragments of what appeared to be a savings bond to the Federal Reserve Bank. It seems the color of the bond resembled the color of the dog's food. Fido had a tasty little snack, leaving only bits of a president's face.

If peace of mind comes best to you through a safe-deposit box, keep your bonds there. This may make sense if you want to restrict a co-owner's access to the bonds. (See Chapter 14, page 176, for additional information on the rights of co-owners.)

Safe-deposit boxes generally cost between $20 and $200, depending on box size and the part of the country you live in. If you only have a few bonds, the safe-deposit box's rental may cost more than the interest you earn.

If you choose to keep the bonds at home, keep them together in an organized fashion. If they are spread out in books, drawers, under the bed, and sewn into jacket linings, your heirs may never find them. Leave directions with your will detailing where the bonds are kept.

How Should Bonds Be Organized?

There is no exact rule on how bonds should be organized. Certain guidelines, however, will make life easier for you and anyone else who has to deal with your bonds (such as the Federal Reserve Bank, if your bonds have to be re-titled). Several different patterns of organization are possible, the worst being the "fifty-two card pick-up" method, which confuses everyone. One way to sort bonds is by series. There are six common series of bonds: E, EE, H, HH, I, or SN/FS (Savings Notes or Freedom Shares). Within each series, bonds can be further sorted by issue date (top right-hand corner), face value, or registration.

Where Should Your Bond Record Be Kept?

Keep one copy of your records with your bonds. An identical copy should be kept in a place safe from fire and theft. This second copy is very important. If the bonds are lost, stolen, or destroyed, that record will make the replacement process much easier.

Inventory Checks Are Critical

It is important to periodically check your bond holdings and here's why: The government will only search their records back ten years from the current date for bonds that have been cashed. The following is a situation you will want to avoid:

> *A couple had purchased hundreds of bonds through the 1970s and 1980s. They had been out of the country for over ten years and upon their return took inventory of their bond holdings. Much to their dismay, they discovered that some of the bonds were missing and unaccounted for. They had no record or recollection of cashing the bonds, so they filed a Lost Bond Claim Form. The BPD wrote and explained that because the bonds had been cashed*

*over ten years ago, they would not research or provide copies of the signa-
tures used to cash the bonds. Consequently, these bond owners had no recourse.*

Though government information states that "if your bonds are ever lost, stolen
or destroyed they will be replaced" (see Chapter 6, page 58, "Filing a Lost Bond
Claim Form"), there clearly needs to be a disclaimer. If someone steals and
cashes your bonds and more than ten years pass from the time of redemption,
you have no recourse.

"To Do" List

- Organize your bonds by series, then by issue date, face value, or registration.

- Use the Savings Bond Record Keeping Sheet to note social security number, serial number, registration, issue date, and face value for each bond.
Or use the Do-It-Yourself Worksheet, Table 7.1, page 80.

- Make a photocopy of the completed bond record.

- Put one copy of the bond record with the bonds; file the other somewhere else.

- Store the bonds in a safe place.

- Keep bond information with your will, stating the location of the bonds
and bond records.

- Do periodic checks of your holdings.

Figure 5.2 U.S. Savings Bond Record Keeping Sheet

U.S. Savings Bond Record Keeping Sheet

Name(s) of Savings Bond Owner(s)

Issue Date (Top right-hand corner)	***Face Value*** Front of bond	***Series*** E, EE, H, HH, SN, FS	***Serial Number***	***Social Security Number***

40

To receive an analysis for each bond you own, use the order form at the back of this book.

Chapter 6

RECOVERING LOST BONDS

▶ *Replacement Is Possible*
▶ *Filing a Lost Bond Claim Form*
▶ *What If I Never Received the Bond?*
▶ *Time Limitations on Claims*
▶ *Bonds Found after a Replacement Has Been Issued*
▶ *Whether or Not to File a Form*
▶ *Quick Tips for Recovering Lost Bonds*

Throughout a series of seminars the author conducted for the American Association of Retired Persons (AARP), a common concern was encountered:"When I was in the service I remember getting bonds, but I don't know whatever happened to them. I assume they are gone forever and I'm out of luck."If you or a family member have bonds that"they don't know whatever happened to,"this section may help you more than the lottery—but watch out for the"fine print."

Replacement Is Possible

Any validly issued Bond that is lost, stolen, destroyed, mutilated, or not received will be replaced either by a substitute Bond bearing the same issue date or by a check for the current redemption value, provided sufficient information and evidence in support of a claim is supplied.

—"Book on U.S. Savings Bonds"

57

U.S. Savings Bonds are not like cash. If you lose money, you stand very little chance of regaining it. Savings bonds, however, are a registered security. The government maintains records on all bonds that have been issued and will research those records for legitimate requests *free of charge*. There are two ways that the government classifies missing bonds:

1. **Bonds received and subsequently lost:** The bond owner received the bond, but at some point in time the bond was lost, stolen, or destroyed.

2. **Bonds purchased but never received:** A bond was purchased, but the purchaser never received it.

Filing a Lost Bond Claim Form

If there are bonds that you wish to locate, the first step is to get a copy of PD F 1048 ("Application for Relief on Account of Loss, Theft or Destruction of United States Savings and Retirement Securities," Figure 6.1, page 62). This form is available from four sources: commercial banks; the Federal Reserve Bank (FRB) that services your area; the Bureau of the Public Debt (BPD), phone (304) 480-6112; and the government's web site at www.savingsbonds.gov. If you attempt to obtain the form from your bank, call first to make sure they have it in stock.

Note: Only requests from persons who are entitled to research the bonds will be honored. You cannot research a friend's or relative's bonds unless you are in some way entitled and can document that entitlement. A copy of the police report must be supplied when bonds with a face value of $1,000 or more have been stolen.

The time it takes to research the bonds will be reduced if the Social Security and serial numbers that appear on the bonds have been provided. **Very important:** In some cases the bonds may not be located if this information has been left out.

The cover page of PD F 1048 has specific instructions for completion and return to the BPD. Allow up to a month or more for a response from the BPD.

A Nice Surprise for Those Who Have Lost Bonds

If you lose bonds and replace them, there is a nice surprise in store for you. The replacement bonds will carry the same issue date as the lost bonds. This means that if the bonds have not yet reached final maturity, they were earning interest the entire time they were lost. Not bad!

What If I Never Received the Bond?

> If a Bond is not received by its purchaser or a person designated by the purchaser to receive it, the buyer should contact the organization or institution which accepted the purchase application. . . .
>
> —"The Book on U.S. Savings Bonds"

Now that a majority of the bonds that are issued are coming from the FRB Regional Processing Sites, researching bonds that were purchased but never received has been streamlined.

When the bond was acquired through a Payroll Savings Plan and issued by a FRB, the purchaser's employer should be informed. The employer, in turn, should immediately notify the FRB.

The FRB will complete all of Part I of the claim form PD F 3062, "Claims for Relief on Account of Loss, Theft, or Destruction of United States Savings Bonds After Valid Issue But Prior to Receipt by Owner, Co-owner or Beneficiary." FRBs are expected to keep information for six months after bonds are issued and provide it on a claim form for the purchaser. The remainder of the form should then be completed and signed by all persons named on the missing bond. Both parents should sign on behalf of a minor registrant, and a court-appointed representative should sign on behalf of the estate of a deceased or incapacitated person named on the missing bond. If one or both parents cannot sign on behalf of a minor, or if there is no representative appointed for an estate, contact your FRB for instructions.

> Once completed and signed, the claim form should be sent to the servicing FRB. If a bond was not received and more than six months have passed since that bond was issued, the servicing FRB should be contacted for instructions.
>
> —Adapted from "The Book on U.S. Savings Bonds"

Time Limitations on Claims
a.k.a. Beware of the Fine Print

> If the records show that the Bonds have been redeemed, the claim usually will be denied unless someone other than the owner or co-owner has cashed the Bonds. In such cases, an investigation of the payment may be appropriate. However, **a Bond for which no claim has been filed within ten years**

of the recorded date of redemption is presumed to have been properly paid. Film records of paid Bonds are maintained for ten years following the recorded redemption date. In addition, **no claim filed six years or more after the final maturity of a Bond will be considered unless the claimant can supply its serial number.**

—"The Book on U.S. Savings Bonds"

This last line is critical. Series E bonds from the 1940s and 1950s reach final maturity forty years from the date of purchase. If you want to file a claim on a Series E bond that is over forty-six years old, you must have the serial number. In addition, we now have Series E bonds that have been issued December 1965 and after, that are thirty-year bonds. Bonds issued in 1966 and 1967 have already stopped earning interest, so the "six-year" clock is ticking. Once it is six years beyond the final maturity date, the government will only research a bond if the serial number is supplied.

Author's question: How many bond owners from the 1940s and 1950s do you think actually recorded the serial numbers of each bond they owned?

The government has devoted a tremendous amount of technological effort into developing their web site and offering the sale of bonds on-line. And while researching old bonds is a time-consuming and costly effort, it would be nice to see the Treasury devote the same energy, time, and ingenuity to helping investors—many of them older Americans—and their heirs recover what is rightfully theirs. Instead, time and effort is spent on just the opposite—developing and implementing rules that will ultimately restrict owners from their money. As previously stated, the government is holding $5.3 billion of Americans' money and using it interest-free. If a private company did the same thing, they would be subject to considerable government regulation and scrutiny.

Swiss banks are being rightfully chastised and held accountable for returning money that they acquired from victims of World War II. What about returning the money to the Americans who helped finance the war?

Author's concern: Recently upon inquiring about a lost bond claim form, the author was told that the BPD only searches by Social Security number, not by name (for bonds issued January 1974 and after). This is a great problem for investors who received bonds as gifts and subsequently lost them. Their own Social Security number may not appear on the bonds, and they may not remember who gave the gift. This is also a problem when bonds carry an incorrect Social Security number (due to a clerical error). If a bond search is limited to Social Security and/or serial numbers, the BPD may not locate legitimate claims.

Bonds Found after a Replacement Has Been Issued

If a lost Bond is found after a substitute or a check has been issued, the owner must return the original Bond immediately to the Savings Bond Operations Office, with a full explanation.
—"The Book on U.S. Savings Bonds"

Important note: When you replace a bond, the original bond becomes the property of the United States. If the original is recovered, it must be surrendered for cancellation. Sometimes heirs get excited when they discover bonds hidden in a relative's house, only to learn that the bonds had been replaced years ago and the replacements subsequently cashed.

Whether or Not to File a Form

When in doubt, fill out the forms and have the research done. The worst case scenario is that the bonds to which you thought you were entitled are not found. The best case scenario: "You're in the money!"

When a relative dies, encourage the personal representative of their estate to file a lost bond claim form. Maybe they had bonds that no one knew about.

Allow up to a month or more for a response from the BPD. It takes a little time, but the price is right.

Quick Tips for Recovering Lost Bonds

- The government will research lost bonds free-of-charge. Whether they can locate them will depend largely on the information you provide.

- To have bonds replaced, a lost bond claim form (PD F 1048) must be filed; it can be obtained from a bank, the FRB that services your area, the BPD—(304) 480-6112—or downloaded from the government's web site at www.savingsbonds.gov

- Once it is six years beyond the final maturity date, the government will research bonds only if a serial number is supplied.

- It is important to record key data which is found on each bond, including Social Security and serial numbers.

- Chapter 5, page 56, has a Savings Bond Record Keeping sheet that you can use to record your information.

- For bonds cashed over ten years ago, the BPD will provide no evidence of who cashed the bond.

Figure 6.1 Lost Bond Claim Form (PD F 1048)

PD F 1048
Department of the Treasury
Bureau of the Public Debt
(Revised June 1997)

OMB No. 1535-0013

APPLICATION FOR RELIEF ON ACCOUNT OF LOSS, THEFT OR DESTRUCTION OF UNITED STATES SAVINGS AND RETIREMENT SECURITIES

IMPORTANT: Follow instructions in filling out this form. You should be aware that the making of any false, fictitious or fraudulent claim to the United States is a crime punishable by imprisonment of not more than five years or a fine up to $250,000, or both, under 18 U.S.C. 287 and 18 U.S.C. 3571. Additionally, 31 U.S.C. 3729 provides for civil penalties for the maker of a false or fraudulent claim to the United States of an amount not less than $5,000 and not more than $10,000, plus treble the amount of the Government's damages as an additional sanction.
PRINT IN INK OR TYPE ALL INFORMATION

INSTRUCTIONS

("Bonds" in these instructions refers to savings bonds, savings notes, retirement plan bonds and individual retirement bonds.)

1. This form should be filled out and signed in ink.

2. (a) If the bonds are registered in the name of only one person as owner, whether or not another person has been named as beneficiary, the owner should execute Part I. If the bonds are registered in the names of two persons as coowners, Part I must be signed by both coowners and sworn to or affirmed by the one having knowledge of the facts concerning the loss, theft or destruction, except as indicated in (b). If it is not convenient for both coowners to join in one application, each should submit a separate application. If separate applications are furnished, the information provided in items 8 and 9 on the forms should agree. If the bonds are registered in beneficiary form, the beneficiary will be required to execute PD F 2243, unless the beneficiary signs Part II of this application. (If any person named on the bonds is deceased, a certified copy of the death certificate must be submitted.) If the registered owner is deceased, the beneficiary should complete and sign Part I.

   (b) MINOR OWNERS, COOWNERS, OR BENEFICIARY NOT UNDER LEGAL GUARDIANSHIP. A minor owner, coowner, or beneficiary not under legal guardianship should execute this application if, in the opinion of the officer before whom the minor appears for that purpose, the minor is of sufficient competency and understanding to comprehend the nature of the transaction. Otherwise it should be executed on the minor's behalf by both parents if living, *and*, in the event the minor does not reside with either parent, also by the person who furnishes the minor's chief support. The minor's social security account number should be furnished. If any parent is unable to sign on behalf of any such minor for any reason, a statement should be provided explaining the reason why this parent is unable to sign, whether or not this parent would have had access to the bonds and whether it is believed that this parent may now have possession of the bonds.

   (c) OWNER DECEASED OR UNDER LEGAL DISABILITY. If there is a legal representative in the case of (1) a deceased owner not survived by a coowner or beneficiary, (2) a minor owner or coowner, or (3) an incapacitated owner or coowner, Part I should be executed by the representative. The representative should submit a court certificate or certified copy of letters, under seal of the court, showing that the appointment is still in force, unless his/her name and official capacity appear on the bonds, in which case no evidence of the appointment will ordinarily be required. If there is no legal representative in the case of a deceased owner or incompetent owner, the Department of the Treasury should be fully informed as to the facts so that further instructions may be given.

3. *If any person other than the applicant had custody or possession of the bonds at the time of loss, theft or destruction or has first hand knowledge of the circumstances under which the bonds were lost, stolen or destroyed, the applicant should have such person furnish a statement on Part II of this form or a separate supporting affidavit. If the space provided in Part II is not sufficient in any particular case, the statement should be continued on a separate sheet which should be attached hereto.*

4. Part I (and Part II when required by Instruction 3.) must be signed before an authorized certifying officer or before a notary public or other officer authorized by law to administer oaths for general purposes. Authorized certifying officers are available at banking institutions, including credit unions, in the United States, and as further provided in the current revisions of Department of the Treasury Circular No. 530 and Public Debt Series, Nos. 1-63, 1-75 and 3-80. A certifying officer must impress or imprint the seal or stamp which he/she is required to use in certifying requests for payment. A notary public or similar officer must impress his/her official seal and show the expiration date of his/her commission .

5. If any investigation of the loss or theft was made by the police or other local law enforcement agency or by any insurance, transportation or similar business organization, please attach to this form a copy of the report of such agency if the amount of the bonds/notes involved exceeds $5000.

6. Ordinarily a substitute bond or check will be issued as soon as practicable after the Bureau of the Public Debt receives a report of the loss, theft or destruction. However, if its records disclose that the bonds have been cashed and it becomes necessary to refer the case to the United States Secret Service for investigation, substitute bonds or a check will not be issued until the investigation is completed.

7. The application and correspondence relating thereto should be sent to the Bureau of the Public Debt, Parkersburg, West Virginia 26106-1328.

8. The applicant should make and retain a copy of this form, or some other statement, with other important papers. This record should serve as a reminder to the applicant and to others who may have occasion to take care of the applicant's affairs that when relief is granted on account of lost, stolen or destroyed bonds, the original bonds become the property of the United States and must be surrendered to the Department for cancellation if they are recovered.

SEE INSTRUCTIONS FOR PRIVACY ACT AND PAPERWORK REDUCTION ACT NOTICE

Figure 6.1 Lost Bond Claim Form (PD F 1048) *continued*

For BPD use only:
Case File Name _____ Case Identification No. _____

PART I

The undersigned hereby severally affirm and say that the following-described bonds have been lost, stolen or destroyed and that the information given herein is true to the best of their knowledge and belief: (If application is made on account of destroyed bonds, any charred, scorched or undestroyed pieces should be submitted herewith.)

ISSUE DATE (If a specific date is not known furnish an approximate range of issue dates)	DENOMINATION (FACE AMOUNT)	SERIAL NUMBER	INSCRIPTION (Please type or print names, including middle names or initials, social security account number, if any, and addresses as inscribed on the bonds.)

(If space is insufficient, use a continuation sheet, sign it, and refer to it above. PD F 3500 may be used for this purpose.)

1. Are you the registered owner of the bonds? _____ If so, go to number 6., unless a minor is named on the bond with you. If a minor is named on the bond, go to number 5.

2. If you are not the registered owner, in what capacity are you acting? _____
   (See Instruction 2.)

3. If you are acting as a guardian or legal representative, have you been court appointed? _____
   [See Instruction 2. (c)]

4. What is your relationship to the registered owner? _____

5. If you are acting on behalf of a minor for whose estate there is no court-appointed guardian or other representative and the minor is not of sufficient competency and understanding to complete the questions in this application, answer the following questions: [See Instruction 2. (b)]

   (a) What is the minor's age _____ , Social Security Number _____ and your
       relationship to the minor? _____

   (b) Does the minor live with you? _____ If not, give the name and address of the person with whom
       he/she lives _____.

   (c) If you are not the father or mother of the minor, who furnishes his/her chief support? _____

6. (a) Were the bonds (1) lost? _____ (2) stolen? _____ (date of theft) _____ or (3) destroyed? _____
       (See Instruction 5.)

   (b) On what date was this discovered? _____

   (c) Who had them last, and for what purpose? (See Instruction 3.) _____

(2)

Figure 6.1 Lost Bond Claim Form (PD F 1048) *continued*

(d) Give the result of inquiry made of other persons as to their knowledge of the loss, theft, or destruction of the bonds. (e.g., who, besides you, had access to the bonds, where were they last placed, and on what date were they last seen?) _____

_____

_____

(e) List any identification documents (i.e., driver's license) lost or stolen with the bonds. _____

_____

7. (a) Has the owner, or anyone on the owner's behalf, received reimbursement from any source on account of the loss, theft or destruction of the bonds?_____

(b) If any reimbursement has been received, explain fully. (If reimbursement was by an insurance agency provide the agency's name and address.) _____

_____

_____

8. Do you wish: (a) bonds _____ or (b) a check _____ ? If you wish a check and the bonds are in the names of living coowners, state the name of the coowner to whom the check is to be drawn. Otherwise, if both coowners have signed this form, the check will be drawn to both coowners and the entire interest reported under the first-named coowner's social security number.

_____

(Series EE and HH savings bonds are not eligible for payment until six months from their issue dates.)

9. Mail bonds or check to: Name _____

Address _____
          (Number and street or rural route)   (City or town)   (State)   (ZIP Code)

    We, the undersigned, hereby severally petition the Secretary of the Treasury for relief as authorized by law, and if such relief is granted, hereby acknowledge that the original bonds shall thereupon become the property of the United States. Upon the granting of relief, we assign all our right, title and interest in the original bonds to the United States and hereby bind ourselves, our heirs, executors, administrators, successors, and assigns, jointly and severally: (1) to surrender the original bonds to the Department of the Treasury should they be recovered; (2) to hold the United States harmless on account of any claim by any other parties having, or claiming to have, interests in these bonds; and, (3) upon demand by the Department of the Treasury, to indemnify unconditionally the United States and to repay to the Department of the Treasury all sums of money which the Department may pay on account of the redemption of these original bonds, including any interest, administrative costs and penalties and any other liability or losses incurred as a result of such redemption. The undersigned hereby consent to the release of any information contained herein, or regarding the bonds described herein, to any party having an ownership or entitlement interest in these bonds.

Signature _____   Signature _____
                  (Name)   (Name)

Home   Home
Address _____   Address _____
         (Number and street or rural route)   (Number and street or rural route)

_____   _____
(City or town)   (State)   (ZIP Code)   (City or town)   (State)   (ZIP Code)

☐☐☐ – ☐☐ – ☐☐☐☐   ☐☐☐ – ☐☐ – ☐☐☐☐
Social Security Account Number   Social Security Account Number

☐☐☐ – ☐☐☐☐ – ☐☐☐☐   ☐☐☐ – ☐☐☐☐ – ☐☐☐☐
Daytime Telephone Number   Daytime Telephone Number

THE CERTIFICATION AT THE TOP OF THE NEXT PAGE MUST BE COMPLETED. SEE INSTRUCTIONS 2 (a) and 4. ON PAGE 1.

(3)

Chapter 7

TRACKING YOUR INVESTMENT

▶ *Options for Tracking Your Investment*
▶ *The Most Important Information to Know
   about Your Bonds*
▶ *How to Build a Savings Bond Statement*
▶ *Understanding Your Savings Bond Statement*

While money management became an increasingly hot topic throughout the 1990s, tracking your savings bond investment may be a new concept to you. Over the years, investors have been led to believe that all they need to know about their savings bond holdings is each bond's value and when it stops earning interest. Those are two important pieces to the puzzle, but if you are serious about getting the most from your investment, there is much more. U.S. Savings Bonds should be treated with the same scrutiny and attention as you would any investment. Therefore, this chapter provides options for analyzing your bonds and outlines the necessary components of a savings bond statement—a tool created by the author in 1990 to assist owners in evaluating their savings bond holdings.

Options for Tracking Your Investment

To determine the interest rates, timing issues, values, and maturity dates for each bond you own, you will need a little knowledge, a few resources, and some time. There are basically two options.

Option #1: Use the "Do-it-Yourself Worksheet" (Table 7.1, page 80) and follow the steps in this chapter to complete a statement of your savings bond holdings. Part of worksheet can be compiled through using the government tables alone, or in combination with the government's software program, the Savings Bond Wizard. (A review of the Savings Bond Wizard is included Chapter 19.) The costs include a phone call or letter to request the current government tables (these can also be downloaded from the government's web site) and the time to select and compute the information that applies to your bonds. The average estimate for completing a bond statement for 50 bonds manually is three hours.

Option #2: Contact The Savings Bond Informer, Inc. (TSBI) and let them do the work for you. You will need to send a list of your bonds (month/year of purchase, face value, and series) or a photocopy of all bonds, and they will produce a report that, in the words of *Newsweek* (October 4, 1993), is "... easy-to-read, easy-to-understand." An example of a TSBI statement is shown in Figure 7.1 (page 79). The cost for the service depends on the number of bonds to be analyzed, starting at $15. A complete price list and an order form have been included at the back of the book. Each bond statement addresses all of the primary questions outlined below. The TSBI bond statement also includes the exclusive "Savings Bond Informer Rating System.℠" This system provides a rating of each bond for the next two- and five-year period.

The remainder of this chapter is designed to help bond owners who prefer to do their own research and crunch their own numbers. And if you like working with numbers, this can be both challenging and enlightening.

Following are the important questions that must be answered about each bond you own.

The Most Important Information to Know about Your Bonds

Detailed Questions

1. What are my bonds worth now?

2. How much interest has accrued to date?

3. When will my bonds reach final maturity?

4. When do my bonds increase in value?

5. What is the guaranteed interest rate on my bonds?

6. How long is the guaranteed rate good for?

7. What are the current earnings?

8. How did my bonds perform the last twelve months?

9. When will my bonds reach face value?

Summary Questions

10. What is the total value of my bond investment?

11. How much did I pay for my bonds?

12. What is the total interest earned on my bonds?

An answer to each question is critical for wise management of your bond investment. The following is a brief explanation of why each answer is important.

1. **What are my bonds worth now?**
   Your bond holdings may be worth as little as half or as much as seven times their face value. Knowing the exact value of each bond will provide you with an accurate assessment of this vehicle within your investment portfolio. Practically speaking, if you want to cash some bonds next month, knowing the values will help determine how many you need to cash.

2. **How much interest has accrued to date?**
   For most bond owners, interest becomes a tax liability in the year the bond is cashed or reaches final maturity (exceptions may include bond owners who report interest annually, bonds that are eligible for the tax-free feature, and bonds exchanged for HH upon final maturity). For tax-planning purposes, this information is essential. (See Chapter 10 for more on tax issues.)

3. **When will my bonds reach final maturity?**
   Plan ahead. Remember: *Americans are holding over $5.3 billion in bonds that have stopped earning interest.* Don't join that crowd. Know when each of your bonds will stop earning interest, and have a plan for exchange or redemption. Chapters 12 and 15 will help you do this.

4. **When do my bonds increase in value?**
   Would you want to give away five months of interest on each investment you have? If you do not know the timing issues on your bonds, you will unknowingly end up making another contribution to Uncle Sam. Each bond issued before May 1997, that is over five years old, will increase in value twice a year. *Cash a bond one day before an increase and you will forfeit six months of interest.* For bonds purchased prior to December

1973, the increases do not always fall on the issue date and six months later. You will need a table to help you determine the correct dates.

5. **What is the guaranteed interest rate on my bonds?**
As was discussed in Chapter 3, each bond purchased prior to May 1, 1995, has a unique guaranteed and average market rate. Knowing these rates will help you determine whether to fold or hold.

6. **How long is the guaranteed rate good for?**
A guaranteed rate is not good for the life of the bond. Bonds purchased prior to May 1, 1995 assume a new guaranteed interest rate when they enter an extended maturity period. Many bonds that were earning 7.5% dropped to a new guaranteed rate of 4% as they entered extended maturity periods. You need to know which bonds are affected when. See Chapter 4 for details on maturity and extended maturity periods.

7. **What are the current earnings?**
This is the rate your bond will receive in the current six month earnings period. The earnings period varies from bond to bond. This rate is not a predictor of future performance beyond the current earning period. This rate does tell you what is happening "now." The best tool for assessing future performance is the Savings Bond Informer Rating System[SM] which rates each bond for the next two and five years.

8. **How did my bonds perform the last twelve months?**
Many investors like to evaluate their investments at least once a year. Determining how a particular bond or the entire bond portfolio performed over the previous twelve-month period informs an owner of the "actual" recent performance.

9. **When will my bonds reach face value?**
Five years? Seven? Ten? Twelve? Eighteen? Any of those answers could be correct depending on when your bond was purchased. The length of time depends on the purchase price and the interest rates assigned to a particular bond. The most important issue related to this question is the date that your bond reaches the end of the original maturity period (at which point the bond will be worth at least face value). At that time it enters an extended maturity period. For bonds purchased prior to May 1, 1995, entering an extended maturity period results in a new guaranteed rate being assigned to the bond.

10. **What is the total value of my bond investment?**
If you are looking at a large purchase, your bonds might provide just the money you need, so it is important to know exactly how much they are

worth. This will also give you an accurate number to put into your net worth statement.

11. **How much did I pay for my bonds?**

   This is your original cost, what you actually paid for the bonds (it is the cost basis even if you received the bonds as a gift). Face values can be misleading. Remember the ads on TV, "Buy this or that and get a free $200 U.S. Savings Bond." That $200 EE bond was bought for $100.

12. **What is the total interest earned on my bonds?**

   If you cash all of your bonds at one time, this is the amount you would have to report as interest income. Your tax bracket would then determine how much you pay in taxes.

How to Build a Savings Bond Statement

Resources

In order to build a bond statement, you will need several tables. The first two are a "Do-It-Yourself Worksheet" (Table 7.1, page 80) and a "Summary Statement" (Table 7.2, page 81). In addition, you will need to obtain the following government tables which have been reproduced at the end of this chapter for illustrative purposes only:

✓ Guaranteed Minimum Rates and Original Maturity Periods (see sample, Table 7.3, page 82)

✓ Table of Redemption Values for Series E and EE bonds (see samples, Table 7.7, page 86). The entire table for September 1998 to March 1999 (including Savings Notes/Freedom Shares) can be found in Appendix C.

✓ The United States Savings Bonds/Notes Earnings Report (Table 7.4, page 83)

Optional:

✓ If you would like to calculate the net yield for the past twelve-month period, you will need a redemption table that is one year old from the date you calculate your redemption values.

Important: All of the above tables will change over time, so the ones printed in this book will become outdated. *For this reason, use these tables only for the practice exercises in this chapter.* Before you calculate the information for your bonds, obtain the most recent versions. They may be ordered from the Bureau of the Public Debt or your regional Federal Reserve Bank or downloaded from the web. See Chapter 19 for addresses, phone numbers, and web sites.

Once you have gathered the above aids, you will need a pencil, calculator, scratch pad, and a big cup of strong coffee—and you are ready to begin. That is, assuming you have already organized your bonds. If not, it would be advisable to quickly review and follow the directions outlined in Chapter 5, "Organizing Your Bonds."

Instructions for the Do-It-Yourself Worksheet

Friendly hint: You may find it helpful to read through the instructions that follow, Steps 1 through 12, before you begin to enter information from your bonds onto your worksheets. This will save you from numerous u#n@p!r*I#n@t*a%b#l@e outbursts and give you a general sense of direction. In addition, you may decide that you only want to calculate the value and maturity dates and so choose to skip some of the steps. *The following instructions only apply to Series E, EE, and Savings Notes/Freedom Shares (SNs/FSs), not to H, HH or I bonds.* (See Chapter 12 for information on H and HH bonds and Chapter 18 for the I bond.)

Step 1: Locate the "Do-It-Yourself Worksheet," Table 7.1, page 80, and complete the information above the table (i.e., "This information is being calculated as of . . ."; this is the month you will refer to when you get to Step 5).

Step 2: Fill in the first three columns of the worksheet with information taken from your bonds as described below—series, date of purchase (month and year), and face value. The bond pictured in Figure 7.2 and the first line of the worksheet will serve as an example.

Figure 7.2   Series EE Savings Bond dated September 1986

Column A: *Series.* The series identification is listed on the front of the bond, usually in an upper corner. You will record either E, EE, or SN in column A. (It does get more exciting, really.)

Column B: *Date of Purchase (Month and Year).* This is also referred to as the "issue date" and can be found in the top right-hand corner of your bond, just below the series identification. (Ignore the issue *stamp* which includes a specific day of the month. It is below the issue date.) The issue date will determine which set of information applies to your bond. Record this in column B.

Column C: *Face Value of Bond.* The face value of the bond is the amount printed in the upper left-hand corner. The face value of the bond is *not* the purchase price. List this in column C.

> **Summary:** The bond pictured on the previous page, is a Series EE with an issue date of September 1986 and a face value of $75. This has already been recorded in columns A, B, and C of your worksheet. (Older bonds may not have the series and face value in the same place as that of the EE bond previously pictured. That information will, however, appear somewhere on the front of the bond.)

Step 3: Locate the table called "Guaranteed Minimum Rates and Original Maturity Periods" Table 7.3, page 82. It has been included as a reference for practice purposes.

In column B of the "Do-It-Yourself Worksheet," you have listed the issue date of each one of your bonds. **Note:** If an issue date is May 1995 or after, list N/A (not applicable) for that bond in column D and skip to Step 5. Otherwise, using each issue date, go to the left-hand column of the "Guaranteed Minimum Rates Table," under the section for your series, and find the range of dates within which your bond was purchased. Using that line look across the table under the heading of "Guaranteed Through Current Maturity Period." This is the guaranteed rate that currently applies to your bond: Insert this number into column D.

> **Summary:** From Table 7.3, we can see that the September 1986 bond has a current guaranteed rate of 4% (in the second edition of this book the rate was still 7.5%: that shows how important it is to track your investment). This is recorded in column D of your worksheet.

Step 4: To determine the Guaranteed Interest Rate Until . . . (GIRU) or, in other words, the date your next extended maturity period begins, go to Table 4.2, page 49, "Guide to Extended and Final Maturity Periods." Again, using the issue date, locate the range of dates within which your bond would fall. Next, move across the table to the right adding the number of years in each maturity period (original, first extended, etc.) **to the year** on your bond until you have sur-passed the present date. The end of the next extension is your GIRU date.

> **Example**: September 1986 shows an original maturity of ten years. This bond, then, entered its first extension on September 1996. Since September 1996 is past, the next date the bond will enter an extension is found by adding the number of years (10) found in the next extended period. The GIRU date for this bond is September 2006.

$$1986 + 10 = 1996$$
$$1996 + 10 = 2006$$

Step 5: To determine the current earnings for each of your bonds you will need the "United States Savings Bonds/Notes Earnings Report."

Again, using the issue date, move down the first column and locate the range of dates within which your bond would fall. Next, staying on the same line, move across the table to the right until you are under the column heading "Current Earnings." The percentage listed here is what your bond will earn for the six-month period covered by the table.

> **Example:** The bond from September 1986 is earning at any annual rate of 3.96% during this six month period. This is recorded in column E of the example line on your worksheet.

Remember: The current yield is not a predictor of future performance. It is the actual representation of current performance.

Step 6: Locate the "Interest Accrual Dates Tables," Tables 7.5 and 7.6 (pages 84 and 85). Once again, using the month and year of issue, locate the interest accrual date within the box that accommodates your issue date. Then, match the month that your bond was purchased to the month below the issue date. The two months listed to the right of your month are those in which your bond will increase in value. List these two months in column F on your worksheet.

> **Summary:** On the interest accrual table, the increase dates listed for the September 1986 bond are September and March. This is recorded in column F of your worksheet.

Skip column G for now, it is an optional step that can be done to answer the last of the detailed questions.

Step 7: Now it is time to calculate the redemption value for your bonds. For Steps 7 and 8 you will use the "Table of Redemption Values," Table 7.7. (To see the complete table that includes information for Series E, EE, and SNs for September 1998 to March 1999, consult Appendix C, page 253.) This table has been chosen for two reasons: First, it is the most common redemption value table available; second, it is free. (See the government web site for other free options www.savingsbonds.gov.)

Locate the year your bond was purchased (in the left-hand column of the table). Note that spot and look at the top of the table: There are six consecutive months listed (with year). Find the column that gives the date in which you wish to value your bonds: This is the "as of" date that you wrote at the top of the worksheet. Staying within the year that the bond was purchased, go down the column and find the month that your bond was issued (there may be a range of months without listing your specific month; if that is the case, find the range for your bond). Note the point where these two come together (intersect, collide, converge, join—you get the picture).

The value listed to the right of this point is the value of the smallest denomination for that particular series—a $50 Series EE bond or a $25 Series E bond or SN. **If you are valuing bonds other than a $50 EE or a $25 E, some calculations will be necessary to arrive at the correct value.**

If you have a Series E bond and the face value is other than $25, divide the face value of your bond by 25. Multiply that number by the value you identified in the redemption table. Copy the result into column H on your worksheet.

If you have a Series EE bond and the face value is other than $50, divide the face value by 50. Multiply that number by the value you identified in the redemption table. Copy the result into column H on your worksheet.

Summary: For our September 1986 bond, locate 1986 in the Issue Date column (the first column on the left). Note that spot and then find the "calculated as of" date which, in this case, is September 1998. As you move across the top of the page, you will see that September 1998 is the first column of data. Go down that column to the where the column and row intersect. You see the following months listed:

Nov.-Dec.	49.34
Oct.	55.42
Apr.-Sep.	56.54
Jan.-Mar.	57.66

Since the bond was issued in September 1986, we want the range of "Apr.-Sep." The value of a $50 EE bond issued September 1986 is $56.54 as of September 1998. However, the example bond has a $75 face value. Using the instructions above, divide the bond's face value—$75 —by 50. The result is 1.5. Now multiply the $56.54 by 1.5. The result is the value you see listed in column H on the example line, $84.81.

Step 8: Once you have determined the value of your bonds, you can calculate the interest. The basic formula is this:

Current Value - Purchase Price = Interest Accrued

The current value has been written in column H as a result of Step 7. The purchase price is different for each series, so make sure you use the number that applies to your series:

> *Series EE:* Purchase price is 50% of face value
> *Series E:* Purchase price is 75% of face value
> *Savings Notes:* Purchase price is 81% of face value

The face value has been recorded in column C of your statement. Once you have calculated the interest accumulated, list it in column I.

> **Summary:** The current value of the bond in the example is $84.81. Since this is an EE bond with a face value of $75, the purchase price was $75 x 50% = $37.50. Using the formula noted above, one can conclude:
>
> Current Value - Purchase Price = Interest Accumulated
> $84.81   - $37.50   = $47.31

Step 9: If your bond was purchased in November 1965 or before, add forty years to the issue date to determine the final maturity date. If your bond was purchased in December 1965 or after, add thirty years to the issue date to determine the final maturity date. List the results of your calculations in column J for each bond.

> **Summary:** The September 1986 bond will reach final maturity in thirty years; therefore, the final maturity date is September 2016. List this in column J.

Optional Step: To calculate the net yield for the last twelve months, two redemption values are needed—the current redemption value, which was calculated in Step 7 and recorded in column H of your statement, and the redemption value as of twelve months ago. To see how your bonds have performed, then, you must obtain a redemption table that reflects values for twelve months prior to your "as of" date. Use this table to calculate the bond's value as of a year ago. Subtract it from the present value and then divide the bond's one-year-old value by the difference. The outcome is the net yield for the previous twelve-month period.

> **Example**: On the example line of your worksheet (Table 7.1), you will find a value of $84.81 for the September 1986 bond. Assuming a Sep-

tember 1998 "as of" date has been used, a September 1997 redemption table (not pictured) reveals that the value of the bond was $81.51 twelve months ago ($54.34 x 1.5 because the face value is $75). The net yield for the past twelve months is 4.05%.

Subtract: $84.81 - $81.51 = $3.30
Then divide: $ 3.30 / $81.51 = 4.05%

Remember: The net yield for the past twelve months is a historic figure. It does not predict future returns, but rather represents a bond's actual performance over the previous year.

Another Optional Step: The last column on the "Do-it-Yourself Worksheet" has space to write the serial number for each of your bonds. Recording your serial numbers is not critical to determining interest rates, values, or timing issues. However, if they have not been recorded on any other documents, this column will provide a useful place for that information. The serial number can be invaluable in getting lost bonds replaced.

Instructions for the Summary Statement

The summary information will be written in on the "Summary Statement," Table 7.2 (page 81). This sheet will reflect the total redemption value of your bonds, the total interest accumulated, and the total purchase price.

Step 10: To determine the total redemption value of your bonds, add all of the numbers in column H of your worksheet. Note this on the summary sheet.

Step 11: For the total interest accumulated on your bonds to date, add all of the numbers in column I of your worksheet. Record the total on the summary sheet.

Step 12: If your calculations are correct, the difference between the totals you calculated in Steps 10 and 11 will be the total purchase price of all of your bonds. Subtract the total interest accumulated on your bonds from the total redemption value. Write this number on your summary page for "Total Purchase Price."

Want to double check? All E bonds were purchased for 75% of face value; EE bonds, for 50% of face value; and Savings Notes, for 81% of face value.

Congratulations. You have finished! (Or you cheated and skipped to this line!)

If you loved it, then the author recommends repeating this process every one to two years. The only columns of your report that will remain the same are columns F and J. Columns D, E, G, H, and I will change over time.

If you hated it, or quit, do not despair. Get a list of your bonds together (or photocopy the bonds) and send them to The Savings Bond Informer, Inc. As mentioned, they will perform the calculations for a small fee.

Understanding Your Savings Bond Statement

The following is a brief explanation of the information that you have listed in each column. **Disclaimer:** *This explanation does not assure that the calculations you perform are accurate.*

Column A: Series identification

Column B: The month and year in which you purchased your savings bond

Column C: The face value of the bond, that is, the dollar amount printed on the front of the bond (**Note:** A bond may be worth more or less than its face value. The current worth of your bond is given in column H.)

Column D: This is the guaranteed interest rate, published by the government, for your bond in the *current maturity period*. **If your bond is less than five years old, read the interest rate rules that apply to your bond later in this chapter**. It is possible to receive an interest rate higher than the guaranteed rate. There is no guaranteed rate for Series EE bonds purchased after April 30, 1995.

GIRU = Guaranteed Interest Rate Until is the date that your bond will enter the next extended maturity period, or if there are no extensions left, the date the bond will stop earning interest. When a bond enters an extended maturity period it will be assigned a new guaranteed interest rate (this applies only to Series E, EE, and SNs issued prior to May 1, 1995). The new guaranteed rate is the floor, or the minimum amount the bond can earn throughout the entire extended maturity period. Although Series EE bonds purchased after April 1995 still have extended maturity periods, the Treasury has yet to announce what rules will govern these bonds as they enter extensions.

Column E: This is your current earnings. This rate is only good for the current six-month earnings period covered by the table that you used. It measures the difference in the value of your bond between the last semi-annual increase and the next semi-annual increase. This is displayed as your annualized yield for that six-month period.

Column F: Interest is added to your bond on the first business day of the two months listed in this column. If you are planning to redeem or exchange bonds, remember that the value of your bond increases only twice a year: on the first business day of the month listed for that bond and again six months later. (This may or may not be the same month as your issue date.) If your bond was purchased after February 1993, read the new rate information on the following page.

Column G: Net yield for the last twelve months. This is an optional column. It represents the actual performance of your bond over the previous twelve-month period.

Column H: This is the redemption value of your bond as of the date listed above your name.

Column I: This is the interest income that you have earned on your bond. If you redeem a bond, the bank reports this to the IRS.

Column J: The month and year listed in this column represent the last time this bond will increase in value. Continuing to hold the bond after the first business day of the month listed will result in no additional interest.

Summary Statement Explanation

Total redemption value is the total value of all the bonds listed on your worksheet as of the date on your statement.

Total interest accumulated on bonds is the total interest accumulated on all the bonds in your worksheet(s). If you were to redeem all the bonds in your statement, the bank that redeemed the bonds would report this amount to the IRS on a 1099-INT.

Total purchase price is the amount that was actually paid for the bonds listed in your statement.

Rate Information for Bonds Purchased March 1993 to April 1995

All EE bonds purchased between March 1, 1993, to April 30, 1995, will carry a guaranteed interest rate of 4% for the original maturity period. They will increase in value monthly until they are five years old. If, at that point, the average of the market rates is greater than 4% (which it is, since none of the individual rates have been lower than 4.25% for the history of the market rate program), then the increase will convert to a semi-annual schedule from the fifth year on. These bonds will also receive a hefty yield (often over 10%), in the year they turn five years old.

Interest Rate Information for Bonds Purchased May 1995 to April 1997

These rules are easier to understand and follow because only one interest rate applies to a bond at any given point in time. (Under the old system, a guaranteed rate and a blend of market rates are assigned to each bond). If the bond is less than five years old, a market rate (based on 85% of the six-month T-bill yields) will be assigned to it every six months. If the bond is held five years or longer, a market rate (based on 85% of five-year Treasury yields) is assigned to it every six months. Under this system, what you see is what you get. There is no guaranteed rate under these rules. There is no retroactive feature attached to any of the market-based rates.

Interest Information for Bonds Purchased after April 1997

At any given point in time, only one interest rate will apply to a bond. The rate is based on 90% of the five-year Treasury yields. Under this system, what you see is what you get. There is no guaranteed rate or retroactive feature attached to any of the market-based rates.

As you can see, tracking your bonds provides information essential to understanding and managing your investment. You can now make decisions based on facts and knowledge rather than opinion and hearsay.

Figure 7.1 Sample: The Savings Bond Informer, Inc. Summary and Detail Listing

The Savings Bond
Informer, Inc.

Account #:CS00000106

Savings Bond Statement For:

NAME OF BOND OWNER

August 1998

P.O. Box 9249
Detroit, MI 48209
Phone: (313) 843-1910
Fax: (313) 843-1912

Statement Summary:

Number of Bonds on this Statement:.............	3
Total Purchase Price:...............................	$2,656.25
Total Interest Accumulated on Bonds:...........	$3,718.42
Total Redemption Value of Bonds:...............	$6,374.67
Interest Earned Year-to-Date:......................	$261.34

Consumer Notice: This statement reflects the rates, values and rating system in effect as of the date of this statement. The government can change the bond program at any time and TSBI, Inc. makes no guarantee of any future returns. The "Bond Statement Explanation Sheet" (enclosed with your order) provides a detailed description of each column including the exclusive Savings Bond Informer Rating System (columns G and H). Thank you for using our service.

Detail Listing of Savings Bonds:

A	B	C	D	E	F	G	H	I	J	K	L	M	N
Line Number & Series	Issue Date	Face Value	Guaranteed Rate	Guar. Rate Until	Current Yield	2-Year Rating	5-Year Rating	Increase Dates	Last 12-Month Yield	Current Value	Interest Accumulated to Date	Bond Stops Earning Interest	Notes
1 E	NOV 1960	$75	4.00 %	NOV 2000	4.00 %	D	NR	AUG & FEB	6.09 %	$540.03	$483.78	NOV 2000	
2 EE	JUL 1986	$5,000	4.00 %	JUL 2006	3.96 %	D	D	JUL & JAN	4.05 %	$5,654.00	$3,154.00	JUL 2016	
3 EE	AUG 1988	$200	6.00 %	AUG 2000	6.02 %	A	C	AUG & FEB	6.06 %	$180.64	$80.64	AUG 2018	

Page Totals: $6,374.67 $3,718.42   Page: 1

To order a savings bond statement, see the last page of this book.

Sort Order: Bond Order

Table 7.1
Do-It-Yourself Worksheet

This information is being calculated "as of" _____ (month/year)

Name of Bond Owner _____ page # _____

A	B	C	D		E	F	G	H	I	J	Optional
Series	Date of Purchase Month/Year (Issue Date)	Face Value of Bond	Current Guaranteed Interest Rate	GIRU	Current Earnings	Months that Bond Increases in Value	Net Yield Past 12 Months	Redemption Value as of Date Listed Above	Interest Accumulated on Bond to Date	Date that Bond will Stop Earning Interest	Serial Number or Notes
EE	Sep/86	$75	4.0	9/2006	3.96	Sep & Mar	4.05	$84.81	$47.31	Sep/2016	

Table 7.2

A DO-IT-YOURSELF SUMMARY STATEMENT
OF U.S. SAVINGS BONDS HELD BY:

_____

"As of" _____

Total redemption value of bonds listed on worksheets: $ _____
(total of column H)

Total interest accumulated on bonds listed on worksheets: $ _____
(total of column I)

Total purchase price: $ _____

Table 7.3 Guaranteed Minimum Rates and Original Maturity Periods
For Series EE, E, and Saving Notes
(This table is for September 1998 and is for practice only. Obtain the most recent chart for your own calculations. To order the table for the present month, see Chapter 19)

Issue Date	Original Maturity Period	Guaranteed Through Current Maturity Period	Life of Bond (years)
SERIES EE			
May 1995 to present	17 yrs	no guaranteed rate	30
March 1993 to April 1995	18 yrs	4.0	30
November 1986 to February 1993	12 yrs	6.0	30
March 1983 to October 1986	10 yrs	4.0	30
November 1982 to February 1983	10 yrs	6.0	30
May 1981 to October 1982	8 yrs	6.0	30
November 1980 to April 1981	9 yrs	6.0	30
January 1980 to October 1980	11 yrs	6.0	30
SERIES E			
March 1978 to June 1980	5 yrs	4.0	30
December 1973 to February 1978	5 yrs	6.0	30
December 1972 to November 1973	5yrs 10 mos	6.0	30
June 1969 to November 1972	5 yrs 10 mos	4.0	30
October 1968 to May 1969	7 yrs	4.0	30
December 1965 to September 1968		no longer earning	30
June 1965 to November 1965	7 yrs 9 mos	4.0	40
January 1961 to May 1965	7 yrs 9 mos	6.0	40
June 1959 to December 1960	7 yrs 9 mos	4.0	40
October 1958 to May 1959	8 yrs 11 mos	4.0	40
May 1941 to September 1958		no longer earning	40
SAVINGS NOTES			
October 1968 to October 1970	4 yrs 6 mos	4.0	30
May 1967 to September 1968		no longer earning	30

Table 7.4 U.S. Savings Bonds/Notes Earnings Report May 1, 1998 through April 1, 1999

VALUES AND YIELDS FOR $100 SERIES EE BONDS
May 1998 Thru April 1999

The table shows semiannual values for $100 Series EE Bonds.* Values for other denominations are proportional to the values shown. For example, the value of a $50 bond is one-half the amount shown and the value of a $500 bond is five times the amount shown. The Current Earnings Column shows the annual yield that the bonds will earn during the period indicated. The Earnings From Issue is the bond's yield from its issue date to the date shown or date adjusted as shown in the footnotes.

Series EE Bond Issue Dates	Earning Period		Earnings to Date when held 5 years***				Redemption Value***	
	Start Date**	End Date**	Start Value	End Value	Current Earnings	Earnings From Issue	Start Value	End Value
5/1998 -10/1998	5/ 1/1998	11/ 1/1998	50.00	51.28	5.12%	5.12%	50.00	50.64
11/1997 - 4/1998	5/ 1/1998	11/ 1/1998	51.40	52.72	5.14%	5.37%	50.68	52.04
5/1997 -10/1997	5/ 1/1998	11/ 1/1998	52.88	54.20	4.99%	5.45%	52.16	53.56

Series EE Bond Issue Dates	Earning Period		Start Value	End Value	Current Earnings	Earnings From Issue
	Start Date**	End Date**				
5/1987 -10/1987	5/ 1/1998	11/ 1/1998	95.84	98.68	5.93%	6.00%
11/1986 - 4/1987	5/ 1/1998	11/ 1/1998	98.68	101.64	6.00%	6.00%
5/1986 -10/1986	5/ 1/1998	11/ 1/1998	113.08	115.32	3.96%	6.80%
11/1985 - 4/1986	5/ 1/1998	11/ 1/1998	115.32	117.64	4.02%	6.69%
5/1985 -10/1985	5/ 1/1998	11/ 1/1998	117.64	120.00	4.01%	6.59%
11/1984 - 4/1985	5/ 1/1998	11/ 1/1998	120.00	122.40	4.00%	6.50%
5/1984 -10/1984	5/ 1/1998	11/ 1/1998	123.44	126.44	4.86%	6.50%
11/1983 - 4/1984	5/ 1/1998	11/ 1/1998	129.32	132.44	4.83%	6.60%
5/1983 -10/1983	5/ 1/1998	11/ 1/1998	134.96	138.04	4.56%	6.66%
3/1983 - 4/1983	9/ 1/1998	3/ 1/1999	142.48	145.76	4.60%	6.80%

*Monthly increases in value, applicable to some bonds, are not shown in the table.

**Each "Start Date" and "End Date" is for the first date of the range in the "Issue Dates" column. Add one month for each later issue month. For example, a bond issued 1/1997 would be worth $53.56 on 7/1/1998 and $54.75 on 1/1/1999.

***A bond issued on or after May 1, 1997, is assessed a three-month interest penalty if redeemed less than five years after its issue date. "Redemption Value" shows bond values without penalty. "Earnings to date when held 5 years" shows the amount upon which future earnings will compound.

Adapted from "United States Savings Bonds/Notes Earnings Report May 1, 1998 thru April 1, 1999," Bureau of the Public Debt.

83

Table 7.5 Interest Accrual Dates for Series E Bonds
•Bonds over 40 years old no longer earn interest•
•Bonds issued December 1965 and after earn interest for 30 years•

Issued September 1958 to May 1959	Interest Accrual Dates	Issued October 1968 to May 1969	Interest Accrual Dates
January	June & December	July	July & January
February	July & January	August	August & February
March	August & February	September	September & March
April	September & March	October	October & April
May	October & April	November	November & May
June	November & May	December	December & June
July	December & June	**Issued June 1969 to**	
August	January & July	**November 1973**	
September	February & August	January	May & November
October	March & September	February	June & December
November	April & October	March	July & January
December	May & November	April	August & February
Issued June 1959		May	September & March
to November 1965*		June	October & April
January	April & October	July	November & May
February	May & November	August	December & June
March	June & December	September	January & July
April	July & January	October	February & August
May	August & February	November	March & September
June	September & March	December	April & October
July	October & April	**Issued December**	
August	November & May	**1973 to June 1980**	
September	December & June	January	January & July
October	January & July	February	February & August
November	February & August	March	March & September
December	March & September	April	April & October
Issued October 1968		May	May & November
to May 1969		June	June & December
January	January & July	July	July & January
February	February & August	August	August & February
March	March & September	September	September & March
April	April & October	October	October & April
May	May & November	November	November & May
June	June & December	December	December & June

Adapted from "Interest Accrual Dates," SBD 2082, U.S. Government Printing Office, 1993.
*December 1965 to September 1968 Series E bonds no longer accrue interest as of September 1998.

Table 7.6 Interest Accrual Dates for Series EE Bonds and Savings Notes
•Savings Notes over 30 years old no longer earn interest•

SERIES EE		SAVINGS NOTES	
Issued January 1980 to April 1997*	Interest Accrual Dates	Issued October 1968 to October 1970	Interest Accrual Dates
January	January & July	January	January & July
February	February & August	February	February & August
March	March & September	March	March & September
April	April & October	April	April & October
May	May & November	May	May & November
June	June & December	June	June & December
July	July & January	July	July & January
August	August & February	August	August & February
September	September & March	September	September & March
October	October & April	October	October & April
November	November & May	November	November & May
December	December & June	December	December & June

Adapted from "Interest Accrual Dates," SBD 2082, U.S. Government Printing Office, 1993.
*Series EE Bonds purchased from March 1993 to April 1995 will increase in value monthly for the first five years.
Series EE bonds issued May 1997 and after increase in value monthly.

Table 7.7 Tables of Redemption Values (EE)

TABLES OF REDEMPTION VALUES FOR $50 SERIES EE SAVINGS BONDS

ISSUE YEARS	SEPTEMBER 1998		OCTOBER 1998		NOVEMBER 1998		DECEMBER 1998		JANUARY 1999		FEBRUARY 1999		ISSUE YEARS
	ISSUE MONTHS	$50	ISSUE MONTHS	$50	ISSUE MONTHS	$50	ISSUE MONTHS	$50	ISSUE MONTHS	$50	ISSUE MONTHS	$50	
1993	Dec.	30.18	Dec.	30.28	Dec.	30.38	July-Dec.	32.34	Aug.-Dec.	32.34	Sep.-Dec.	32.34	**1993**
	Nov.	30.28	Nov.	30.38	June-Nov.	32.34	May-June	33.12	May-July	33.12	May-Aug.	33.12	
	Oct.	30.38	May-Oct.	32.34	May	33.12	Mar.-Apr.	33.16	Mar.-Apr.	33.16	Mar.-Apr.	33.16	
	May-Sep.	32.34	Mar.-Apr.	33.16	Mar.-Apr.	33.16	Jan.-Feb.	34.62	Feb.	34.62	Jan.-Feb.	35.66	
	Apr.	32.30	Jan.-Feb.	34.62	Jan.-Feb.	34.62			Jan.	35.66			
	Mar.	33.16											
	Jan.-Feb.	34.62											
1992	Oct.-Dec.	34.62	Nov.-Dec.	34.62	Dec	34.62	July-Dec.	35.66	Aug.-Dec.	35.66	Sep.-Dec.	35.66	**1992**
	Apr.-Sep.	35.66	May-Oct.	35.66	June-Nov.	35.66	Jan.-June	36.72	Feb.-July	36.72	Mar.-Aug.	36.72	
	Jan.-Mar.	36.72	Jan.-Apr.	36.72	Jan.-May	36.72			Jan.	37.82	Jan.-Feb.	37.82	
1991	Oct.-Dec.	36.72	Nov.-Dec.	36.72	Dec.	36.72	July-Dec.	37.82	Aug.-Dec.	37.82	Sep.-Dec.	37.82	**1991**
	Apr.-Sep.	37.82	May-Oct.	37.82	June-Nov.	37.82	Jan.-June	38.96	Feb.-July	38.96	Mar.-Aug.	38.96	
	Jan.-Mar.	38.96	Jan.-Apr.	38.96	Jan.-May	38.96			Jan.	40.12	Jan.-Feb.	40.12	
1990	Oct.-Dec.	38.96	Nov.-Dec.	38.96	Dec.	38.96	July-Dec.	40.12	Aug.-Dec.	40.12	Sep.-Dec.	40.12	**1990**
	Apr.-Sep.	40.12	May-Oct.	40.12	June-Nov.	40.12	Jan.-June	41.34	Feb.-July	41.34	Mar.-Aug.	41.34	
	Jan.-Mar.	41.34	Jan.-Apr.	41.34	Jan.-May	41.34			Jan.	42.58	Jan.-Feb.	42.58	
1989	Oct.-Dec.	41.34	Nov.-Dec.	41.34	Dec	41.34	July-Dec.	42.58	Aug.-Dec.	42.58	Sep.-Dec.	42.58	**1989**
	Apr.-Sep.	42.58	May-Oct.	42.58	June-Nov.	42.58	Jan.-June	43.84	Feb.-July	43.84	Mar.-Aug.	43.84	
	Jan.-Mar.	43.84	Jan.-Apr.	43.84	Jan.-May	43.84			Jan	45.16	Jan.-Feb.	45.16	
1988	Oct.-Dec.	43.84	Nov.-Dec.	43.84	Dec.	43.84	July-Dec.	45.16	Aug.-Dec.	45.16	Sep.-Dec.	45.16	**1988**
	Apr.-Sep.	45.16	May-Oct.	45.16	June-Nov.	45.16	Jan.-June	46.52	Feb.-July	46.52	Mar.-Aug.	46.52	
	Jan.-Mar.	46.52	Jan.-Apr.	46.52	Jan.-May	46.52			Jan.	47.92	Jan.-Feb.	47.92	
1987	Oct.-Dec.	46.52	Nov.-Dec.	46.52	Dec	46.52	July-Dec.	47.92	Aug.-Dec.	47.92	Sep.-Dec.	47.92	**1987**
	Apr.-Sep.	47.92	May-Oct.	47.92	June-Nov.	47.92	Jan.-June	49.34	Feb.-July	49.34	Mar.-Aug.	49.34	
	Jan.-Mar.	49.34	Jan.-Apr.	49.34	Jan.-May	49.34			Jan.	50.82	Jan.-Feb.	50.82	
1986	Nov.-Dec.	49.34	Nov.-Dec.	49.34	Dec.	49.34	Nov.-Dec.	50.82	Nov.-Dec.	50.82	Nov.-Dec.	50.82	**1986**
	Oct.	55.42	May-Oct.	56.54	Nov.	50.82	July-Oct.	56.54	Aug.-Oct.	56.54	Sep.-Oct.	56.54	
	Apr.-Sep.	56.54	Jan.-Apr.	57.66	June-Oct.	56.54	Jan.-June	57.66	Feb.-July	57.66	Mar.-Aug.	57.66	
	Jan.-Mar.	57.66			Jan.-May	57.66			Jan.	58.82	Jan.-Feb.	58.82	
1985	Oct.-Dec.	57.66	Nov.-Dec.	57.66	Dec	57.66	July-Dec.	58.82	Aug.-Dec.	58.82	Sep.-Dec.	58.82	**1985**
	Apr.-Sep.	58.82	May-Oct.	58.82	June-Nov.	58.82	Jan.-June	60.00	Feb.-July	60.00	Mar.-Aug.	60.00	
	Jan.-Mar.	60.00	Jan.-Apr.	60.00	Jan.-May	60.00			Jan.	61.20	Jan.-Feb.	61.20	
1984	Nov.-Dec.	60.00	Nov.-Dec.	60.00	Dec	60.00	Nov.-Dec.	61.20	Nov.-Dec.	61.20	Nov.-Dec.	61.20	**1984**
	Oct.	60.16	May-Oct.	61.72	Nov.	61.20	July-Oct.	61.72	Aug.-Oct.	61.72	Sep.-Oct.	61.72	
	May-Sep.	61.72	Jan.-Apr.	64.66	June-Oct.	61.72	May-June	63.22	May-July	63.22	May-Aug.	63.22	
	Apr	63.00			May	63.22	Jan.-Apr.	64.66	Feb.-Apr.	64.66	Mar.-Apr.	64.66	
	Jan.-Mar.	64.66			Jan.-Apr.	64.66			Jan	66.22	Jan.-Feb.	66.22	
1983	Nov.-Dec.	64.66	Nov.-Dec.	64.66	Dec	64.66	Nov.-Dec.	66.22	Nov.-Dec.	66.22	Nov.-Dec.	66.22	**1983**
	Oct.	65.74	May-Oct.	67.48	Nov.	66.22	July-Oct.	67.48	Aug.-Oct.	67.48	Sep.-Oct.	67.48	
	May-Sep.	67.48	Mar.-Apr.	71.24	June-Oct.	67.48	May-June	69.02	May-July	69.02	May-Aug.	69.02	
	Apr.	69.38	Jan.-Feb.	72.30	May	69.02	Mar.-Apr.	71.24	Mar.-Apr.	71.24	Mar.-Apr.	71.24	
	Mar.	71.24			Mar.-Apr.	71.24	Jan.-Feb.	72.30	Feb.	72.30	Jan.-Feb.	74.46	
	Jan.-Feb.	72.30			Jan.-Feb.	72.30			Jan.	74.46			
1982	Nov.-Dec.	72.30	Nov.-Dec.	72.30	Dec.	72.30	Nov.-Dec.	74.46	Nov.-Dec.	74.46	Nov.-Dec.	74.46	**1982**
	Oct.	78.78	May-Oct.	81.14	Nov.	74.46	July-Oct.	81.14	Aug.-Oct.	81.14	Sep.-Oct.	81.14	
	Apr.-Sep.	81.14	Jan.-Apr.	83.58	June-Oct.	81.14	Jan.-June	83.58	Feb.-July	83.58	Mar.-Aug.	83.58	
	Jan.-Mar.	83.58			Jan.-May	83.58			Jan.	86.08	Jan.-Feb	86.08	
1981	Oct.-Dec.	83.58	Nov.-Dec.	83.58	Dec	83.58	July-Dec.	86.08	Aug.-Dec.	86.08	Sep.-Dec.	86.08	**1981**
	May-Sep.	86.08	May-Oct.	86.08	June-Nov.	86.08	May-June	88.66	May-July	88.66	May-Aug.	88.66	
	Apr	88.18	Jan.-Apr.	90.82	May	88.66	Jan.-Apr.	90.82	Feb.-Apr.	90.82	Mar.-Apr.	90.82	
	Jan.-Mar.	90.82			Jan.-Apr.	90.82			Jan.	93.54	Jan.-Feb.	93.54	
1980	Nov.-Dec.	90.82	Nov.-Dec.	90.82	Dec	90.82	Nov.-Dec.	93.54	Nov.-Dec.	93.54	Nov.-Dec.	93.54	**1980**
	Oct.	95.28	May-Oct.	98.14	Nov.	93.54	July-Oct.	98.14	Aug.-Oct.	98.14	Sep.-Oct.	98.14	
	May-Sep.	98.14	Jan.-Apr.	100.10	June-Oct.	98.14	May-June	101.10	May-July	101.10	May-Aug.	101.10	
	Apr.	97.18			May	101.10	Jan.-Apr.	100.10	Feb.-Apr.	100.10	Mar.-Apr.	100.10	
	Jan.-Mar.	100.10			Jan.-Apr.	100.10			Jan	103.10	Jan.-Feb.	103.10	

Adapted from Tables of Redemption Values, Department of the Treasury, Bureau of the Public Debt.

Chapter 8

MAKING THE DECISION TO HOLD OR FOLD

▶ *The Best and Worst Performing Bonds*
▶ *The Maybes*
▶ *What About the Rest of the Bonds You Are Holding?*
▶ *Quick Tips on Holding and Folding*

Over the last two years, one question has been asked of the author more than any other, "Should I cash my bonds or keep them?" As with many investments, some savings bonds are winners and some are losers. Like playing a hand in a card game, there is a time and reason to hold certain bonds and to fold others. Determining which is which is the key to playing a good game, but an attempt at this kind of evaluation does not always provide clear-cut answers. Therefore, in addition to revealing which bonds to hold and which to fold, this chapter will help you sort out the "maybes."

The Best and Worst Performing Bonds

Hold These

EE bonds purchased between November 1993 and April 1995 should be held until they turn five years old. Why? They carry the distinction of being the top performers in the savings bond program over the next one to two years. This is because these bonds will provide short-term yields that make other conservative products jealous.

What is so magic about five years? These bonds earn 4% a year for the first four years, eleven months. However, when they turn five years old, they receive a market rate average (currently between 5% to 5.5%) retroactive to the date of purchase. Because this rate is taken retroactive over five years, the net effect is a short-term yield of over 9% in the year that the bond turns five years old. That's a great return on a *conservative* investment and worth waiting for.

Once the bonds turn five years old, the rate of interest they earn will drop back down to 4.5% to 5.5% if market rates remain relatively flat. Here's an example:

> *Josiah has $15,000 in savings bonds that were purchased in November 1993. They have been increasing in value about $300 to $325 every six months. On November 1, 1998, his bonds received a retroactive credit based on the average market rate of interest. This increase will be over $700 more than its value six months ago. The yield for this period—more than 9%.*

Any bond issued May 1995 and after does not get this five-year, retroactive bonus. The reason: The (Gatt-cha) rules implemented in May 1995 did away with the retroactive bonus that was offered for older bonds.

Fold These

As incredible as this may sound, it is true—the government is holding more than $5.3 billion of American's money (in savings bonds) that have stopped earning interest. Because they are not notified, many unsuspecting investors hold their bonds past their final maturity date. Therefore, Uncle Sam is able to continue to use their money as an interest-free loan.

Savings bonds that no longer earn interest should be cashed or exchanged. (If a bond is one year past final maturity, it cannot be exchanged. See Chapter 12, "Exchanging for HH Bonds.") But before examining the list of bonds that fall in this category, you should familiarize yourself with the tax issues.

Tax Consequences

- When you cash a bond, you receive a 1099-INT for all the interest earned during the life of the bond. This interest is to be reported as interest income in the year the bond is cashed (unless previously reported and you can provide proof). The interest is subject to federal tax, but exempt from state and local tax.

- If you received bonds as a gift or through an inheritance, the possibility exists that some of the interest may have already been reported. You should check (whenever possible) with the people involved with the transaction (attornys, CPAs, executor of the estate, living relatives) to see if any of the savings bond interest was previously reported. If it was, obtain written proof (since IRS won't "take your word" for it). This may reduce your tax liability when cashing the bonds.

A fuller description of tax at redemption is provided in Chapter 10 "Taxation Issues for U.S. Savings Bonds," page 107. If you are considering a redemption, take time to learn about the tax issues before, not after, the event.

Savings Bonds that No Longer Earn Interest

- Any E bond issued before December 1965 and that is over 40 years old

- Any E bond issued after November 1965 and that is over 30 years old

- Any Savings Note/Freedom Share issued after November 1965 and that is over 30 years old

- Any H bond over 30 years old

Pass this list to your friends, relatives, co-workers, and anyone else who may own savings bonds.

The Maybes

Hold These???

How does 6% on a conservative investment sound? At the time of writing, it beats most CDs, money market accounts, new savings bonds, and, certainly, savings accounts. Many of your bonds may be earning 6% if they fit the following description.

The Potential Keepers

- Any bond issued from November 1986 to February 1993 will earn 6% until it turns twelve years old. When the bond is twelve, it can pick up a new guaranteed rate that may reduce future earnings. At 6%, you are receiving almost a full point (100 basis points) higher than the current EE bond rate of 5.06%.

- Other older bonds have rates that range from 4% to 6%. Many bonds from the 1960s and 1970s still earn 6%. To identify the rate that each of your bonds is earning, use Chapter 7 to learn how to track your investment or have an independent service, such as The Savings Bond Informer, do it for you. (See the last page of the book for more information.)

Fold These???

There are two groups of bonds that win the prize for poor performance and will continue to do so for quite some time. By cashing these bonds and purchasing new ones (if you want), you will immediately begin to earn a higher rate of interest. Historically this rate has often been over 1.5% higher (150 basis points). Before we tell you which these are, however, here are several facts that could have bearing on your decision.

Important Facts to Consider Prior to Redemption

- When you cash a bond, you receive a 1099-INT for all the interest earned during the life of the bond. This interest is to be reported as interest income in the year the bond is cashed (unless previously reported and you can provide proof). The interest is subject to federal tax, but exempt from state and local tax.

- Because cashing a bond creates a taxable event, you will have less than your redemption value to invest in another bond or financial product.

  Anne wants to cash $10,000 of her EE bonds and plans on purchasing $10,000 of new EE bonds. The $10,000 value of her current holdings is comprised of the $5,000 purchase price and $5,000 of interest. When cashing the bonds, she has to report the $5,000 of interest as income. Because she is in a 15% tax bracket, she will have to pay approximately $750 in taxes. The redemption value ($10,000) minus her taxes ($750) leaves Anne with $9,250 to reinvest in EE bonds.

- Your tax bill is a "pay me now" or "pay me later" proposition. Even when you die, your heirs will have to report all the interest back to the date of purchase when they cash the bonds. (See Chapter 10 for possible alternatives). Even though you may not want to create a taxable event now, by doing nothing you will only defer it until later.

- The limit on new purchases of EE bonds is $15,000 per person per year. If you redeem a large amount of bonds, you may not be able to reinvest the entire amount in new EE bonds in the same year. Consult Chapter 14 on purchasing bonds for ways to buy more than the limit in one year. You can buy up to $30,000 a year in I bonds; however the I bond rate at the time of writing is below 5%.

Your Potential Hit List

- **Bonds Purchased between May 1986 and October 1986:** Congratulations, you beat the system for the first ten years that you held these bonds. During that time, you received 7.5%. The bad news . . . these bonds are currently earning only 4% and that rate is unlikely to change before the year 2006. For a complete explanation of what happened and why see Chapter 3. If 4% is unattractive, but you want to keep your money in savings bonds, consider that the new EE bonds pay 5.06% at the time of writing.

Remember that since these bonds are over ten years old, you may have a hefty tax bill when cashing as illustrated in the following example.

Dave and Debbie bought $15,000 (face value) of October 1986 bonds that are currently worth $16,626. If they cash these bonds now, they will have to report $9,126 of interest income. Their combined income puts them in a 28% tax bracket, making their tax bill $2,555. This leaves them $14,071 to reinvest in new EE bonds. Assuming the couple hold these new EE bonds for eight years and then redeem them, if the EE bonds average 5.25%, that will leave approximately $19,824 after taxes. If, on the other hand, Dave and Debbie hold the October 1986 bonds for the same length of time and then redeem them, they will have approximately $18,855 left after taxes. By cashing now and taking the tax hit, they gain over $1,000. This assumes that their tax bracket is the same today as it will be when they cash the new EE bonds.

Since these bonds have eight years until they receive an interest rate of more than 4% (at time of writing), they are the worst performers in the bond program (except for bonds that have stopped earning interest).

- **Bonds Purchased between May 1995 and April 1997:** These bonds are the infamous result of a rule change that was supposedly for the investor's benefit. Why are these bonds on the "hit list?" You receive only 85% of six-month T-bill yields for the first five years (historically that rate has averaged 1 to 1.5% lower than yields tied to the five year Treasury yield). After five years, you receive 85% of the five-year Treasury yield instead of 90% like that of the current EE bond.

  Since these bonds were recently issued, in most cases you do not have a significant amount of interest to report when cashing them. An increase in the interest rate of 0.5% to 1.5% will result in an increase in your return of $50 to $150 per year per $10,000 invested.

What About the Rest of the Bonds You Are Holding?

Any bond over five years old is earning between 4 and 6.1%. Which ones do you hold and which ones do you cash? The answer is not cut and dried. As you will see in the next chapter, it depends on what you consider to be an acceptable rate of return, what your specific bonds are earning, what your other investment options are, and whether you want to create a taxable event should you decide to cash in.

If your bonds are earning an average of 5% (halfway between the 4% and 6%), they are on a pace to double in value every fourteen years. However, the interest rate can vary from bond to bond.

Knowing which bonds are earning rates of interest below 5% and which are above 5% will allow you to be even more selective in your decisions. For yields that govern the next six months, consult the government yield tables (to order see page 226) or obtain a statement from the Savings Bond Informer, Inc. (see the last page of the book). The Savings Bond Informer Rating System[SM] provides an additional factor in identifying which bonds are better than others—a specific two- and five-year rating for each bond in your portfolio.

You may have turned to this section first, hoping to get a quick and easy answer about whether you should "cash all your bonds or not." If your bonds were not specifically mentioned, do not rush your decision. Spend the extra time (either with this book, the government tables, on the government's web site, or obtaining a report from The Savings Bond Informer, Inc.) to learn the specifics that will enable you to make informed decisions about each of your bonds.

Quick Tips on Holding and Folding

- If your bond is less than five years old, and purchased prior to May 1995, you have the best performing bond in the program: Hold for now.

- Check to make sure that each of your bonds is still earning interest. If not, it's time to fold.

- Always consider the tax consequences before cashing your bonds.

- Many bonds are still earning guaranteed rates of 6%. These will be among the best performers of your holdings.

- If you bought bonds between May 1986 and October 1986, you have the worst performing bonds in the program.

- For many of your older bonds, whether to hold or fold must be based on several factors: potential tax liability, the rate of interest each of your bonds is earning now and will earn in the future, what you feel is an acceptable rate of return, and your other investment options.

Chapter 9

COMPARING SAVINGS BONDS TO OTHER INVESTMENT OPTIONS

▶ *What About Those Who Say, "Just Cash Them All"?*
▶ *Which Savings Bond Rate Should Be Used?*
▶ *Evaluating New Bond Purchases*
▶ *Evaluating an Exchange*
▶ *Savings Bonds vs. Savings Accounts, CDs,*
   and Money Market Funds
▶ *Savings Bonds vs. Treasury Bills, Notes, and Bonds*
▶ *Savings Bonds vs. Pork Bellies*
▶ *Quick Tips on Comparisons*

As stated in the preface, the author's purpose in writing this book is neither to recommend the redemption nor purchase of savings bonds. (Although if people cease to buy bonds there will eventually no longer be a need for this publication!) Rather than try to define for you where to keep your money, then, the intent of this chapter is to provide a framework within which savings bonds can be compared to other investments.

The person who dismisses all bond holdings because you can "do better elsewhere" probably fails to take into account that each investor's financial position is unique and contains elements that are not a part of other portfolios. This would include your personal tax standing (i.e., the tax bracket that you are currently in and the one you anticipate being in during the next five to ten years); risk tolerance (i.e., the amount of sleep you are able to get in direct relation to the amount of money you have in riskier investments); and asset allocation (i.e., the amount of money invested in savings bonds in relation to your overall portfolio—10%, 25%, or 50%, etc.). Before introducing the structure you need for a fair comparison, we will take a brief look at how to spot bad advice.

What About Those Who Say, "Just Cash Them All"?

The author has conducted hundreds of interviews for radio, television, and print media. He has also worked with thousands of financial professionals. The vast majority work hard to provide accurate, useful information. Occasionally, however, someone will make a bold statement that is not in the best interest of the bond owner. For example, anyone who says, "you don't need to do a comparison, just cash all your bonds," without reviewing a written analysis of your holdings is not giving sound counsel. In this case, it is best to ask the following questions: Does the person making the suggestion have a vested interest in your action, that is, "cashing all your bonds?" Have they provided you with the specific analysis and data to support their recommendation? (**Note:** The Savings Bond Wizard, although a good program for determining the worth of your bonds, is not a sufficient tool for evaluating bonds. If someone tells you the values of your bonds and then concludes with advice to cash them, they have not provided you with an analysis.) Do they have a systematic plan for redemption that will minimize tax consequences and take advantage of the bond increase date? The following scenarios reveal how bad advice can be financial damaging when comparing bonds to other investment options.

Scenario #1: A couple purchased $30,000 ($60,000 face value) in bonds in October 1986, locking in a guaranteed rate of 7.5% for ten years. On September 15, 1996, a "money expert" advised them to cash all the bonds and invest in mutual funds. The advice was followed and the bonds were redeemed that very week. Unfortunately, they forfeited $2,260 that would have been theirs had the bonds been held for another 15 days (until October 1). If we annualize it, this return equals 90%. Is there a mutual fund that is guaranteed to perform that well? Furthermore, they then had less money to invest in the mutual fund because they cashed just before the bond was to be credited with an increase.

Scenario #2: Once again, assume that the "money expert" mentioned in Scenario #1 gave the same advice about the October 1986 bonds. In this case, however, the bond owner's tax bracket was to change in the next year from 28% to 15% due to retirement. Because all the bonds were cashed, all of the interest was taxed in their then-current bracket of 28%. Had the couple waited until January 1 to cash, some or all of the interest would have been taxed at 15%. Assuming that half the interest was taxed at 15%, an additional $1,489.06 would have been available to invest in some other"hot"option that was proposed.

This sort of advice is generally borne from the fact that the stock market and mutual funds have consistently outperformed savings bonds over the last de-cade. Remember, though, timing and tax issues must be considered before"cash-ing all your bonds."Remember, too, that stocks or mutual funds possess a much greater risk of value fluctuation than do savings bonds (such as an overall mar-ket loss of more than 10% in a four-week period at the time of writing).

Which Savings Bond Rate Should Be Used?

Recently the track and field world was debating who was the fastest man on earth. Was it the winner of the 100-yard dash or the winner of the 220-yard dash? Ultimately a distance was set and the two winners raced to settle the matter. You see, there had to be a common starting and ending point.

To start a comparison process with your savings bonds, it is critical to pick the right"starting point."That is why this chapter examines the three govern-ment-published rates and whether each, or any, of these rates offers a reason-able "starting point." However, since most bond owners are concerned with performance over the next several years, historic data (looking backward) and short-term data (measuring only six-months of performance) are both lacking as a useful starting point. Here are the most common, government-published (free), rates used to analyze savings bonds:

- The average annual yield
- The six-month earnings rate
- The guaranteed rate

A fourth source of data will be described at the end of this section (fee-based):

- The Savings Bond Informer Rating System[SM]

As outlined in Chapter 3,"Understanding Interest Rates," EE bonds bought after April 1995 are governed by a"what you see is what you get"program. But what about older bonds that carry both the guaranteed and average market rates? Which rates should be used to evaluate future earnings? What about the government's new yield tables that show the average annual yield from the date of purchase? What about the yield table that shows the earnings rate for the next six months?

The author's experience has been that most bond owners are not as concerned with the next six months' yield as they are with long range projections. This is because bonds may be part of their retirement planning or the means for funding the educational expenses of that little one. These investors want to make a decision now about whether to stick around for the long haul or move on.

It can be debated which interest rates or yields should be used to predict a bond's long-term performance. Since there are many different interest rates and yields published for savings bonds, it is important to examine each in order to determine which would best represent future performance.

It is important to discern the reliability and usefulness of the savings bond data you use. If those who present the data cannot fully describe the context for any given piece of information, they probably don't understand savings bonds and thus may come to inaccurate conclusions. Let's examine those rates.

The Average Annual Yield

Let's rule out this one. The average annual return over the life of the bond is a good historic number. It shows how the bond *has* performed. However it is *not* a good indicator of future performance. This is particularly true of savings bonds. Why? Interest rates in the early 1980s were high compared to today. Thus, most bonds over ten years old had a much higher return in the past than they do now. When high returns early in the life of a bond are averaged with low returns late in the life of a bond, the overall average is generally much higher than the bond's current yield.

The average annual yield is a "feel good" piece of data. It will typically be 50 to 300 basis points higher than the actual current or future performance of most bonds. It is "feel good" data because it may make you feel good about what "did" happen, but it is of no use in predicting what "will" happen.

Here is the problem with this piece of data—and how it is often being used to arrive at wrong conclusions.

Wrong Conclusion: The government recently added a new column to the redemption tables that are used by many bank tellers. This column is called the "Average Annual Interest Rate." Because older bonds received high interest rates in the 1980s, the "Average Annual Interest Rate" will often overstate the current performance of a particular bond. The trouble is that many tellers are leading investors to believe that the "Average Annual Interest Rate" is the actual rate the bonds are currently earning. (In the fall of 1997, a teller at a bank in Illinois told the author that a bond issued in October 1986 was currently earning 7.34%. That bond was actually earning 4%.)

The Six-Month Earnings Rate

The yield for the next six months is a good short-term indicator in that it projects what return a bond will receive for that six-month period. While this can be helpful for short-term decisions, it can also lead to inaccurate conclusions about long-term performance. It is often a temporary distortion from what the long-term performance will be and may result in an under- or overinflated view of how a bond is performing. Consider the following two examples:

Wrong Conclusion: A bond bought in November 1993 received a flat rate of 4% for the first five years. Once it turned five years old, it received a market-rate of 5.22% retroactive to the date of purchase. Because the retroactive feature is all credited on the bond's fifth-year anniversary, the net yield for the time period that includes that anniversary will be skewed upward. The government table listed this bond as having a yield of 16.47%. What the data did not say, however, is that the same bond would drop back down to a range of 4.5% to 5.5% after the five-year catch-up. A bond owner will look at the yield table, see a great yield, and decide to hold that bond for the next decade—and that bond owner will be disappointed. The future performance of this bond will provide far less than the table indicates due to this one-time "spike."

Another Wrong Conclusion: This example is similar to the previous one, but is on the opposite end of the spectrum. In 1996, the government yield tables revealed that some bonds bought in 1987 and 1988 had short-term yields as low as 2%. Without using this space to detail why, suffice it to say that this "dip" was short-term. The yields did return to a guaranteed rate of 6% for several years before the end of the original maturity. However, upon seeing a low yield, a bond owner could easily assume that these bonds should be cashed. People who made that mistake often redeemed bonds that would have paid 6% over the next several years, while keeping bonds that were paying only 4 to 5%.

Note: Short-term yields are often aberrations (skewed up or down depending on the date the data is analyzed) compared to the long-term performance of a bond. They are not the best indicator of long-term performance.

The Guaranteed Rate

The best choice of the free options is the guaranteed rate. The guaranteed rate of interest in your current maturity period is just that—a guarantee of the minimum you will earn over the entire maturity period. This is the most conservative estimate of what the bond will return. (Bonds may yield higher returns if the market-based average for a given bond results in a greater redemption value than the redemption value produced by using the guaranteed rates.) Since this rate is guaranteed over the entire maturity period that the bond is in, the author views this as the best "free information" representation of future performance (until the bond enters the next extended maturity period). This is also the most conservative estimate. Better to err on the side of being conservative in future estimates than paint a picture that is never achieved. (Here's why: The market rate program received a great deal of fanfare and attention through the 1980s. In fact, the first rate ever published was a whopping 11.09%. Yet due to the complicated way the rates are averaged, no one ever received 11.09% on their bonds.) All bonds purchased prior to May 1995 now carry guaranteed rates of either 6% or 4%.

Exceptions: Series EE bonds purchased between March 1993 and April 1995 will receive a retroactive bonus at the end of the fifth year, if the market rate average exceeds 4%. The result on those bonds will be a one-time spike in the short-term yield at the end of the fifth year that will produce short-term yields of 10% or more.

The Savings Bond Informer Rating System℠

The Savings Bond Informer Rating System℠ provides a rating for each bond, which is based on a projection of two-year and five-year future performance. This system takes into account the specific interest rates and timing periods—thereby revealing exceptions like the spikes and dips mentioned above—and then assigns a rating for each bond. A rating of each bond and a complete description of the rating system is provided with each bond statement prepared by The Savings Bond Informer, Inc. There is a fee for this information. See page 79 for an example.

If you use savings bond information that provides a short-term yield *without also including the guaranteed floor for the current maturity period,* and a future rating, you are not getting the full picture.

Advice should be based on written facts. Those who dismiss savings bond holdings, yet do not demonstrate a working knowledge of how they operate and how mistakes can be avoided, may be more concerned with their own financial welfare than with yours.

Evaluating New Bond Purchases

The new rules for Series EE savings bonds are easy to understand: What you see is what you get. Each May and November the government announces a short-term market-based rate for savings bonds. The most recent published rate is the rate your bond earns for the first six months. Every six months your bond will pick up a new rate that will vary, depending on market conditions.

Example: If you bought a bond in May 1997, you received a rate of 5.68%. That rate was good for the first six months. In November 1997, a new rate of 5.59% was published, so you earned that rate for the second six months that you held the bond. In May 1998, a new rate of 5.06% was published. Thus, you earned 5.06% for the third six-month period. In November 1998, a new rate will be published and the bond will earn that rate until May 1999. Your interest rates can be illustrated as follows:

May 1997 to November 1, 1997	5.68%
November 1997 to May 1, 1998	5.59%
May 1998 to November 1, 1998	5.06%

Under the current system, the new rate published every May and November will always be lower than the average of the five-year Treasury yields for the six months preceding the rate announcement. Why? The government is giving you 90% of the average rate for five-year Treasury yields.

To evaluate whether to buy or not based on current rates, call 1-800-USBONDS. The recorded line will give you the current market rate that will apply to the bond for the first six months. The problem with evaluating bonds as long-term investments is that without a guaranteed rate you can no longer tuck a bond away for ten or twenty years and forget about it. Rates should be monitored to determine whether this investment is meeting your expectations.

For information on the I bond and a comparison of EE and I bonds, see Chapter 18.

Evaluating an Exchange

More than one bond owner has complained to me of the proverbial "rock and a hard place" between which the government has squeezed them with the low 4% rate on HH bonds. This is what they mean. Suppose you have bonds that have reached final maturity and have stopped earning interest. You have a lot of accrued interest that has, to this point, not been reported as interest income and, therefore, has not been taxed. At final maturity you must either redeem the bonds (which creates a taxable event) or exchange them for HH bonds that pay only 4%. Please don't say you will "just hold your bonds." First, you earn no interest on bonds that have reached final maturity. Second, IRS rules state that you must report the interest in the year the bonds reach final maturity, whether you cash them or not. The only exception to this is when you exchange your savings bonds for HH bonds. Why does this upset bond owners? First, because they have kept their bonds for thirty or forty years, they are long-term investors. Yet all they are offered and assigned is an HH bond rate that is paying less than a three-month Treasury bill (often over 100 basis points less). Many opt for the HH bond and the low rate because they want to delay reporting the interest.

Savings Bonds vs. Savings Accounts, CDs, and Money Market Funds

To conduct a fair evaluation, U.S. Savings Bonds must be compared to like investments. Investment options can generally be classified into one of three categories—high, moderate, and low risk. Which investments fit into which categories is often the subject of much debate. Most people, however, would agree that savings bonds fit into the latter. Savings bonds are defined in the marketplace in the following ways: secure/safe, conservative, patriotic, government product, liquid, low-risk/low-return. Consider, for example, that no one has ever received less than what they invested in a savings bond. Over time a bond always has a positive return (we are not factoring in inflation-adjusted returns in this discussion). Thus, for comparison purposes, savings bonds should be grouped with other conservative, safe investments.

Three other popular investment/savings options can easily fit within the range of conservative investments: savings accounts, certificates of deposit, and money market funds. Table 9.1 (page 103) was completed in late 1998 and can be used to compare these investments. A blank copy, Table 9.2 (page 104), is included as a worksheet for future evaluations.

Savings Bonds vs. Treasury Bills, Notes, and Bonds

Comparing these government products is sort of like comparing three brothers. They are distinctly different yet they come from the same family. (Their daddy is like an uncle to us!) Hence they share certain attributes inherent in government products—safe, conservative, debt-financing instruments. The younger brother, savings bonds, has considerably less freedom than the two older: T-bills and T-notes/bonds can be bought at original issue and venture out into the secondary market. The bottom line is that each of these government products is used to round out the conservative end of millions of Americans' portfolios.

Table 9.3 (page 105) highlights the features of each security.

Savings Bonds vs. Pork Bellies

The author once worked at the Chicago Mercantile Exchange (the "Merc"), where futures commodities are traded and fortunes are won and lost—sometimes in the same day. Let's examine the commodities market to see how this investment compares with the conservative nature of savings bonds.

- The place where traders stand to conduct business is called a "pit." The author's experience is that a pit is usually a deep, dark hole from which it is generally difficult to retrieve things, such as . . . oh, let's say . . . money.

- Trades are conducted by hand signals. Many of the hand signals witnessed in the "pit" by the author are those frequently used on the freeway.

- As you look out onto the trading floor, you see coats of many color. This conjures up images of the biblical Joseph who was cast into a "pit" and ended up broke and in prison.

What's the point? The point is that as an investor, you have to determine which investment environment best suits your personality and your needs. For the uninformed, futures commodities are generally a high-risk investment. High risk means you could make a lot of money or, the more likely scenario if you're not on the trading floor, you could lose a lot of money.

When evaluating any investment option, make sure that you understand it. Make sure that you understand the downside—how much you could lose or how low the return could be. (The upside usually receives ample explanation.) Realize that few investments carry the security and backing that savings bonds have. With that security, savings bonds offer a fairly predictable, non-spectacular return.

Quick Tips on Comparisons

- Be wary of those who advise "just cash them all in" without offering a written analysis of your holdings.

- Interest rates, timing issues, tax consequences, and risk tolerance, as well as values, should be considered when comparing savings bonds to other investment options.

- The best representation for projecting the long-term performance of bonds purchased prior to May 1995 is The Savings Bond Informer Rating System.[SM]

- To evaluate whether to buy or not, call 1-800-USBONDS for interest rates on new purchases.

- Other conservative investments against which bonds are often compared include T-bills, notes, and bonds, and CDs and money market funds.

Table 9.1 Comparing Savings Bonds to Savings Accounts, CDs, and Money Market Funds

	Series EE & Series I Savings Bonds	Savings Accounts	CDs	Money Market Funds
Federal Tax	Yes, deferred until bond is cashed or reaches final maturity	Yes	Yes	Yes
State Tax	No	Yes	Yes	Yes
Local Tax	No	Yes, if applicable	Yes, if applicabale	Yes, if applicable
Minimum Investment	*Series EE:* $25 for a $50 face value bond *Series I:* $50 for a $50 face value bond	None, although some accounts have minimum balance require- ments	Usually $500, some may be available for lower initial investment	Usually $500, some accounts may be opened for less initial investment
Maximum Investment	*Series EE:* $15,000 purchase price per person per year *Series I:* $30,000 purchase price per person per year	None	None	None
Interest Rates	*Series EE:* 5.06% first six months for bond purchased 5/98 to 10/98 *Series I:* 4.66% for 9/98 and 10/98	Average of 1% to 3%, depending on bank	Small denomina- tion six-month CDs averaged 4.67% as of 9/9/98 (source: *Bank Rate Monitor*)	Averaged 5.19% as of 9/98
Liquidity	Can cash bond anytime after six months, three- month penalty if cashed prior to five years	Can withdraw money at any time without penalty, although minimum balance require- ments & penalties may apply	Must hold until"official" maturity date or face penalties for early withdrawal	Can usually liquidate at any time without fees or penalty
Safety	Backed by full faith and credit of U.S. government	Are insured up to $100,000 at qualified financial institutions (FDIC insured)	Are insured up to $100,000 at qualified financial institutions	Are usually not insured

Table 9.2 Complete Your Own Comparisons

	Series EE and Series I Savings Bonds	Other Investment Option _____	Other Investment Option _____	Other Investment Option _____
Federal Tax	Yes, deferred until bond is cashed or reaches final maturity			
State Tax	No			
Local Tax	No			
Minimum Investment	*Series EE:* $25 *Series I:* $50			
Maximum Investment	*Series EE:* $15,000 *Series I:* $30,000			
Interest Rates	*Series EE:* 4.60% if purchased 11/98 to 4/99 *Series I:* 5.05% if purchased 11/98 to 4/99			
Liquidity	Can cash bond anytime after six months, three-month penalty if not held five years			
Safety	Backed by full faith and credit of U.S. government			

Table 9.3 Comparing Savings Bonds to Treasury Bills, Notes, and Bonds

	Series EE Savings Bonds	Treasury Bills	Treasury Notes/Bonds
Federal Tax	Yes, deferred until bond is cashed or reaches final maturity	Yes, in the year the bill reaches face value (or matures)	Yes, the semi-annual interest payment is subject to Federal Tax in the year it is received
State Tax	No	No	No
Local Tax	No	No	No
Minimum Investment	$25 for a $50 face value bond	$1,000, receive a discount after issue date once purchase price is established	$5,000 for a two-year note, $1,000 for anything longer
Maximum Investment	$15,000 purchase price per person per year	$1,000,000	$5,000,000
Interest Rates	4.60% first six months for bond purchased 11/98 to 4/99	• 4.63% as of 3/11/99 for three-month T-bill • 4.72% as of 3/11/99 for six-month T-bill • 4.91% as of 3/4/99 for one-year T-bill	Most recent auction prior to 3/99 2 yr: 5% (3/1/99) 5 yr: 4.75% (2/16/99) 10 yr: 4.75% (2/16/99) 30 yr: 5.25% (2/16/99)
Term	Six months to thirty years	three-month six-month one-year	Two-year, five-year, ten-year, thirty-year, other issues may be offered periodically
Liquidity	Can cash bond anytime after six months without penalty	Can sell at any time in secondary market, however, there is a commission or fee to sell, and current market conditions will determine the sale price	Can sell at any time in secondary market, however, there is a commission or fee to sell, and current market conditions will determine the sale price. May receive more or less than the face value if sold prior to maturity.
Safety	Backed by full faith & credit of the U.S. government	Backed by full faith & credit of the U.S. government	Backed by full faith & credit of U.S. government
Where to Purchase	Through payroll deduction with many employers, at financial institutions, at Federal Reserve Banks	Federal Reserve Banks, commercial banks, brokers	Federal Reserve Banks, commercial banks, brokers
Purchase or Redemption Costs	None	None if purchased from a FRB and held to maturity. If purchased from a bank or broker, fees and/or commissions will apply.	None if purchased from a FRB and held to maturity. If purchased from a bank or broker, fees and/or commissions will apply.

Chapter 10

TAXATION ISSUES FOR U.S. SAVINGS BONDS
a.k.a. What Uncle Sam Wants

▶ *Common Tax Mistakes*
▶ *How and When to Report Interest Income*
▶ *Who Has to Report Interest Income*
▶ *Tax Concerns When Transferring Bonds*
▶ *Taxes upon Death*
▶ *Watch Out for Double Taxation*
▶ *Federal Estate Tax*
▶ *Gift and Inheritance Taxes*
▶ *Estate Planning*
▶ *Comments on the 1997 Tax Law Changes*
▶ *Quick Tips on Taxes*

Tax information. . . . A typical chapter on this exhilarating subject will cure even the worst case of insomnia. And quite frankly, this chapter contains quite a bit of technical language. The information presented relies in large part upon the Internal Revenue Service Publications 17 and 550 and the Department of Treasury, Bureau of the Public Debt publications, "Legal Aspects of U.S. Savings Bonds" and "The Book on U.S. Savings Bonds." However, you will find some things that should catch your attention: tax tips; how to avoid tax traps; and information designed to help you recognize your options. And, throughout this chapter, whenever possible, a reader-friendly explanation accompanies the technical explanation.

Note: Since March 1, 1941, the interest on U.S. Savings Bonds has been subject to federal income tax, but exempt from state, municipal, or local income taxes. (See Chapter 16 for possible exceptions.)

Common Tax Mistakes

When evaluating the status of your savings bond holdings, taxation issues should be taken into careful consideration. Here are the four most common tax mistakes bond owners make:

Mistake #1: Cashing savings bonds without first considering how much interest income will be reported and how much tax liability must be paid.

Mistake #2: Gifting or transferring bonds without knowing the tax consequences.

Mistake #3: Paying double tax: Unknowingly paying tax again on bond interest that had already been reported by a previous taxpayer.

Mistake #4: Lower-income retired persons cashing a large number of bonds in one year, causing a substantial portion of their Social Security benefits to be taxable.

How and When to Report Interest Income

In order to determine how interest on savings bonds is taxed, two questions must be answered:

1. Is the taxpayer using the cash basis or the accrual basis of accounting for income tax purposes?

2. What type of savings bond is being analyzed (E, EE, SN, H, HH)?

The cash basis of accounting is used by the majority of individuals owning U.S. Savings Bonds. If you don't know whether you are on the cash or accrual method, most likely you are on the cash method. If you have never specifically elected accrual, the cash method is the automatic default.

The difference between the purchase price of an E or EE bond and its redemption value is considered interest income under IRS Code. At some point in time, this income will have to be reported. When to include (or report) this interest income as taxable income (on a tax return) is an important issue. Interest on Series E and EE bonds and SNs/FSs is not paid on an annual or semi-annual basis to the investor. Instead, the interest is added to the value of the bond, which is paid when the bond is cashed. This is called interest accrual: The bond value is growing as a result of the interest being added to the value of the bond. The taxpayer on the cash basis method must choose between two methods of reporting interest income:

1. *Deferral.* Defer the reporting of the interest income until the year in which the E or EE bonds or SNs/FSs are cashed, disposed of, or reach final maturity, whichever comes first. If you do nothing, this is the option you have chosen. All the interest accrued will be reported in the year the bonds are cashed or reach final maturity.

2. *Annual Reporting.* Report the interest earned each year as it accrues on the bond.

Deferral

When you buy a bond and do nothing about the interest, you have automatically chosen the deferral method. The interest the bond earns causes it to increase in value, but you choose not to be taxed annually on this interest because no cash has been received. It should be emphasized that when bonds are cashed under this method all the interest earned will be taxable in one year.

For older bonds, this could result in a significant amount of taxable income. There have been many instances when a taxpayer cashed bonds without taking into account the *timing* of the transaction for income tax purposes, looking only at the interest rates and liquidity issues. With proper tax planning, cashing bonds can be timed to minimize tax liability. This is especially important if the taxpayer has had an unusually high- or low-income year.

TAX TRAP: *When a bond reaches final maturity, it not only stops accruing interest but any interest accrued is taxable that year.* This is an easy item to overlook since bond owners receive no statement telling them that a particular bond has stopped earning interest. Thus many bond owners unknowingly hold bonds past final maturity. If you hold bonds that are over three years past final maturity, consult a professional tax advisor for your options.

If you discover this situation after your tax returns for the year have been filed, amended returns should be filed to properly report the bond interest income. It is extremely important to know when your bonds are scheduled to reach final maturity so that you can plan for the tax impact on the interest that has accrued on each bond.

Series E bonds issued before December 1965 reach final maturity forty years after their issue date. Series E bonds issued after November 1965 and all Series EE bonds and Savings Notes reach final maturity thirty years after their issue date. **Note**: A special rule permits further deferral if an E bond or Savings Note is exchanged for a Series HH bond no later than one calendar year after final maturity.

A $1,000 Series E bond purchased in June 1958 for $750 has a current value of $7,381.20. If the owner has not reported any of the interest on this bond, the entire difference of $6,631.20 is potentially taxable as interest income in 1998. The only way to avoid liability in 1998 is to exchange it for HH bonds.

TAX TIP: Taxpayers holding Series E bonds that are reaching final maturity should consider whether they want all the interest income taxed in the year of final maturity. If they do not, they should consider exchanging their Series E for HH bonds. The interest on HH bonds is paid every six months and is taxable in the year of receipt. However, the accrued interest on the Series E bonds that have been surrendered will continue to be deferred until the Series HH bonds are either cashed or mature (see Chapter 12 for details on exchanging).

Annual Reporting

Under the cash basis method, the bond holder may choose to report the annual increase in the bond's value (the interest income) on each year's tax return, rather than waiting until the bond is cashed or reaches final maturity.

If a taxpayer wants to report the interest as it accrues, *all* interest accrued and not previously reported on all Series E and EE bonds and SNs/FSs must be included as income for the tax year in which this election is made (that is, the year you start to report interest annually). In other words, if a taxpayer chooses this method, it will apply to all the bonds he or she owns. You cannot pick and choose which bonds you want to report annual interest on and which to leave alone. It should be kept in mind that once you choose to report the interest each year, you must continue to do so for all Series E and EE bonds and SNs/FSs you own and for any you may obtain later, unless you request permission from the IRS to change back to the deferral method. (See IRS Publication 17 for rules on changing methods.)

If the taxpayer is in a low tax bracket, it may make sense to be taxed on interest income each year as it accrues. In some situations, little or no tax is paid if the income is reported each year. If all the income is taxed in the year the bonds are cashed or in the year of final maturity, this "bunching" of the interest income may create a significantly higher total tax than if the tax had been paid each year. This would be especially true for a low-income taxpayer who held a large number of bonds which would come due in one tax year.

For example, a seventy-year old single taxpayer has bonds that are increasing in value at $3,000 per year. The taxpayer also has $5,000 of additional taxable interest income and receives $10,000 in Social Security benefits each year. She plans to cash the bonds in ten years.

Option 1: She decides to report as interest income the $3,000 per year as the bonds increase in value. The total federal income tax due each year using 1998 rates and exemptions would be $0 for each year, resulting in a total federal income tax of $0 for the ten years.

Option 2: She chooses to defer the interest income on these bonds and pick up the whole $30,000 ($3,000 times 10 years) in year ten. The total federal income tax due would then be about $6,645, assuming tax rates similar to 1998 rates.

In this simple situation, the difference in total federal income tax between options 1 and 2 is *$6,645.* This is a considerable amount of money. *The time value of money must be taken into account when making this calculation.* If there were taxes in option 1 they would be paid earlier than in option 2. In many cases the difference is so great that it is better to report the interest each year, even if it meant a small amount of taxes, rather than to defer it until year ten.

TAX TRAP: In the situation above, part of the tax increase occurs in year ten when all the bond interest income is taxable. A portion of the bond holder's Social Security benefits would become taxable, too, because she has a higher total income. This tax bite has surprised many a taxpayer receiving Social Security. In the example above, $2,380 of the $6,645 additional taxes was due to the fact that $8,500 of the $10,000 Social Security benefits received that year were taxed at 28% because of the influx of bond interest.

When you choose the annual reporting methods for a minor, the first year's tax return should report all the interest income accrued through that tax year. In successive years the minor need only file when total income exceeds the IRS level. In 1997, a minor who made less than $650 did not need to file. If you choose this method, please pay special attention to the double taxation discussion later in this chapter to ensure that you avoid reporting the interest twice.

Accrual Basis: E and EE Bonds

If the taxpayer has specifically elected the accrual basis for income tax purposes, the accrued interest on E and EE bonds *must be reported as income each year*.

H and HH Bonds

Interest on Series H and HH bonds is paid semi-annually by check or by direct deposit and must be reported annually for federal income tax purposes.

Who Has to Report Interest Income

Co-owners

When bonds are held by co-owners, there is often a great deal of confusion as to who is liable for the tax on the interest when the bond is redeemed. Irving, a psychologist from the East Coast, called with these examples:

> *Irving's family had a large holding of bonds. They checked with several accountants and an attorney regarding tax liability because they wanted to know who is responsible for the tax if a bond is registered in the name of both parents, or a parent and a child. The answer was unanimous: They were informed that the tax would be reported to the first listed person whose Social Security number is on the bond. All were wrong. The one who cashes the bond is the one who receives the 1099-INT.*
>
> *In a separate incident, Irving's parents wanted to change the co-owner to a child. Some advisors claimed that this would create a taxable event, while others said that it would not. In fact, adding a new co-owner does not normally create a taxable event. Irving's point in sharing these stories is to illustrate the tremendous amount of misinformation that exists regarding tax liability (which also affects estate planning), even among professionals.*

The following chart adapted from "Legal Aspects On U.S. Savings Bonds" states the government's position. As discussed in Chapter 15, the actual reporting method used by the banks, Federal Reserve Banks (FRB), and IRS when documenting Social Security numbers and names to generate a 1099-INT *does not* match the rules outlined:

Bond Purchaser	Tax Liability
"Dad buys a bond in the names of "Dad" and "Son" as co-owners.	Interest is income to "Dad," the person who contributed the purchase price.
"Dad" and "Son" buy bonds in co-ownership, each contributing part of the purchase price.	Interest is income to both "Dad" and "Son," in proportion to their contributions to the purchase.
"Son" and "Daughter" receive bonds in co-ownership as a gift from "Dad."	Interest is income to both "Son" and "Daughter": 50% to each co-owner.
"Mom" buys a bond in the name of "Son," who is the sole owner of the bond.	Interest is income to "Son."

If you buy a U.S. Savings Bond and add a co-owner, the person whose funds were used to purchase the bond is the person who must pay the tax on the interest. This is true even if the purchaser lets the other co-owner redeem the bond and keep the proceeds.

The problem with this situation is that the organization that redeems the bonds will issue a 1099-INT to the person who redeems the bond despite the fact that, according to IRS rules, the interest is taxable to the co-owner who purchased the bond. Since the redeeming co-owner will receive a 1099-INT at the time of redemption, he or she is supposed to provide the purchaser/co-owner (who is to be taxed) with another 1099-INT, showing the amount of interest that is taxable.

The co-owner who redeemed the bond is called a "nominee." If a taxpayer receives a 1099-INT for interest received as a nominee, he or she should list that amount separately below the subtotal of all interest income listed on Schedule B. That amount should be labeled "Nominee Distribution" and subtracted from the interest income subtotal. This procedure ensures that the bond interest will not be added into the nominee's taxable income on his or her tax return.

Author's note: If the previous section seems confusing, don't be alarmed: It is absolutely confusing. The purpose of this chapter is to inform you of the rules—whether they make sense, are being enforced, or even have the capacity to be enforced. The author is not aware of a single case in which the redeeming, non-purchaser co-owner actually issued a 1099-INT to the first-named co-owner and sent a copy to IRS.

This rule leaves room for shady action, as you may realize. According to this rule, Uncle John buys bonds with his nephew as a co-owner. His nephew cashes the bonds and receives a 1099-INT. The young man then turns around and issues a 1099-INT to Uncle John and reports that same 1099-INT to IRS. Nephew is now "in the money" tax-free. The only drawback may be meeting up with his uncle in the near future.

Tax Concerns When Transferring Bonds

There are many situations when bonds are reissued in a different person's name or are reissued to eliminate, or add, a co-owner's name. The question that is often overlooked by the taxpayer and the financial advisor making these changes is, "Does this change cause tax consequences to any of the parties involved?" The answer could be "yes" or "no," depending on the situation. Any time a change in ownership due to the reissue of bonds is recommended, tax consequences must be considered.

Non-Taxable Event

The general rule is that *a change in the registration of a savings bond that does not change ownership will not result in shifting income tax liability*. Here are some examples when changes *do not* result in the shifting of income tax liability and, consequently, are *not* considered a disposition that requires the owner to report interest income.

1. The original owner who furnished 100% of the funds to purchase the bond has it reissued to name the original owner and another person as co-owner.

2. An original owner who furnished 100% of the funds for the bond's purchase has the bond reissued to eliminate a co-owner's name from the bond.

3. If bonds that two co-owners purchased jointly are reissued to each of the co-owners in the same proportion as their original contribution to the purchase price, neither co-owner has to report, at reissue, the interest earned before the bonds were reissued.

4. The owner can continue to postpone reporting the interest earned if a taxpayer owns Series E or EE bonds, and
   a. transfers them to a trust, and
   b. is considered the owner of the trust, and
   c. the increase in value both before and after the transfer continues to be taxable to the owner.

5. If a person who owns Series EE bonds exchanges them for Series HH bonds, and the Series HH bonds are issued in the owner's name and that of another co-owner, the original owner must remain the first listed on the new bonds.

Taxable Event

What action creates a taxable event? These following situations illustrate when a change in registration will cause the interest to become taxable at the time of the change.

1. If a person buys Series E or EE bonds entirely with his own funds and has them reissued in a co-owner's name alone, this is considered a disposition. In the year of reissue, the original bond purchaser must report all interest earned on these bonds not previously reported.

2. If a person buys Series E or EE bonds entirely with his or her own funds and has them reissued in another beneficiary's name alone, this is considered a disposition. In the year of reissue, the original bond purchaser must report all interest earned on these bonds that has not been previously reported.

3. When a person who owns Series E or EE bonds gives the bonds to another person and reissues the bonds in the recipient's name alone, the reissuance of the bonds causes this to be a taxable situation for the person who makes the gift. Any previously unreported interest would have to be included as the giver's income in the year of the reissue. **Note**: Any interest earned on the bond after the reissue would be taxable to the recipient.

4. If a person transfers Series E or EE bonds to a trust and also gives up all rights of ownership, that person must report all the interest earned through the date of transfer (that has not been previously reported). This interest would be taxable in the year of transfer.

Additional Note: Be aware that persons who inherit bonds may create taxable events by removing their names from the bonds. Contact your FRB or a professional tax advisor for more information before taking this course of action.

Taxes upon Death

Many financial professionals and bond owners expect that, as with other investment vehicles, a stepped-up basis applies to U.S. Savings Bonds. This is *not* the case. In fact, there is no automatic stepped-up basis for people who inherit or receive bonds upon the death of another individual.

The manner of reporting interest income on Series E or EE bonds after the death of the owner depends on the accounting and income reporting method the decedent had used. If the bonds transferred at death were owned by a person who used the accrual method (or who used the cash method and chose to report the interest each year), the interest earned in the year of death must be reported on that person's final return. The beneficiary, or new owner, of the bonds includes as income only the interest earned after the date of death.

If the decedent had used the cash basis method (and had not reported the interest each year) and had bought the bonds entirely with his or her own funds, all interest earned before death must be reported in one of the following ways:

1. The surviving spouse or personal representative (executor, administrator, etc.) who files the final income tax return of the decedent can choose

to include on that return all of the interest earned on the bonds before the decedent's death. The person who acquires the bonds then includes as income only interest earned after the date of death.

2. If option 1 is not selected, the personal representative can report all of the interest in the estate and have it taxed at estate income tax rates. If this method is chosen, the interest should not be included in the decedent's final return.

3. If you do not choose options 1 or 2, the interest earned up to the date of death is *income in respect of a decedent* and it should not be included in the decedent's final return. *All of the interest earned both before and after the decedent's death is income to the person who acquires the bonds.* If that person uses the cash method and chooses not to report the interest each year, he or she can postpone reporting any of the interest until the bonds are redeemed or reach final maturity, whichever comes first. In the year that the interest is reported, he or she can claim a deduction for any federal estate tax paid for savings bond interest that was included in the decedent's estate.

In summary, the personal representative of the estate has three options.

1. Elect to report unreported interest on the final income tax return of the decedent under Code Section 454(a) of the Internal Revenue Code.

2. Report all of the savings bond interest in the estate. This can be done by electing to report all previously unreported interest in the estate or by reporting the interest as the bonds are cashed in the estate.

3. Distribute the bonds to the residuary beneficiaries (the person or persons entitled to the estate residue, that is, whatever is left over from the estate's assets and not specifically designated to a particular entity). In this case, the beneficiaries would report the savings bond interest when cashed or in the year an election is made to report previously unreported interest.

It should be noted that beneficiaries who receive bonds can choose to continue deferring interest or to report interest annually on the bonds they receive.

TAX TIP: To see which option provides the lowest federal income tax liability when a large number of bonds are involved, the tax consequences for all three options must be calculated. If the decedent was in a low income bracket, it often makes sense to include the interest in the decedent's final return. See Table 10.1 (page 121) for an example of this calculation.

Watch Out for Double Taxation

Can savings bond interest be double taxed by the Internal Revenue Service? You bet it can! While not intentional, it nonetheless happens due to the confusing nature of the rules. As mentioned earlier, the financial institution that redeems the bond will issue a 1099-INT to the person redeeming it. The 1099-INT shows the difference between the amount the holder receives and the purchase price.

Important note: There are several instances when the 1099-INT may show more interest than the taxpayer is required to include as income on the tax return. This may happen if:

1. You chose to report the increase in the redemption value of the bond each year. The interest shown on your 1099-INT will not be reduced by the amounts previously included as income.

2. You received a bond from a decedent. The interest shown on your 1099-INT will not be reduced by the interest reported by the decedent before death, or on the decedent's final return, or by the estate on the estate's income tax return.

3. The interest shown on your 1099-INT will not be reduced by the interest accrued prior to a transfer of bond ownership.

4. You redeemed a bond on which you were named as a co-owner but which you did not buy; the person who had purchased the bond previously reported interest accrued.

TAX TIP: Any taxpayer or personal representative who chooses to include interest on U.S. Savings Bonds in a year other than the year the bonds are redeemed should keep a detailed worksheet showing the years when the interest was taxed, as well as the amount of interest that was previously included as income. They should also keep copies of the federal tax returns (Form 1040 and Schedule B) on which this interest was reported. These records should be safely stored and available to the co-owners and to persons who may obtain the bonds through reissue transactions.

TAX TIP: If you have received a sizable number of bonds from a decedent and have paid tax on the interest for the entire 1099-INT issued, check prior records to see if any of this income had been previously taxed in the decedent's tax returns or in the estate returns. *If this has happened within the past three years, you may be entitled to a federal income tax refund: You should file amended returns.* Better yet, now that you know what to look for, research the reported interest status of your bonds before you cash them.

Federal Estate Tax

In this section, we will not go into a deep discussion of estate tax rules. We will only discuss issues related to U.S. Savings Bonds. Much of the information in the next few sections is technical and is adapted from the Bureau of the Public Debts (BPD) publication, "The Book On U.S. Savings Bonds."

To begin, the estate is primarily liable for any estate tax that can be attributed to bonds owned by the decedent, even if they pass directly to a co-owner or beneficiary. In the event the estate fails to pay the estate tax, the persons receiving the bonds or other property could be required to pay the estate tax.

Determining Bond Values

When savings bonds are included for estate tax calculation purposes, it is important to use the proper value of the bonds. *The proper value is the redemption value of the bond on the date of the owner's death.* An increasing number of personal representatives and legal counsel are engaging the services of The Savings Bond Informer, Inc., rather than track down old redemption tables and calculate the value of each bond themselves. (See Chapter 7, "Tracking Your Investment.")

Income Tax Deduction for Federal Estate Tax Paid

Under certain conditions, it is possible for a taxpayer to take a deduction for federal estate tax paid on savings bond interest that was included in a decedent's estate for tax calculation purposes. Assume, for example, that the taxpayer acquired the bonds either as surviving co-owner, beneficiary, or distributee of an estate of a (cash basis) taxpayer who had not elected to report interest annually. At the time the accrued interest on the bonds is reported as income, the taxpayer would be entitled to claim a deduction on his or her federal income tax return for the portion of the estate tax paid that was applicable as a result of interest accrued during the decedent's lifetime.

It should be emphasized that this is not a dollar-for-dollar offset. It is a deduction that may or may not equalize the taxes, depending on the respective tax brackets of the estate and the income distributee. Because computations in this area can be very complicated, consult a tax advisor.

Gift and Inheritance Taxes

Federal Gift Tax

Any one taxpayer who gives more than $10,000 to any other person in a calendar year must file a gift tax return (Form 709). The value of any U.S. Savings

Bonds given would be included in this $10,000 computation. The value used for the gift would be the bond's redemption value on the date of the gift. A gift of savings bonds can be made in several ways and is subject to the federal gift tax.

One way to give savings bonds is to purchase the bonds in the name of the person who will receive them (the donee). Another way is to reissue the bonds in the name of the donee. If the value of the bonds given is under $10,000 per year per donee, no gift tax is due. If gifts of more than $10,000 are made in one year to one person, gift tax may be due. *The tax is imposed on the person making the gift*, not the person receiving the gift. (Remember that reissuing bonds to gift them will generate a taxable event to the person giving away the bonds even if the gift is under $10,000.)

A husband and wife may combine their gift tax exemptions to give a third person a total of $20,000 annually. The husband could give $20,000 in savings bonds to the third person without exceeding each spouse's $10,000 annual exemption. Both the husband and wife must consent to the gift-splitting by signing gift tax Form 709, which must be filed for the year the gift is given.

Note: Starting January 1, 1999, the annual gift tax exclusion will be indexed annually for inflation.

State Gift Tax

U.S. Savings Bonds may be subject to state gift tax.

Previous editions of this book had stated that they were not. This statement was based on the government publication "Legal Aspects of United States Savings Bonds." After being questioned, the government acknowledged that its publication contained an inaccuracy about state gift taxes.

That savings bonds may be subject to state gift tax is supported in another government publication, "Dept. Circular No. 1-80, 3rd Revision," that reads, "The Bonds are subject to estate, inheritance, gift or other excise taxes, whether Federal or State. . . ." (*Federal Register*, 55(4):7).

State Inheritance Tax

When bond ownership is transferred by the death of one owner, it is subject to state inheritance tax. In the case of co-owned bonds, many states follow the rule applied under the federal estate tax provisions—measuring each co-owner's taxable interest by the amount each contributed to the purchase price. Other states view the bonds as held in equal shares by each co-owner and require that one-half of their value be reported as part of the gross estate of the co-owner first to die, regardless of who purchased the bonds. Contact your state's tax authorities for current information.

Estate Planning

Remember rule number one of estate planning: You have an estate plan whether you think you do or not. Either you devised a plan that reflects your personal desires and wishes, or the state and federal taxing agencies have one waiting for you. It is highly recommended that you plan now, while you have control, to minimize estate taxes. That way, most of the assets that you have worked a lifetime to accumulate will be passed on to the heirs or charities of your choice.

Estate planning is very complicated. Add the unique tax characteristics of savings bonds to the process and it does not get any easier. The remainder of this section will give you some items to consider during this process, including how income taxes and estate taxes interact with estate tax calculations.

The following example illustrates some of these considerations. The purpose is to show how different choices can change the amount of assets that end up in the hands of the heirs of a 65-year-old taxpayer. Here are the facts of the case, followed by possible courses of action (both before and after Mr. Taxpayer's death), and their outcomes.

Facts

1. Mr. Taxpayer's assets include a personal residence valued at $250,000; certificates of deposit totaling $150,000, invested at 6%; and Series EE savings bonds totaling $800,000, of which $400,000 is accumulated interest.

2. Mr. Taxpayer receives annual Social Security benefits of $10,000.

3. Taxable interest each year is $9,000 ($150,000 x 6% interest rate).

4. 1998 federal tax rates, personal exemptions, and standard deductions are used in tax calculations.

5. All proceeds from cashing any savings bonds, less applicable income taxes, are invested to earn 6% taxable interest.

6. All bonds are cashed on the last day of the year for figuring future year taxable interest income from proceeds.

7. A combined state and local income tax rate of 4% is used to calculate taxes.

8. Mr. Taxpayer dies on the last day of the fifth year of tax calculations.

9. No state inheritance tax or final expenses have been taken into account.

Options

1. Wait until the taxpayer's death and elect to have all of the $400,000 of accumulated savings bond interest taxed on the *taxpayer's final return* and then calculate the estate tax.

2. Cash $200,000 of bonds each year for four years before the taxpayer dies, generating $100,000 of taxable bond interest each year, and then calculate the estate tax.

3. Redeem all the bonds in the estate and have the *estate pay tax* on the $400,000 of accumulated interest in the estate and then figure the estate tax.

4. Wait and distribute the bonds to the beneficiaries (outside the estate) and have the *beneficiaries report the interest* when they cash the bonds.

The result of each option is shown below.

Table 10.1 Savings Bond Estate Planning Options

	Option 1	Option 2	Option 3	Option 4
Asset value left in estate before estate taxes:				
Personal residence	$250,000	$250,000	$250,000	$250,000
Other investments	$150,000	$150,000	$150,000	$150,000
Investments from bonds cashed	$655,935	$661,000	$800,000	0
Savings bonds	0	0	0	$800,000
Total estate value	$1,055,935	$1,061,000	$1,200,000	$1,200,000
Less federal income tax in estate	0	0	($157,215)	0
Estimated federal estate tax after $229,800 credit for year 2002	($138,933)	($141,010)	($198,000)	($198,000)
Net assets to distribute to heirs	$917,002	$919,990	$844,785	$1,002,000
Less estimated income tax for heirs when bonds are cashed (28% federal)	0	0	0	($112,000)
Plus personal tax saved when deducting federal estate tax paid on accumulated savings bond interest included in estate (28% federal)	0	0	0	+$44,800*
Project net value to heirs after taking into account tax effect.	$917,002	$919,990	$844,785	$934,800*

*If heirs are in the 36% federal tax bracket, however, the projected amount left for them would be about $13,000 less than $934,800. If the heirs are in the 39.6% bracket, the amount would be about $18,500 less. This assumes that the heirs itemize deductions and can use the federal estate tax-paid deduction (and that their other income does not limit their itemized deductions).

Use of the Qualified Disclaimer

In some estate planning situations, it may be beneficial for an heir to disclaim the assets. This is especially true when the beneficiary already has substantial assets and has a taxable estate without adding assets from a parent's or relative's estate. Careful consideration should be made before this decision is finalized because it is irrevocable and certain conditions must be met. This is another area where it is important that a competent estate tax advisor be consulted.

Internal Revenue Code Section 2418 defines a qualified disclaimer for federal estate tax purposes as an irrevocable and unqualified refusal by a person to accept an interest in a property if the following four conditions are met:

1. The refusal or disclaimer is in writing,

2. The written disclaimer is received by the transferor of the interest, his legal representative, or holder of the legal title to the property to which the interest relates not later than the date which is nine months after the later of . . .
    a. The day on which the transfer creating the interest in such person is made, or
    b. The day on which such person attains the age of 21,

3. The person has not accepted the interest or any of its benefits, and

4. As a result of such refusal, the interest passes without any direction on the part of the person making the disclaimer and passes either to the spouse of the decedent or to a person other than the person making disclaimer.

> *In 1998, a single person with assets of $1,000,000 receives a call from an attorney stating a distant relative has left her $200,000 in savings bonds. Before receiving the bonds, this single taxpayer has a projected federal estate tax of approximately $143,750. After the $200,000 in bonds have been received and included in her estate, her new projected federal estate tax is $225,750, an increase of $82,000. In this case, the net effect of the transfer of the $200,000, after the estate taxes, is $118,000. This is a situation where a disclaimer might be considered. It is very important that all facts be thoroughly examined before the final decision to disclaim is made, because disclaiming is irrevocable.*

One question that often comes up when considering to disclaim assets is, "Who will receive the assets if I disclaim them?" This can be answered by the decedent's will or living trust. The will treats the person disclaiming the property as if that person had died before the actual decedent (i.e., whose will or trust is being administered). The will or trust would then determine who would receive the assets on that basis. It is important to know how assets will be transferred even though the disclaiming person has no control over it, because that information may have an impact on the decision to disclaim.

Comments on the 1997 Tax Law Changes

The Taxpayer Relief Act of 1997 was signed into law on August 5, 1997. It contains the largest tax cut in more than sixteen years. There is nothing in the law that specifically changes the income taxation of U.S. Savings Bonds interest. However, there are several provisions where deductions and credits begin to be phased out at various adjusted gross income (AGI) levels for individual taxpayers.

When investors cash savings bonds, they increase their adjusted gross income by the amount of the taxable bond interest income. Without proper tax planning, this additional interest income could cause the taxpayer to exceed AGI phase-out limits. The new deductions and credits (which may be affected when cashing bonds) are listed in the chart below. The numbers represent the level where AGI phase-out begins.

Table 10.2 1997 Tax Law Deduction and/or Credit Phase-Out Levels

Deduction or Credit Description	Levels at which adjusted gross income phase-out begins	
	Single Taxpayer	**Married Filing Jointly**
Hope credit for higher eduction	$40,000	$80,000
Lifetime learning eduction credit	$40,000	$80,000
Higher education loan interest deduction	$40,000	$60,000
Child tax credit	$75,000	$110,000
First-time home buyer credit	$70,000	$110,000
Roth & educational IRAs	$95,000	$150,000

One additional factor that effects many investment decisions is the new lower capital gains rate. The maximum capital gains rate (for long-term capital gains) was reduced from 28% to 20%. Taxpayers in the 15% tax bracket may be entitled to a 10% capital gain rate instead of the 20% rate. Consult with a tax advisor if you need to determine which rate applies to you. When considering an investment in savings bonds, remember that bond interest will be taxed at ordinary income rates, not at the capital gain rate and the advantages of a lower capital gain rate are not applicable to bond interest.

Quick Tips on Taxes

- Interest earned on savings bonds is subject to federal tax, but exempt from state and local taxes.

- When savings bonds are inherited or received due to a retitling, past records should be scrutinized to determine if any interest was previously reported. This can help the bond owner avoid double taxation.

- When savings bonds are part of an estate, the redemption value of the bonds as of the date of death is the proper value to use.

- Bond owners who receive Social Security payments may cause a portion of their benefits to be taxed—and that previously may *not* have been taxed—when cashing in a large amount of savings bonds in one year.

- Most bond owners have not reported interest annually, thus they must report it when the bond is cased or when the bond reaches final maturity (exchanging for HH bonds can provide additional deferral).

The information in this chapter is based on current tax laws. Be aware that tax laws are constantly changing and that the information in these pages may become obsolete. It is not our intent to offer legal or tax advice. The author strongly suggests that anyone with a specific savings bond tax issue or legal issue consult a competent and experienced professional for advice.

Chapter 11

SAVINGS BONDS AND RETIREMENT
What To Do

▶ *Pre-Retirement Issues*
▶ *Retirement Issues*
▶ *Spending Your Hard-Earned Money*
▶ *Quick Tips on Retirement*

U.S. Savings Bonds: You purchased them faithfully for years. They may represent a portion of the income you plan to use in retirement, or they may constitute your rainy day fund. Regardless of your intent, one thing is certain: You received no manual outlining the important strategies for maximizing your investment. As retirement nears, however, it is important that you thoughtfully examine your savings bond investment.

Part of making the most of this investment is to avoid serious pitfalls. Another aspect is to have a systematic plan for the use of your bonds, one based on your specific needs and goals. In this chapter, we will consider both, in addition to common retirement questions.

Note: This chapter is not meant to replace a qualified financial advisor. In fact, the information presented is best utilized by integrating the savings bond portion of your investments into an overall strategy for funding your retirement years. A qualified financial professional may be able to help you integrate this information into your comprehensive plan.

Pre-Retirement Issues

Let us assume that you will be retiring in the next two to ten years. What savings bond issues should be concerning you? First, you must start with the basics. You should know how much your bonds are worth now, what interest rates they are earning, how much deferred interest has not yet been reported, when they will stop earning interest, and how long the bonds will earn interest at their current rates. All of this information is readily available by ordering a bond statement from The Savings Bond Informer, Inc. (see the last page of the book); most of the information is available by creating a statement yourself (see Chapter 7). Once you have this information, Table 11.2 (page 138) will help you project approximately how much your bonds will be worth by the time you retire.

Bonds that Stop Earning Interest Before You Retire

If any of your bonds are to reach final maturity prior to your retirement, you will need to decide whether to redeem them or exchange them for HH bonds. Even though the HH bond pays a stingy 4% (at the time of writing), it may still make sense to exchange for them. This is especially true for those in high tax brackets who are close to retirement. If you anticipate that you may be in a lower tax bracket after retirement, deferring the interest from old Series E and EE bonds could provide a nice tax savings, as demonstrated in the following example:

> *Sam Jones is 63 years old. He plans to retire in two years. Next year, at age 64, $20,000 of his old Series E bonds will reach final maturity. Of the $20,000 redemption value, approximately $17,500 is deferred interest, income that would have to be reported should he cash the bonds. Since Sam is in a 28% tax bracket, his tax bite would be $4,900 if he cashes them before retirement. Thus he would have only $15,100 to invest or live on after taxes.*
>
> *Sam anticipates that his income will drop after retirement. He has figured he could take about $4,000 a year in income that would be taxed at a lower rate of 15%. Sam is trying to decide if he should roll over to HH bonds and cash some ($4,000) each year, or if he should cash all the bonds now and reinvest the proceeds in something else.*

Table 11.3 (page 139) outlines the options that Sam is considering. Option #2 will provide a higher income stream over the next five years and the greatest amount left to reinvest after taxes (Option #1= $15,100 vs. Option #2= $17,375).

Several variables will affect each bond owner's situation. The most significant is, "What is the expected return on the other investment options?"

Common Pre-Retirement Questions

Should I keep investing in bonds?
Examine this question in light of your other investment alternatives (see Chapter 9). The advantages and disadvantages, like those presented for savings bonds, need to be determined for your other investment options. Let's examine the savings bond pros and cons for the two series currently available—Series EE and Series I.

Advantages

1. Savings bond growth is tax-deferred. Just prior to retirement, you are probably in the highest income period of your life; additional income during these peak earning years will be taxed at a rate that will likely be higher than your retirement rate. Thus, for most wage earners nearing retirement, tax-deferral is often desirable. It means your dollars are growing and compounding without a tax bite until the bonds are cashed. Income from a certificate of deposit, for example, will be taxed annually, which means you are reinvesting after-tax dollars (this means fewer dollars to reinvest than a tax-deferred compounded interest investment). This is particularly important if you anticipate that your tax bracket will change downward after retirement.

2. Savings can be systematic. You may already belong to a payroll deduction program and have witnessed first-hand the growth of your savings bond portfolio through these systematic purchases. For most Americans, a disciplined form of savings beats the "I'll save when I have extra money" approach. (**Note:** The I-bond may not yet be available through payroll deduction at your company.)

3. No fees, no commissions. All your money begins to work for you immediately. If you invest in something that has a 3% front end load, only $970 of $1,000 begins to work for you from day one. You would need to earn slightly more than 3% just to get back to your original $1,000. For those who will need the money in one to three years, a steep commission could result in a lower yield.

4. Your investment in savings bonds is liquid; that is, you can cash the bonds anytime after the first six months. You don't have to wait until you are 65 or 70½) or whatever other age the government decides upon. But remember, there is a three-month interest penalty if you cash in before the bond turns five years old.

5. Purchase as little or as much (almost) as you want: $15,000 per person per calendar year for EE bonds and double that for I bonds. See Chapter 14 for more information on purchase options and limitations.

Disadvantages

1. The current interest rate structure does not provide a guaranteed minimum return on your investment in EE bonds. The first rate for EE bonds purchased between May 1, 1998 and October 30, 1998 is 5.06%. That is good for the first six months only. This rate, always lower than the preceding six-month average of five-year Treasury yields, may not meet investor demands for a reasonable return. The rate changes every six months. The I bond interest rate is based on a fixed rate (3.4%) and a rate that is tied to inflation. The combination of the two provided an initial rate of 4.66% on I bonds purchased in September and October 1998. Both rates are reset every May and November. Current rates can be obtained by calling 1-800-USBONDS.

2. Investments in savings bonds are made with after-tax dollars. With several other investment options available through employers, you can invest pre-tax dollars. Pre-tax investing means more of your money is working for you sooner. Investing pre-tax dollars is not currently available with U.S. Savings Bonds.

3. Savings bonds do not receive a stepped-up basis at the time of death. If bonds are passed on to children who are in higher tax brackets, the interest will be taxed at that higher rate when the bonds are redeemed or reach final maturity. (See Chapter 10 for more tax information.)

4. The deferred reporting of interest income, usually an advantage, can also be viewed as a ticking tax bomb. At some point (redemption or final maturity), the bomb goes off and decades' worth of deferred interest has to be reported. Often this causes some or all of the interest to be taxed at a higher rate.

Should I cash my bonds now?

Most taxpayers are in a higher tax bracket during their working years than they will be in retirement. The exception would be a person who has a lower income in the later working years, but who has significant income potential from investments in retirement plans (401(k) plans, Individual Retirement Accounts, and other qualified retirement pension plans). If a taxpayer is in a lower tax bracket in his final working years than he thinks he will be in after retirement, he should consider cashing some bonds while in the lower tax bracket.

It often makes sense to defer income tax if it is anticipated that the income tax rate before and after retirement is projected to be the same or lower.

Throughout this book one theme has been emphasized: Do not cash your bonds without first evaluating each and every one. In the evaluation process you learn what your bonds are earning. That must be compared with your other investment options. Keep in mind that cashing bonds creates a taxable event. Thus, your redemption value minus the taxes due is the amount that truly is available to spend or invest in another option.

Should I convert to HH bonds?
As long as the guaranteed rate on HH bonds is 4%, and your E or EE bonds still have interest-earning life left, do not exchange for HH bonds. (See Chapter 12 for more on the concept of selective redemption.) HH bonds are paying only 4%; when you exchange, the rate is fixed for the first ten years with no upside potential. If you exchange now, you also forfeit the opportunity to exchange these same Series E or EE bonds two or three years from now should HH bond interest rates go up to 5% or 6%.

Can I gift these bonds away?
The real question is, "Can I gift these bonds without a taxable event?" The book answer is no, with one gray area. To gift bonds to a charity, you must cash the bonds and then give the money to the charity. Cashing the bonds creates a taxable event. Bonds that are titled to you cannot just be handed over to a charity or another person. Savings bonds are non-transferable, so you cannot sign them over to someone else. The one gray area is created by the reporting system used by the IRS to collect data when bonds are cashed. This gray area is outlined in the tax discussion in Chapter 10 (see pages 112 and 113).

I want to gift bonds to my grandchildren so they can use them tax-free for education. Can I do this?
I hope you are sitting down. The answer is no for several reasons. First, only bonds purchased January 1, 1990, and after qualify. Chances are that many of your bonds were purchased prior to that date. Second, the bonds must be registered in the name of the parent or parents of the child. Since your bonds are registered in your name, they will not qualify. And, you cannot simply "get the name changed." Taking your name off the bond (assuming you are listed first) would make a taxable event for you. For more on the educational feature of savings bonds, see Chapter 16.

I'm two years from retirement and someone is telling me to cash all of my bonds and put the money into a better paying investment.

Since the author doesn't know what this "better paying" investment is, the question cannot be answered. However, here are some considerations. How critical is this money to your retirement? Since you are only two years from retiring, a high-risk investment may jeopardize some or all of your principal. Can you afford to lose this? What are the real risks associated with the "better paying investment?" For most investments, past performance does not guarantee future return. If this money is critical to your retirement, you may be better off plugging along at a safe 4% or 5%.

I want to systematically convert to HH bonds over the next five years. How can I do that?

As has been stated repeatedly, HH bonds currently earn a rate of 4%. If you are still interested, here are some options for converting. First, convert to the lowest denomination of HH bond—$500; this makes redeeming your holdings easier (much easier than if you have your money locked into $10,000 bonds). Second, identify the increase dates for the E and EE bonds that you want to convert. Time your exchange for right after the bonds have been credited with an increase. Third, since you want to systematically convert some bonds each year for the next five years, pick bonds with the lowest interest rates and convert them first. Fourth, determine if you want an income stream monthly, quarterly, or semi-annually. Remember that HH bonds pay interest every six months (it does not accumulate as with E or EE bonds). Thus, if you want a monthly income stream, you will need to convert bonds every month for six months in a row.

Retirement Issues

Steps to Managing Bonds in Retirement

Step #1: *Know where you stand.*

What you have: Take inventory of your holdings. Your plan should include all your assets—your house, car(s), 401(k), IRAs, savings bonds, Treasury securities, etc. Although this book will not advise you on how to maximize your investment in these areas, you do need to know which assets are available to convert to income so that you can determine when in your retirement (if ever) you will need to cash some bonds.

Chapter 7 explains how to create or purchase a savings bond statement of your holdings. This is an indispensable tool for your financial plan. The statement provides the value of your holdings, the interest rates you are earning, and the dates your bonds will change interest rates. It also shows when each bond will stop earning interest.

What you need: The key here is to evaluate what your needs are going to be. This should include both ongoing living expenses and one-time big-ticket items (car, vacations, weddings). Table 11.4 (page 140) will help you begin to think and plan. However, a comprehensive evaluation of your needs by a qualified financial professional may also prove helpful. And you might want to purchase one of the many retirement planning publications available in bookstores.

When you need it: Many people have investments that they do not access until a certain age (65 or 70½). This means you may have to take more from your other investments in the meantime. Consider this example:

> *Mary Johnson and her husband will both retire at the age of 63. They choose not to start withdrawing from their 401(k) until the age of 70½. For seven and a half years, they will need to supplement their income. Fortunately, they own more than $200,000 in U.S. Savings Bonds and they plan to cash about $20,000 a year once they retire. The savings bonds will provide the "bridge" they need to keep a level income stream until they start to withdraw their 401(k) plan.*

Step #2: *Make a plan.*

The author has witnessed bond owners forfeiting thousands upon thousands of dollars because they had no plan for handling their savings bonds. Suddenly one day they decide, for whatever reason, to redeem a substantial portion of their bond holdings. If they do not consider tax issues, timing issues, and interest rates, it is highly unlikely that they will pick just the right bonds to redeem at just the right time.

As you formulate your plan, the following components should be incorporated: tax issues, timing issues, and estate planning issues. Once again, these areas are often best understood and developed with the help of a financial professional. For instance, the author does not do all his own tax planning and preparation. Why not? Because he wants someone who knows every in and out of taxation to advise him. Likewise estate planning is complex. As outlined in Chapter 10, you have an estate plan whether you drew one up or not. Since most of us would rather not default to the government's plan for our money, we need to be about the business of establishing an estate plan. Working with a competent attorney, one familiar with estate planning options and tools, is very worthwhile.

Step #3: *Follow the plan.*

If you were building a house, you would not spend considerable time and money drafting blueprints and then not refer to them during the building process. Your plan is your blueprint.

Step #4: *Evaluate your plan and revise as needed.*

Periodically meet with the financial professionals who helped to draft your plan to review any significant changes in your life, such as, you hit the lotto; the National Football League is starting a senior division and you signed a multi-million dollar contract to play quarterback (you may want to look at that disability coverage); your kids have all become financially independent; Social Security finds $500 trillion dollars and quadruples everyone's monthly checks.

Actually many factors can affect our plans, including the tragic, yet inevitable, loss of a loved one. As your circumstances change, keep your plan up to date. Make sure the proper paperwork is available for your heirs. Communicate the necessary information to those who need to know.

Common Questions from Retirees

The author has conducted dozens of seminars on retirement issues. The lines of people waiting to ask questions after these sessions reveal several things. First, each person has a different scenario, thus they need information specific to their situation. Second, many bond owners make a point of voicing their frustration at not being able to get good answers to their questions (usually they are asking the wrong people; for example, expecting a bank teller to address a retirement tax question). They seem grateful to receive information that addresses their particular concerns.

In this section the most common retirement questions and concerns will be examined. If you don't find the answer to your question, please write to the author so that it can be considered for a future edition.

Will cashing in savings bonds cause some or all of my Social Security to be taxed?
Possibly. This often happens when bond owners are in a very low tax bracket: they have little or no income and, as a result, little or no tax. However, they may have a large cache of U.S. Savings Bonds, which has accrued a considerable amount of interest over the years. Redeeming a large number of bonds at one time may cause a substantial portion your Social Security income to be taxed. Again, consult a competent tax professional for counsel.

Can I gift the bonds to someone else?
Sometimes bond owners find they do not need their savings bonds. They have ample income from other investments and they would like the savings bonds to be taken out of their name and given to children, grandchildren, or some other important persons. The rules regarding transfer of ownership state: If the principal owner (generally the first-named owner or co-owner) removes their name, it creates a taxable event. Thus you cannot just "sign the bonds over, by signing

the back of the bond" to the relative of your choice. See Chapter 10 and Chapter 13 for more detail.

Is there an automatic stepped-up basis on bonds?
No. See Chapter 10 for more detail.

What tax consequences will my heirs face when they inherit these bonds?
If the interest has not been previously reported (and in most cases it has not), they will inherit the liability for all the interest earned from the date of purchase. See Chapter 10, page 115.

Will these bonds end up in probate?
Not if you have a co-owner or beneficiary listed on the bonds and you predecease that person. However, the person who receives the bonds from you should then have the bonds retitled into their name and add a co-owner or beneficiary of their choosing. This way when they die, should their estate go through probate, the bonds will again pass directly to the co-owner or beneficiary they have listed on the bonds.

May I list a charity as the co-owner or beneficiary of my bonds?
No. You cannot have an entity (organization, charity, trust) listed as a co-owner or beneficiary of a bond.

Maximizing Family Wealth

Choosing which asset to liquidate can make a difference when it comes to maximizing family wealth.

> *A 65-year-old woman has $80,000 of stocks, $40,000 of which is capital gain that will be taxed if sold. She also has $80,000 of savings bonds that have $40,000 of untaxed interest income. Her tax bracket is 28% or less. She would like to sell one group of assets to supplement her retirement plans. The second group of assets will likely be passed on to her heirs.*

Prior to 1998, if she had liquidated either group of assets the federal tax would have been the same. In 1998, due to the new lower capital gains rate, she would pay $8,045 in federal taxes if she cashed the savings bonds and only $5,590 if she sold the stock. In 1998, her taxes would be $2,455 lower if she sold the stock rather than cashing the bonds. At first glance, this appears to be the best approach and this would be true if these assets were treated the same at her death.

Note: In most states, there would also be tax on the capital gain of the stocks. The treatment of these two assets upon the death of the owner is different and has a significant impact upon family wealth. If this woman leaves the savings bonds to her heirs, they will inherit the liability for all the interest and will be taxed at their own rate when the bonds are cashed. If she leaves the stocks to her heirs, they are liable only for the gain in the value of the stock from the time of her death until the stock is cashed. The $40,000 gain that took place during her life is excused due to the stepped-up basis that the stocks receive. Assuming the heirs are in the 28% tax bracket, they will pay $11,200 more in taxes if they receive the bonds rather than the stocks. So the family unit is $8,745 ($11,200 minus $2,455) better off in this case if she cashes in the bonds during her lifetime rather than selling the stock. By paying $2,455 more in taxes in 1998 her family will save $11,200 later after her death.

As demonstrated, tax issues for savings bonds are unique and very different from those for stocks. The reporting of interest earned on your bonds has probably been deferred (that is, it has never been reported and so you have never paid any tax on your accrued interest). If you die while still in possession of the bonds, your children can, of course, inherit the bonds (unless you have named someone else as a co-owner or beneficiary). But, guess what else they inherit? The tax liability. If the interest is not reported on the last return of the deceased, or if it is not reported within the estate, the full amount of interest income becomes a liability to the recipients of the bonds when the bonds are cashed or reach final maturity. Consider another example:

> Jonathan Smith, an only child, inherited $50,000 in bonds from his mother. The accrued interest on the bonds was $40,000. At the time of her death, his mom had been in the 15% tax bracket—and had been for the last decade of her life. Jonathan, a successful businessman, was in the 39.6% tax bracket. If the bonds had been cashed during her lifetime, the $40,000 could have been taxed at her 15% rate. (Note: This may have required cashing the bonds over several years to avoid reporting all the income in one year, which would have thrown her into a higher tax bracket.) The tax bill would have been approximately $6,000. If Jonathan cashes the bonds now, his tax rate will be used to calculate the tax, resulting in a bill of $15,840—almost $10,000 more than had his mother cashed the bonds.

From the standpoint of maximizing "family" wealth, it often makes sense to cash bonds in order to utilize the lower tax brackets of older parents.

There is one other strategy for Jonathan to consider. Upon his mother's death, he could disclaim his interest in the bonds (assuming the other heirs are Jonathan's children) and let the bonds be titled directly to his children. Once his children are 14 years old, they can cash the bonds and be taxed at their rate. This may result in an even lower tax bite. See Chapter 10, page 122, for further explanation. Consult with a competent attorney and/or CPA before attempting to invoke this strategy.

Author's note: If your calculations reveal that cashing your bonds rather than passing them on to your heirs results in a lower family tax hit, communicate your intentions to your children. Make sure you receive competent legal and financial advice before you act. Then (and this is just the author's opinion) spend a little bit of what you saved on yourself for being so smart.

Spending Your Hard-Earned Money

You have worked hard. You have saved well. If you have a stash of bonds, maybe you should consider a little reward for yourself. It could be a trip to that special place you always dreamed of visiting or a unique purchase. Anyway we look at it, we are not going to take it with us.

The following true story illustrates that you could spend a portion of your savings bond investment without affecting its current value.

A couple in Michigan had over $400,000 in bonds, representing half of what they had saved for early retirement. The wife called and was afraid that by cashing some of the bond they might deplete their holdings. After having her investment analyzed, she discovered that the holdings were growing at over 5% a year. This meant they could redeem $20,000 a year and still have over $400,000 left for retirement.

If they cashed $20,000 a year, this couple wouldn't even touch their principal. If they chose to redeem $50,000 a year over the next ten years, they would still not deplete the entire portfolio. Educate yourself so that the fear of cashing does not keep you from using money that could be helpful to you.

In the table below, you will find data that will help you determine how much you could cash each year for the next ten, fifteen, or twenty years before your bond holdings would be exhausted, assuming you are earning an average return of 5%.

Remember: To effectively use this strategy, you should get the details on each of your bonds (see page 66 for alternatives) and cash the bonds earning the lowest interest rates first.

Table 11.1 Spending Your Hard-Earned Money

Current total value of your bonds	An annual redemption that will not affect your principal	An annual redemption that will leave $0 in 10 years	An annual redemption that will leave $0 in 15 years	An annual redemption that will leave $0 in 20 years
$10,000	$500	$1,295	$963	$802
$50,000	$2,500	$6,475	$4,815	$4,010
$100,000	$5,000	$12,950	$9,630	$8,020
$250,000	$12,500	$32,375	$24,075	$20,050
$500,000	$25,000	$64,750	$48,150	$40,100

©1998 The Savings Bond Informer, Inc. All Rights Reserved.
Assumptions and Comments:
1. Overall holdings will grow at a constant rate of 5%. Your bonds will vary and a specific analysis is recommended before invoking this strategy.
2. Money will be removed at the end of a given year.
3. This is the amount prior to taxes.
4. Before you use this strategy, consult with a compettent financial professional or trusted advisor to confirm your strategy and your calculations.

While some people won't cash any of their bonds, others rush in and redeem them all at once.

Opps, The Opposite Extreme

A TSBI client from the Midwest wrote the following letter describing a case of the "panic and do something" method of bond ownership. Hopefully, you have seen a couple of themes repeated in this book, that is, don't rush your decisions and you don't have to cash all your bonds at once.

> *We had a close friend who cashed in all his bonds in the year of his retirement and thus ended up paying a large amount of taxes. He was so afraid that "he and his wife would not be able to make ends meet." This, in spite of the fact that he was to receive a large pension, social security, plus investment income from other sources. We talked ourselves blue in the face trying to convince him that he should wait and see if he would actually need the money from the bonds. He cashed them all and put the proceeds into a savings account where it is still drawing interest of 3% or less!*
>
> *For "conservative" people like this who suffer from retirement phobia, perhaps you could stress in your book that it is not a "do it now or never"*

situation, since savings bonds can be redeemed at least twice a year or more often. . . . So the retiree can easily wait until the situation arises where he may actually need the money, and even then it may not be necessary to cash all the bonds at one time.

Well said.

Quick Tips on Retirement

- Before implementing a retirement plan, make sure you know the following for each of your bonds: how much they are worth now, the interest rates they are earning, how much deferred interest has not yet been reported, when they will stop earning interest and how long they will earn interest at their current rates.

- If financial planning is difficult for you, consider hiring a competent financial advisor to help you integrate the savings bond portion of your retirement savings into a plan that will be adequate for your retirement needs.

- Before determining whether or not you should keep investing in bonds, you should examine the advantages and disadvantages.

- The first step to managing your bonds in retirement is knowing where you stand: what you have, what you need, and when you will need it.

- For bond owners in low tax brackets who plan to leave bonds to heirs in high tax brackets, cashing the bonds during their lifetime, rather than passing them on to heirs, can maximize their family's wealth.

- Leave documentation for your family of your bond transactions. This will save the family from trying to "piece" together what action you did or did not take.

Table 11.2 Projected Value of Bond Portfolio at Retirement

Current Value of Bond Holdings & Avg Projected Interest Rate	Value in 3 Years	Value in 5 Years	Value in 10 Years	Value in 20 Years
$10,000 at 4%	$11,262	$12,190	$14,859	$22,080
$10,000 at 5%	$11,597	$12,801	$16,386	$26,851
$10,000 at 6%	$11,941	$13,439	$18,061	$32,620
$25,000 at 4%	$28,154	$30,475	$37,149	$55,201
$25,000 at 5%	$28,992	$32,002	$40,965	$67,127
$25,000 at 6%	$29,851	$33,598	$45,153	$81,551
$50,000 at 4%	$56,308	$60,950	$74,297	$110,402
$50,000 at 5%	$57,985	$64,004	$81,931	$134,253
$50,000 at 6%	$59,703	$67,196	$90,306	$163,102
$100,000 at 4%	$112,616	$121,899	$148,595	$220,804
$100,000 at 5%	$115,969	$128,008	$163,862	$268,506
$100,000 at 6%	$119,405	$134,392	$180,611	$326,204
$250,000 at 4%	$281,541	$304,749	$371,487	$522,010
$250,000 at 5%	$289,923	$320,021	$409,654	$671,266
$250,000 at 6%	$298,513	$335,979	$451,528	$815,509
$500,000 at 4%	$563,081	$609,497	$724,974	$1,104,020
$500,000 at 5%	$579,847	$640,042	$819,308	$1,342,532
$500,000 at 6%	$597,026	$671,958	$903,056	$1,631,019

Table 11.3 Two Options for Cashing Bonds that Stop Earning Interest Before Retirement

	Option #1: Cash all the bonds when they reach maturity	**Option #2:** Exchange E &EE bonds for HH bonds, deferring all interest until after retirement. Then cash $4,000 of bonds per year over a five-year period.
Value of bonds at final maturity	$20,000	$20,000
Amount of accrued interest	$17,500	$17,500
Tax bracket	28%	Can take $4,000 a year and be taxed at 15% rate
Current year	Cash in all bonds, all interest taxed at 28%. Received $20,000 cash. Pays $4,900 in taxes. Net left is $15,100.	Roll over to HH bonds, deferring all interest until HH bond is cashed. HH bonds pay interest at 4% a year.
Years one through five after retirement	$15,100 is put into the investment of choice to produce income. Assume a conservative 5% return.	Cash $4,000 of bonds each year. $3,500 interest income to be taxed at 15%, Annual taxes on savings bond interest is $525. Over five years, $2,625.
Income stream	$15,100 x 5% = $755 a year	HH bond interest + interest from other 5% investment: yr 1 $20,000 $800 + 0 = $800 yr 2 $16,000 $640 + 174 = $814 yr 3 $12,000 $480 + 348 = $828 yr 4 $ 8,000 $320 + 521 = $841 yr 5 $ 4,000 $160 + 695 = $855
Amount left at the end of five years	$15,100	$17, 375

Important assumptions:
1. The bond owner will spend the income stream that is received each year.
2. In Option #1, money from bonds after tax is invested at 5%, a different interest rate (higher or lower) would obviously change the income stream.

   In Option #2, the bond owner would save $2,275 in taxes by exchanging for HH bonds and creating a systematic redemption pattern over a five-year period. This tax savings is significant provided the other investment option yield is close to the HH bond yield.

Table 11.4 Anticipated Expenses in Retirement

Category	Monthly Cost	Annual Cost
Food		
Utilities		
Rent or Mortgage		
Transportation		
Medical/Dental		
Charitable Giving		
Savings Investment		
Insurance		
Entertainment		
Clothing		
Child Support/Alimony		
Gifts/Presents		
Loan Payments		
Miscellaneous		
Other:		
Other:		
TOTAL:		
Big Ticket Expenses	**Estimated Cost**	**Projected Date**
Car		
House/Condo		
Wedding		
Vacation		
Other:		

Chapter 12

EXCHANGING FOR HH BONDS

▶ *HH Bonds: What They Are and How They Work*
▶ *What Can Be Learned by Looking at an HH Bond*
▶ *Tax Consequences of an Exchange*
▶ *Points to Consider*
▶ *Where to Exchange Bonds and the Process Involved*
▶ *Are HH Bonds Right for You?*
▶ *Selective Redemption: An Alternative to Exchange*
▶ *Timing Your Exchange*
▶ *Latest Rule Changes Do Not Affect H/HH Bonds*
▶ *Additional Technical Guidelines Covering Exchange*
▶ *Quick Tips on Exchange*

"To exchange, or not to exchange?" That is the question which plagues many owners of E and EE bonds. "Should I keep my E and EE bonds or exchange them for HH?" On the one hand, current income, tax deferment, and direct deposits of interest payments seem very tempting. On the other hand, consider the guaranteed interest rate of only 4% (as of September 1998), with no upside potential for ten years and no tax deferment of the yearly interest income, and the proposition begins to look slightly bleak. After presenting various points for you to weigh in making your decision, this chapter will not only supply instructions on the exchange process, but also tips that will ensure you maximize your return whether you exchange or not.

HH Bonds: What They Are and How They Work

Series HH bonds are called "current income bonds." As the name suggests, these bonds produce an interest income stream that is paid to the bond owner every six months. The HH bond replaced the Series H bond in January 1980. Many Series H bonds are still earning interest, although the issuing of new Series H bonds ended in December 1979.

Series HH bonds cannot be purchased for cash. They are only available through the exchange of Series E, EE, and Savings Notes. They can also be obtained through the reinvestment of Series H bonds that have reached final maturity.

HH bonds come in denominations of $500, $1,000, $5,000, and $10,000. Bond owners must have a minimum redemption value of $500 from any combination of bonds they wish to exchange. Since the HH bond pays interest every six months, the bond is always worth the face value upon redemption.

HH bonds obtained through exchange as of March 1, 1993, will pay a guaranteed interest rate of 4%. The interest is paid semi-annually, direct deposit to the bank account of the bond holder's choice. This rate is fixed for the first ten years. For the second ten-year period, the bonds will earn the guaranteed rate that is in effect the day they enter the extended period. The market-based rate does not apply to HH bonds. The total life of the HH bond is twenty years. See Table 12.2 (page 154) for interest rates for H and HH bonds.

All H and HH bonds that are still paying interest have an initial maturity of ten years. H bonds receive two ten-year extensions for a total life of thirty years. HH bonds receive one ten-year extension for a total life of twenty years. Many investors are surprised (and disappointed) that the bonds pick up the current guaranteed rate in effect each time a new ten-year extension is started. This new rate stays in effect for the full ten-year period. Retirees on fixed incomes, who exchanged for bonds in the mid-1980s at 7.5%, have been upset to find that the semi-annual interest payment they are used to has been cut almost in half (to 4%) as their HH bonds enter a new ten-year extension in the mid-1990s. Typically no notice is sent, so suddenly they start receiving smaller payments. See Table 12.2 (page 154) for Series H and HH bond interest rates.

What Can Be Learned by Looking at an HH Bond

The following is an HH bond:

Figure 12.1 HH Bond

Here is what you can know by looking at the bond:

1. The bond is worth the face value. If the bond pictured above were cashed, the bond owner would receive a check or direct deposit for $500.

2. The first interest payment will occur six months after the exchange. Interest payments thereafter will always be on the anniversary of the issue date and six months later. In this example, the bond owner receives the interest payments every July 1st and January 1st. If he or she cashes before an interest payment, they will forfeit up to six months of interest.

3. If the bond owner cashes the bond, they will receive a 1099-INT for the amount of deferred interest printed on the face of the bond—$175 in this example. This is reported as interest income and subject to federal tax, but exempt from state and local tax. When this bond was issued, the funds likely came from Series E or EE bonds. The value of the E or EE bonds was a combination of the purchase price and the accrued interest. This accrued interest from the old bonds is "rolled" into the HH bond, thus it is part of the HH bond face value. However this interest has never been reported, so cashing an HH bond causes this amount to become taxable income. Because deferred interest was part of the redemption value ($500), the bond owner will not receive additional dollars.

4. An HH bond will stop paying interest twenty years from the issue date. (See top right-hand corner.)

5. If the bond was issued May 1989 or after, the bond owner is receiving direct deposit of the interest payments. If issued prior to that date they may be receiving a check or direct deposit.

6. As of the date of this publication, all HH bonds are paying either 4% or 6%. There is no market rate. Table 12.2 on page 154, will provide the rate structures as of the date on the table.

Tax Consequences of an Exchange

Because most bond owners do not report the interest accruing on their E and EE bonds annually, they must report it when the bonds are redeemed. When exchanging for HH bonds, the bond owner has the option of (a) reporting all interest accrued for the bonds presented for exchange, or (b) deferring the reporting of interest until the HH bond is cashed, reaches final maturity, or is disposed of so as to create a taxable event. By electing to defer the interest reporting, a bond owner may receive up to twenty years of additional deferment (the life of the HH bond is twenty years).

The option of whether to report or defer accrued interest is the bond owner's choice. If a bank teller is assisting you, advise him or her of your choice. Do not allow anyone to assign you an option without your consent.

How to Know the Amount of Deferred Interest

If the bond owner chooses to defer the accrued interest from the bonds they exchanged, the amount deferred will be printed on the face of the HH bonds. (See the example on page 143.)

For instance, consider a holder who exchanges $20,000 (redemption value) of Series E bonds for Series HH bonds. Of that $20,000, the purchase price was $6,000 and the interest accrued was $14,000. The bond owner receives two $10,000 HH bonds. On the face of older HH bonds is a statement similar to the following:

> Deferred interest $7,000 on Savings Bonds/Savings Notes exchanged for this bond and included in its issue price is reportable for federal income tax purposes, for the year of redemption, disposition, or final maturity of this bond, which ever is earlier.

The $7,000 mentioned on the two bonds adds up to the $14,000 of accrued and deferred interest. When the bond owner redeems the HH bonds, he will receive $20,000 and a 1099-INT for $14,000 in interest income.

Points to Consider

You only have to hold your Series E and EE bonds and SNs for six months before they are eligible to be exchanged for HH bonds. At final maturity (i.e., the date the bond stops earning interest), the investor has one year to exchange those bonds for HH bonds. One year past final maturity, the bonds are no longer eligible for exchange.

You may defer reporting interest earned on Series E, EE, and SNs until the HH bonds received in exchange are redeemed, disposed of (for example, taxable reissue), or have reached final maturity, whichever comes first. The deferred interest will be reported to the bond owner and to the IRS at the time the HH bonds reach such a taxable event. Since HH bonds have a total life of twenty years, bond owners can receive up to twenty years of additional tax deferment when they exchange to HH bonds.

The semi-annual interest payments from HH bonds must be reported as interest income. This interest is subject to federal income taxes, but exempt from state and local taxes.

Unlike Series EE bonds which have a purchase limit, you may exchange for an unlimited dollar amount of HH bonds. (Refer to Chapter 14, "Purchasing U.S. Savings Bonds," for additional information on purchase limits.)

If you exchange a substantial dollar amount, consider requesting smaller denominations of HH bonds, such as $500 or $1,000 instead of $10,000. Why? At a later date if you want to cash a few thousand dollars here or there, you can select the exact number of bonds you need. You can, in fact, cash part of a $10,000 bond and have the remainder reissued; needless to say, this requires more paperwork.

Where to Exchange Bonds and the Process Involved

The exchange process is a simple transferal of the value of your E or EE bonds into HH bonds. The transaction can be handled at most commercial banks. If your bank handles the redemption of savings bonds, they should be familiar with the exchange procedure.

The form to use for exchanging is PD F 3253 (Figure 12.2, page 153). The bank will record the redemption value of the bonds you present for exchange on PD F 3253. (If you want to double-check their calculations, see Chapter 7 for options.) The value of the bonds you present for exchange will probably not exactly match the $500 increments of HH bonds. You may add money to the transaction, up to the next $500 increment, or you may take money back, down to the next $500 increment. This is your choice—do not let the bank teller make it for you. If you choose to receive money, thus rounding down to the nearest $500 denomination of HH bond, some or all of the money you receive is interest from the old bonds. The amount of interest will be reported as interest income for the year in which the exchange takes place.

The PD F 3253 includes an authorization for direct deposit of interest payments to an account at the financial institution of your choice. The direct deposit feature has been required for all HH bonds issued since October 1989.

Are HH Bonds Right for You?

When might HH bonds be a good investment? They might be attractive when you have money in a savings account paying only 2% to 3% or when you could use the semi-annual interest payments to supplement your income.

If you have at least $500, and can afford to tie it up for one year, this HH bond scenario might work. Buy an EE bond for $500 ($1,000 face value). Hold the bond for six months and then exchange it for an HH bond (you will forfeit three months interest on the EE bond since it is being cashed in before five years). At the time of exchange, you can receive the interest you earned on the EE bond. Once you have held the HH bond six months, your semi-annual payment will be direct deposited to your bank account. If you are only earning 2% on your savings account, this is a quick way to double your earnings. You can cash the HH bond anytime after holding it six months.

Another option bond owners use is to exchange at final maturity if they need another one or two years of deferment before they report interest income. By exchanging, the bond owner now has up to twenty years in which to time the redemption to suit their specific situation.

When are HH bonds *not* a good idea? If locking up money for ten years at 4% makes you a bit queasy, consider some of the other conservative investment options presented in Chapter 9, "Comparing Savings Bonds to Other Investment Options." To summarize, each bond owner's situation is unique. A case can be made for or against HH bonds, depending on the variables of an individual's situation. Five- and ten-year Treasury notes have yielded in a range from 5 to 7% over the last several years.

Author's note: Most bond owners who obtain HH bonds have been in the bond program for twenty, thirty, or forty years. If this were a company, we would say these are the "best" customers. Yet, how does the government treat these customers? By giving them not only the lowest rate in the bond program, but a rate that has consistently been 75 to 150 basis points below that of three-month T-bills. This makes no sense—thousands of investors have said that they are leaving the bond program rather than accept a 4% rate—unless, of course, the government is trying to discourage the purchase of HH bonds, forcing people into redemption, and thus creating more immediate tax revenue.

Selective Redemption: An Alternative to Exchange

Millions of Americans bought savings bonds with the intent of exchanging them for HH bonds to supplement their retirement income. This strategy was more attractive when HH bonds paid 6%. On March 1, 1993, however, HH bonds began paying only 4%. Here is what most bond owners fail to realize:

1. Many E and EE bonds may still have a guaranteed rate of 6%. Exchanging them would result in forfeiting 2% interest on many bonds. A 2% drop in the interest rate results in a loss of $200 per $10,000 per year.

2. When you exchange during the 4% rate period that was enacted March 1, 1993, the 4% rate is locked for ten years. Even if rates increase after you exchange, you will remain at 4% for the first ten years. You can cash your HH bond after six months, but then you have to report any interest that was deferred from the E or EE bonds when you exchanged—which is probably what prompted you to exchange in the first place.

Selective redemption is a process wherein the bond owner chooses which bonds to redeem or exchange based on interest rates and timing issues. When bonds need to be cashed or exchanged, the goal is to divest the lower-paying bonds and hold on to those earning higher interest rates. Selective redemption is not grabbing a handful of bonds and redeeming or exchanging with no forethought.

How does it work? Let's suppose you were going to exchange your bonds for HH bonds. To use selective redemption instead of exchanging, you would cash bonds that would equal the dollar amount you would have received in interest had you exchanged for HH bonds. This allows you to keep the majority of your E and EE bonds at the higher rates of interest. When selecting which E and EE bonds to cash, choose those earning the lowest rate of interest.

One advantage of this strategy is that it puts off the exchange decision for an indefinite period of time. Thus, if rates on savings bonds increase in 2000 or 2001, you could then exchange for HH bonds at the new higher rate, which would be in effect for the next ten years.

Consider this example. An investor has Series E bonds with a redemption value of $10,000. If he exchanges the E bonds for HH bonds, he will receive one $10,000 HH bond that is paying 4%. The annual interest earned on that bond is $400. The entire $400 will be reported as interest income for tax purposes.

Instead of exchanging his bonds, this bond owner uses the selective redemption system. First, he determines the exact interest rate that applies to each of his bonds. He learns that some of his bonds are earning 4%, and most of them 6%. On average he is earning about 5.8% on his Series E bonds. After identifying the bonds earning 4%, he decides to cash a few of them and receives approximately $400.

What is the result? A comparison at the end of one year is illustrated in Table 12.1.

Table 12.1 Comparison of Exchange and Selective Redemption

AFTER ONE YEAR	EXCHANGING FOR HH BONDS	SELECTIVE REDEMPTION
Value of remaining bonds	$10,000	Approximately $10,180
Proceeds	$400 from interest payments	$400 from redemption
Tax consequence	All $400 is interest income	$400 minus original purchase price of E bonds is interest income
Future options	Locked in at 4% for ten years, have to cash HH bonds if you want to exercise other options	Can continue selective redemption for an indefinite period, or can exchange for HH bonds at any time, if the HH bond rate is increased to more attractive levels. Keeps options open.

©1995 The Savings Bond Informer, Inc. All Rights Reserved.

In this example, selective redemption resulted in an even flow of dollars (redemption proceeds) to the bond owner and an increase in the bond holdings by $180. The actual numbers will vary in each case. The primary numbers that may make this option attractive are the interest rates on the E and EE bonds. If the guaranteed rates are 6%, then selective redemption makes a lot of sense.

To effectively use this strategy, you need to know the exact interest rates, values, and timing issues for each bond you own. Chapter 7 outlines the options for obtaining this information for your bonds. The Savings Bond Informer Rating System[SM] may be especially helpful in comparing one bond to another (see the last page of the book for more information).

If a bond has reached final maturity, your only option is to redeem or exchange it (if the bond is less than one year past final maturity).

Timing Your Exchange

The more you can get from your E and EE bonds and SNs, the more you have to invest in HH bonds. Since most E and EE bonds and SNs increase in value semi-annually, exchanging right after a semi-annual increase will maximize the amount available for exchange. Tables 7.5 and 7.6, pages 84 and 85 provide the date of increase for your E and EE bonds.

You will receive an interest payment every six months after the initial exchange. If you exchanged in January, your interest payment will be deposited to your account every July and January. Thus, if you want payments twice a year, transact all your exchanges in the same month. (More than likely this will not maximize the timing on the bonds being presented for exchange.) Or if you prefer to receive an interest payment every month, spread your exchange requests over a consecutive six-month period. This will insure that you receive an interest payment twelve months of the year.

Latest Rule Changes Do Not Affect H/HH Bonds

New rules implemented May 1, 1995, and May 1, 1997, have no impact on any new or old issues of H or HH bonds. H/HH bonds have never been affected by the market-based rates and this is still the case. The new I bond rules do not affect HH bonds. In addition, you cannot exchange I bonds for HH bonds.

Under the current rules that apply to H/HH bonds, any future announcements of a change in the guaranteed interest rates would affect H/HH bonds as they entered extended maturity periods. For more information on extended maturity periods, see Chapter 4.

Additional Technical Guidelines Covering Exchange

The remainder of this chapter is fairly technical; if you have had your fill, move on to the next chapter. If you want more details, indulge yourself. The information in this section, some of which has been adapted for your benefit, is from The Department of Treasury, The Bureau of the Public Debt's (BPD) publication, "The Book on U.S. Savings Bonds."

There are some situations where bond owners have reported the interest on their bonds and SNs annually. These bonds and SNs may also be exchanged for Series HH bonds.

When further deferment of tax liability is elected in the exchange, the rules on the registration of the bonds are as follows:

1. If the accrual bonds and SNs are registered in single ownership or ben-
    eficiary form, the person named as owner must also be named as owner
    or first-named co-owner on the HH bonds. A beneficiary may be added,
    changed, or removed or a co-owner may be added to the registration.

2. If the accrual-type bonds and SNs are registered in co-ownership form,
    the "principal co-owner" (the one whose funds were used to purchase
    the bonds and SNs) must be named as owner or first-named co-owner
    on the HH bonds. The other co-owner could be changed or removed
    or a beneficiary added. If both co-owners shared equally in the pur-
    chase or received them jointly as gifts of a legacy, the registration on
    the Series HH bond must name both persons as co-owners.

3. If the owner or "principal co-owner" of the older bonds and SNs is
    deceased, and there is a surviving beneficiary or co-owner, the latter
    must be named as owner or first-named co-owner on the HH bonds.
    The person submitting the bonds and SNs for exchange must submit
    evidence establishing entitlement (for example, the beneficiary must
    furnish proof of death of the registered owner). Another co-owner or
    beneficiary could be named.

Advice on how to resolve difficult situations can be obtained from the BPD.
(See Chapter 19 for address and phone number.)

Who May Request Exchange and Changes in Registration

The Owner. The term "owner" means: (1) the registered owner of a security
registered in single ownership or beneficiary form, whether or not a natural
person, or (2) a beneficiary or co-owner named on a security with a deceased
owner or co-owner. The beneficiary would be required to furnish proof of the
owner's death. An owner may request the exchange and have the HH bonds
issued in his or her name in any authorized form of registration permitted under the Department of the Treasury Circular, Public Debt Series 3-80, provided
he or she is owner or first-named co-owner.

The Co-owner. A "principal co-owner" is one who (1) purchased the securities
with his or her own funds, or (2) received them as a gift, legacy, or inheritance,
or as a result of judicial proceedings, and had them reissued in co-ownership
form, provided that he or she received no contribution in any manner from
the other co-owner for being so designated. (Those processing the exchange
subscription form PD F 3253 are not required to go beyond a person's certification on such form that he or she is the principal co-owner of the securities
presented.)

The principal co-owner of the securities presented for exchange must be named as owner or first-named co-owner on the Series HH bonds and his or her Social Security number must be provided.

Co-owners Who May Request An Exchange

Either co-owner may request the exchange, that is, if there is no change in registration and the HH bond is to be registered exactly the same way the securities surrendered had been.

If a tax-deferred exchange is requested, the Social Security account number of the "principal co-owner" (whose name must be shown first in the inscription) must be used for bonds to be inscribed in the names of two persons as co-owners.

If the principal co-owner is not the person requesting the exchange, the principal co-owner must complete Form W-9 to certify the correctness of his or her Social Security account number and that he or she is not subject to backup withholding. In such cases, the co-owner requesting the exchange must also strike the statement on PD F 3253 above his or her signature that he or she is the principal co-owner.

Only the principal co-owner may request an exchange if the HH bonds are to be registered differently from the securities surrendered. Such HH bond registration may be in any form permitted by Department of the Treasury Circular, Public Debt Series 3-80, but must include the principal co-owner as the owner or first-named co-owner.

Legal Representative (Named in Registration on the Bond)

A legal representative means the court-appointed (or otherwise qualified) person, regardless of title, who is legally authorized to act for the estate of a minor, incompetent, aged person, absentee, et al. The legal representative would be required to show full title and provide appropriate identification. Legal representatives of decedents' estates should not conduct exchanges, but should request distribution on PD F 1455 so that persons entitled to the estate may do so.

More than One Form of Inscription Requested

Subject to the limitations stated above, a subscriber may request that the HH bonds be issued in several inscriptions. A note to that effect should be made on the face of the form with the additional inscriptions recorded, together with the appropriate amounts for each, on the back of the blue (A) copy of Form PD F 3253. The person authorized to request the exchange must execute the requests for payment on the bonds.

HH bonds can be useful if you have specific financial goals in mind. To exchange, or not to exchange? Only you can answer that!

Quick Tips on Exchange

- EE bonds only need to be held for six months to be eligible for exchange.

- You only have one year past the time a bond stops earning interest to exchange for HH bonds.

- Selective redemption is an alternative to exchanging that can maximize your investment.

- Because many E and EE bonds are currently earning a guaranteed rate of 6%, exchanging these would mean a loss of 2% of interest earnings per bond.

- To effectively use selective redemption, you must know the exact interest rates, values, and timing issues for each bond you hold.

- If you choose to defer reporting the interest you have earned on your E or EE bonds or SNs/FSs when exchanging for HH bonds, you can defer reporting that interest for up to twenty years.

- Since most E and EE bonds and SNs/FSs increase in value semi-annually, exchanging right after a semi-annual increase will maximize the amount available for exchange.

- I bonds cannot be exchanged for HH bonds.

Figure 12.2 Exchange Application (PD F 3253)

PD F 3253
Department of the Treasury
Bureau of the Public Debt
(Revised February 1994)

OMB No. 1535-0005

EXCHANGE APPLICATION FOR U.S. SAVINGS BONDS OF SERIES HH
Follow the attached instructions and use the worksheet when completing the application.

1. For Federal income tax purposes, I ☐ (a) wish to defer reporting ☐ (b) will report this year or have reported the interest earned on my bonds/notes surrendered in this exchange transaction.

2. $	3.	4. $	5.	6. $
Redemption Value	Interest Earned	HH Bonds To Be Issued	Payment Returned	Interest Deferred

7. Number Of Each Denomination	@ $500	@ $1,000	@ $5,000	@ $10,000

FRB USE ONLY	Increment On Each Bond				
	Bond Serial Numbers				

8. REGISTRATION INFORMATION

OWNER OR FIRST-NAMED COOWNER (of Series HH bonds)

TAXPAYER
IDENTIFICATION NO.:   —   —   – OR –   —

Social Security Number   Employer Identification Number

NAME

NUMBER AND STREET
OR RURAL ROUTE

CITY   STATE   ZIP CODE

COOWNER OR BENEFICIARY (OPTIONAL). Coownership will be assumed if neither block is checked. The following person is to be named as   coowner   beneficiary. See reverse for additional registrations.

NAME

Delivery Instructions for HH
bonds (if different than above): _____

9. DIRECT DEPOSIT AUTHORIZATION REQUIRED FOR U. S. RESIDENTS. (READ ITEM 9 BEFORE COMPLETING THIS SECTION).

NAME(S) ON
DEPOSITOR ACCT.: _____

ROUTING/ TRANSIT NO.:
—   —   —

DEPOSITOR
ACCT. NO.:   TYPE OF ACCOUNT: CHECKING   SAVINGS

To owners of Series H/HH Bonds issued before October 1989:
I request that semiannual interest payments on all Series HH/H bonds purchased prior to October 1989 and bearing the above taxpayer identification number also be deposited directly to this account. If neither block is checked, yes will be assumed.   YES   NO

10. Under penalty of perjury, I certify that I am the owner or principal coowner of any savings bonds and notes submitted herewith; that the number shown on the form is my correct taxpayer identification number; and that I am not subject to backup withholding either (i) because I have not been notified that I am subject to backup withholding (as a result of a failure to report all interest and dividends) or (ii) because I have been notified by the Internal Revenue Service that I am no longer subject to backup withholding, unless I check this block:
☐ I am subject to backup withholding.

Daytime
Telephone No.: _____ Serial Number of one of the savings bonds/notes submitted in this exchange: _____

Applicant's Signature: _____   Date _____

11. FINANCIAL INSTITUTION AUTHORIZATION AND CERTIFICATION	As representative of the financial institution named in this item, I certify that the account name(s) and number shown in Item 9 are correct and that the financial institution agrees to receive and deposit the semiannual interest payments on the Series HH bonds issued pursuant to this form in accordance with applicable regulations.
NAME, ADDRESS, AND TELEPHONE NO.:	
PURCHASE METHOD: ☐ Charge Reserve Account * ☐ Check	
* R/T NUMBER:	

Payment Stamp

(Authorized Signature)   (Date)

FRB USE ONLY CASE I.D. NO.: _____

A. Federal Reserve Bank Copy

Table 12.2 Interest Rates for Series HH and H Bonds
Valid for September 1998 only

Issue Date	Original Maturity Period	Guaranteed Through Current Maturity Period	Date Next Extension Begins	Life of Bond
SERIES HH				
March 1993 to...	10 years	4.0	March 2003 to...	20 years
October 1988 to February 1993	10 years	6.0	October 1998 to February 2003	20 years
March 1983 to September 1988	10 years	4.0	Currently in final extension	20 years
January 1980 to February 1983	10 years	6.0	Currently in final extension	20 years
SERIES H				
October 1978 to December 1979	10 years	6.0	October 1998 to December 1999	30 years
March 1973 to September 1978	10 years	4.0	Currently in final extension	30 years
October 1968 to February 1973	10 years	6.0	Currently in final extension	30 years
June 1952 to September 1968		0.0	Bonds have reached final maturity	30 years

Adapted from Department of Treasury, Bureau of the Public Debt, U.S. Savings Bond Marketing Office. For a current table, call (304) 480-6112.

Chapter 13

REISSUING U.S. SAVINGS BONDS

►*Common Reissue Cases*
►*When Bonds Do Not Need to Be Reissued*
►*How to Reissue Bonds*
►*Who Can Help with the Forms: Cost for Assistance*
►*Which Reissue Transactions Create a Taxable Event*
►*What Reissue Forms Are Available and From Where*
►*Where to Send the Reissue Forms*
►*Quick Tips on Reissue*

"Reissue" is the term used by the Federal Reserve Banks (FRB) and the Bureau of the Public Debt (BPD) to describe the change of a registration on a U.S. Savings Bond. The public often uses the word "retitled."

There are literally hundreds of variables that can affect any given reissue case. This chapter will attempt to deal with some of the most common cases and questions, as well as to present resources available to the bond owner.

As you will see in the following story, knowing your reissue options is vital to managing your bond investment.

The year was 1992, the state, Arkansas—and no, this story is not about a presidential election. A wife and mother had just suffered the loss of her husband. They had been married for several decades.

Over the years they had purchased a stack of U.S. Savings Bonds worth over $200,000. Both of their names were on the bonds as co-owners. After *several months, she began to attend to her financial matters and, in the process, took the bonds to her bank to ask what she should do. After listening to her situation, the bank representative told her she "must redeem the bonds."*

Cashing the bonds would mean having to report $150,000 of interest income, with a minimum tax bite of over $50,000. Fortunately, this woman sought a second opinion and received an answer that was totally different from what the bank had told her.

A written analysis of this woman's bonds from The Savings Bond Informer, Inc., revealed that they all had over eight years of interest-earning life left. She was listed as a co-owner on the bonds and in *no way* did she have to redeem them. She could simply have them reissued. This means that she would have her deceased husband's name removed and her name put first, adding the co-owner or beneficiary of her choice. Reissuing, in this case, is not a taxable event. Once the bonds are reissued she could hold them to final maturity, exchange them for HH bonds and continue the tax deferment, or selectively redeem them over a period of years to spread the tax liability. When appropriate, reissuing savings bonds can often provide advantageous financial and/or timing options to the bond owner.

Reissuing may also assure that your wishes are carried out appropriately and in a timely manner. Consider these two real life stories:

A mom and dad were on the bonds as co-owners. Dad died many years ago and Mom never had the names changed on the bonds. Mom died in 1990 and her estate went into probate. Due to variety of factors, the assets in the estate have been tied up for over eight years, savings bonds included. If Mom had simply had the bonds retitled, removing her deceased husband's name and adding her daughter as a co-owner, the daughter, who was left to care for a disabled sister, could have used the savings bonds at will. As it is now, the daughter still hasn't received the bonds.

After the death of a loved-one, consider who you would want to have the bonds when you are gone and begin the reissue process as soon as you are able. When seeking answers to reissue questions, never take the verbal advice of anyone without confirming what they say with the FRB or the BPD (see Chapter 19 for phone numbers and addresses).

Common Reissue Cases

There are hundreds of reasons why a bond might need to be reissued. Here are some of the most common:

- To add a co-owner or beneficiary to a bond that is presently in one name only (see Figure 13.1, page 163, PD F 4000)

- To change the beneficiary that is presently listed on the bond to co-owner (see Figure 13.1, page 163, PD F 4000)

- To correct an error in the way the bond was inscribed by the issuing agent

- To eliminate the name of a deceased co-owner or beneficiary and add another person in his/her place (see Figure 13.1, page 163, PD F 4000)

- To have the bonds retitled into a trust (see Figure 13.2, page 164, PD F 1851)

- To remove the name of a living person from the bond (**Note:** This may create a taxable event and may require the consent of the party being removed.)

When Bonds Do Not Need to Be Reissued

U.S. Savings Bonds do not need to be reissued for the following cases.

1. The government will not reissue Series E and EE bonds or Savings Notes/ Freedom Shares for a change of address. The average American moves five to eight times over a thirty- to forty-year period. Your address has no bearing on your bond. **Note:** Owners of Series H and HH bonds *are* required to notify the BPD so that interest account records can be updated. Current addresses are needed to deliver the forms 1099-INT to these bond owners.

2. A savings bond does not need to be reissued for a change of name due to marriage. The bond may still be redeemed with proper identification. The person named on the bond will sign her married name, "changed by marriage from," and then sign her maiden name.

3. If a bond is within two months of final maturity it will not be reissued by the BPD. Contact your local FRB if they will be processing your reissue as their guidelines may differ slightly.

How to Reissue Bonds

This section will briefly examine the steps needed to have your savings bonds reissued. If you choose to have a professional handle your transaction, you can let him or her worry about them.

1. Identify and order the proper reissue form. One of the FRB regional sites or the BPD can assist you. A brief description of each form is given later in this chapter.

2. Read the instructions that come with each form. They are in small print, but hang in there. The instructions will address most of your questions.

3. Complete the form in full. The author suggests working on the form on a weekday during normal business hours, if possible. Then, if you have a question or a quandary, a phone call to the BPD or your regional FRB can be made immediately. (They do not staff their phones on the weekends or in the evenings.) Be prepared for a lengthy process; most forms require listing the serial number, issue date, face value, and registration information for each bond.

4. Secure the necessary signature guarantees, certifications, or notarizations.

5. Once you are satisfied that you have completed the form properly, make a photocopy for your own records.

6. Send the form, the bonds, and any additional paperwork required to the FRB, or take the bundle to your bank and ask that they forward it for you. (See "Where to Send the Reissue Forms," page 161.)

Special note: For most reissue transactions, you will *not* need to sign the bonds. In all cases, however, the appropriate person(s) must sign the form and their signatures must be certified, guaranteed, or notarized.

Who Can Help with the Forms: Cost for Assistance

The bond owner has several avenues for assistance when completing reissue forms. If you choose to do it yourself, you can call the appropriate regional FRB site or the BPD. They will answer your questions, but it will be your responsibility to enter the correct information onto the appropriate reissue form. There is no cost for this assistance.

If you would prefer to have someone else complete the paperwork, here are several options.

Commercial Banks. Banks are free to create their own policies regarding what work they will do and how much they will charge when reissuing bonds for investors. Many will not charge a fee to complete the forms, although this may be limited to bank customers. Other banks will charge as much as $5 a bond: $1,000 if you have 200 bonds. Ask for a quote in writing before you let them begin. **Caution:** If your bank seldom completes reissue forms, they may not be the best choice. If they frequently process reissue requests and there is no charge, that could be a winning combination.

Financial Professionals. With the increase in personal trusts and total financial planning, many people in the financial professional community provide assistance on reissue forms. As with banks, price and level of service will vary. If you choose a financial professional (attorney, accountant, financial planner, or bank representative) to handle your reissue transaction, once again, ask for a price quote in writing. If they are familiar with bonds, they should be able to estimate the time this task will take and provide a quote.

Which Reissue Transactions Create a Taxable Event

Certain types of reissue transactions generate a taxable event for the bond owner. A detailed review of which transactions create taxable events is covered in Chapter 10, "Taxation Issues for U.S. Savings Bonds."

Don't be taken by surprise (for instance, an unwanted 1099-INT, resulting in a taxable event). Erika from Illinois called with this story:

In the 1970s Erika's husband worked for a company that pushed the purchase of U.S. Savings Bonds. They purchased over 70 bonds in a seven-year period. The first forty-eight were titled in her name first with her husband as a co-owner. Then the company said that the bonds had to list her husband's name first, so twelve of the last twenty-two bonds were registered as such with Erika as the co-owner, and ten were purchased in his name alone.

Later, the couple decided to have some of the remaining bonds retitled into Erika's name (to help distribute their assets more equally). Erika called all over and could find no one to tell her the procedure for getting the bonds retitled. The government's literature made her blurry-eyed, but she finally called the BPD and received the explanation she needed. Just when she was about to hang up, the consultant asked, "How are the bonds titled now?" It was then that she learned this procedure would create a taxable event. Erika's frustrated response: "Nowhere in the government literature did it suggest that doing this would result in a tax bill—I found out by accident!"

One reissue question that appears with regularity is, "Can I remove my name and give my bonds to someone else (e.g., grandchildren, spouse, relative)?" Yes, you can, but do you want to? The case just described creates a taxable event for the bond owner. If Erika's husband is removed from the bonds where he is listed first, he will have to report all the interest earned on the bonds up to that point in time, even though he will receive no money from the bonds.

Even worse, when the recipient of the bond cashes it ten or twenty years later, he or she will receive a 1099-INT for all the interest it ever earned. If they do not know that some of the interest had already been reported, they will report all the interest themselves. Thus, part of the interest will be taxed twice (see in Chapter 10, "Watch Out for Double Taxation," page 117). When reporting interest income from U.S. Savings Bonds, the specific bonds and serial numbers are not listed on the 1099-INT. The IRS has no easy way of knowing or tracking the fact that interest on a particular bond may have been reported twice.

Removing the principal co-owner (normally considered the first-named party, unless both parties on the bond confirm otherwise) from a bond while that person is still living creates a taxable event for the principal co-owner.

Beware: A recent change in policy by the BPD will create problems for many bond owners. It used to be that the BPD would notify you if a transaction were to result in a taxable event. Now the transaction will simply be processed, and the bond owner notified "after the fact."

What Reissue Forms Are Available and From Where

The following list of Public Debt (PD) forms are available from the five regional FRBs and from the BPD (listed in Chapter 19). Commercial banks may carry some of the forms, particularly the ones that are requested most often. Some of the forms can be downloaded from the government web site at www.publicdebt.treas.gov.

PD F 1455
Request by Fiduciary for Reissue of United States Savings Bonds/ Notes

PD F 1851
Request for Reissue of United States Savings Bonds/Notes in Name of Trustee of Personal Trust Estate

PD F 1938
Request for Reissue of United States Savings Bonds/Notes During the Lives of Both Co-owners

PD F 3360
Request for Reissue of United States Savings Bonds/Notes in the Name of a Person or Persons Other Than the Owner (Including Legal Guardian, Custodian for a Minor Under a Statute, etc.)

PD F 4000
Request by Owner for Reissue of United States Savings Bonds/Notes to Add Beneficiary or Co-owner, Eliminate Beneficiary or Decedent, Show Change of Name, and/or Correct Error in Registration

PD F 5336
Application for Disposition—United States Savings Bonds/Notes and/or Related Checks Owned by Decedent Whose Estate is Being Settled Without Administration

Where to Send the Reissue Forms

All reissue transactions are processed by a regional FRB or the BPD. You may submit your transaction to your local commercial bank for forwarding or you may mail directly to the appropriate regional FRB processing site. (See Chapter 19 for address and phone number.)

If your commercial bank is an authorized issuing and paying agent (that means they sell and redeem bonds), they will probably be familiar with the appropriate regional FRB site and thus be willing to forward your transaction. The advantages of this are (1) you will save postage, and (2) should there be a problem, the bank can verify that the transaction was submitted. The disadvantage is that, in some cases, it may take a little longer to travel through the bank's mailing or delivery system.

The second option is to submit your transaction directly to the appropriate FRB regional processing site. If you choose this option, it is best to send your transaction by registered or certified mail, return receipt requested. The receipt becomes important in case there is any problem in locating the transaction: It will verify whether your paperwork reached the FRB or not. Should special handling or rulings be required for a particular reissue case, the FRB may forward the case to the BPD.

Unfortunately, the need to reissue bonds can come at a time that is less than ideal, that is, after the death of a loved one. If you follow the suggestions in this chapter and are patient in pursuing the correct avenues of assistance, reissuing bonds can be a relatively easy, although time-intensive, process.

Quick Tips on Reissue

- In some cases, having savings bonds reissued can provide advantageous financial and/or timing options.

- Begin the reissue process as soon as you are able following the death of a loved-one who is named on the bond with you. Otherwise, your wishes may never be carried out.

- When seeking answers to reissue questions, never take the verbal advice of anyone without confirming what they say with the FRB or the BPD.

- You do not need to have bonds reissued if your address has changed, you have had a change of name due to marriage, or if the bonds are within two months of final maturity. (For H and HH bonds, submit your change of address to your regional FRB. See Chapter 19 for addresses.)

- There are three choices for having bonds reissued: you can do it yourself, secure the services of a bank, or hire a financial professional.

- Reissue forms are available from all of the FRBs, the BPD, and some commercial banks.

- When hiring someone to complete your reissue forms, seek to find out their level of experience with this transaction and always get a quote in writing before they begin the work.

- Be aware that certain types of reissue transactions create a taxable event.

Figure 13.1 Reissue Form PD F 4000

PD F 4000
Department of the Treasury
Bureau of the Public Debt
(Revised October 1995)

**REQUEST BY OWNER FOR REISSUE OF UNITED STATES
SAVINGS BONDS/NOTES TO ADD BENEFICIARY OR COOWNER,
ELIMINATE BENEFICIARY OR DECEDENT, SHOW CHANGE
OF NAME, AND/OR CORRECT ERROR IN REGISTRATION**

OMB No. 1535-0023

IMPORTANT: Follow instructions in filling out this form. You should be aware that the making of any false, fictitious or fraudulent claim to the United States is a crime punishable by imprisonment of not more than five years or a fine up to $250,000, or both, under 18 U.S.C. 287 and 18 U.S.C. 3571. Additionally, 31 U.S.C. 3729 provides for civil penalties for the maker of a false or fraudulent claim to the United States of an amount not less than $5,000 and not more than $10,000, plus treble the amount of the Government's damages as an additional sanction.
PRINT IN INK OR TYPE ALL INFORMATION

To: Federal Reserve Bank
The undersigned hereby presents and surrenders for reissue the following-described United States Savings Bonds.
Total face amount _____

ISSUE DATE	DENOMINATION (FACE AMOUNT)	SERIAL NUMBER	INSCRIPTION (Please type or print names, including middle names or initials, social security account number, if any, and addresses as inscribed on the bonds.)

(If space is insufficient use continuation sheet on page 4, sign it and refer to it above - or use Form PD 3500 for this purpose.)

I hereby certify _____ is the principal coowner of any bonds registered in coownership form
(Name of coowner)

submitted herewith and is responsible for any federal tax liability arising from this transaction (SEE TAX LIABILITY NOTICE), and I hereby request that said bonds be reissued in the following form of registration:

Mr. ☐   Mrs. ☐   Miss ☐ _____
(First name)   (Middle name or initial)   (Last name)

Address _____
(Number and street or rural route)   (City or town)   (State)   (ZIP Code)

If a coowner or beneficiary is desired, complete the following line:

With Mr. ☐   Mrs. ☐   Miss ☐ _____ as { ☐ coowner
(First name)   (Middle name or initial)   (Last name)   ☐ beneficiary

TAXPAYER IDENTIFYING NUMBERS (See General Instructions, page 3)

☐☐☐-☐☐-☐☐☐☐   ☐☐☐-☐☐-☐☐☐☐   ☐☐-☐☐☐☐☐☐☐
(S.S. No. - Owner or first coowner)   (S.S. No. - Second coowner or beneficiary)   (Employer Identification Number)

If new bonds are not to be delivered to address shown thereon, give delivery instructions here.

Name _____
Address _____
(Number and street or rural route)   (City or town)   (State)   (ZIP Code)

Reissue is requested for the reason(s) below:

**IN ALL CASES
THIS FORM MUST BE SIGNED
ON THE REVERSE SIDE**

1. ☐ To add a coowner or beneficiary.
2. ☐ To change present beneficiary to coowner.
3. ☐ To eliminate a living beneficiary and reissue the bonds in either single ownership form or with another person as coowner or beneficiary. (For Series E and H bonds and savings notes, the present beneficiary must consent on page 2.)
4. ☐ To reissue in the name of a surviving owner, coowner, or beneficiary or in his/her name and that of another person as coowner or beneficiary. (Proof of death of owner, coowner, or beneficiary named on Series E or H bonds or savings notes, and owner or coowner named on Series EE or HH bonds, must be furnished.)
5. ☐ Change of name by: (a) ☐ marriage   (b) ☐ divorce   (c) ☐ court order   (d) ☐ naturalization   (e) ☐ otherwise
   if (e) is checked, furnish explanation: _____
6. ☐ Correct error in registration. (See specific instruction No. 6) Provide following information:
   (a) The bonds were purchased by: _____
   (b) The funds belonged to: _____
   (c) Explanation of error _____

Figure 13.2 Reissue Form PD F 1851

PD F 1851
Department of the Treasury
Bureau of the Public Debt
(Revised February 1995)

**REQUEST FOR REISSUE OF UNITED STATES SAVINGS BONDS/NOTES
IN NAME OF TRUSTEE OR PERSONAL TRUST ESTATE**

OMB No. 1535-0009

IMPORTANT: Follow instructions in filling out this form. You should be aware that the making of any false, fictitious or fraudulent claim to the United States is a crime punishable by imprisonment of not more than five years or a fine up to $250,000, or both, under 18 U.S.C. 287 and 18 U.S.C. 3571. Additionally, 31 U.S.C. 3729 provides for civil penalties for the maker of a false or fraudulent claim to the United States of an amount not less than $5,000 and not more than $10,000, plus treble the amount of the Government's damages as an additional sanction.
PRINT IN INK OR TYPE ALL INFORMATION

TO: Federal Reserve Bank

BEFORE FILLING OUT THIS FORM, READ TAX LIABILITY NOTICE ON PAGE 3
(The applicable statement(s) below MUST be completed. Failure to furnish this information could cause rejection of the transaction. See instructions.)

1   I (we) hereby request reissue of the bonds described on the reverse hereof in the form set out in item 7 below to the extent of
$ _____ (face amount).

2. In support of this request, I (we severally) certify that the trust estate described in item 7 below is a personal trust estate as defined in item 1 of the instructions on page 3 of this form, and

   a. ☐   was created by _____
   (Name(s) of owner, coowner, or both coowners creating trust)

   b. ☐   was created by some other person and

   (i) ☐   I am (one of us is) a beneficiary of the trust.

   (ii) ☐   _____ , a beneficiary of the trust, is related
   (Name)

   to _____ as _____
   (Name of owner or coowner)   (Give exact relationship)

3   You must check box a or b. (SEE "TAX LIABILITY" SECTION OF INSTRUCTIONS).

   a ☐   I (we) certify that, for federal income tax purposes, I (we) will be treated as owner(s) of the portion of the trust represented by **any** tax-deferred accumulated interest on the surrendered bonds.

   b ☐   I (we) certify that, for federal income tax purposes, I (we) will not be treated as owner(s) of the portion of the trust represented by **any** tax-deferred accumulated interest on the surrendered bonds, and therefore, I (we) <u>will include</u> the tax-deferred accumulated interest in gross income for the taxable year in which the bonds are reissued to the trust. I (we) am aware that a 1099 INT will be issued and the interest will be reported to the Internal Revenue Service by the agent that processes the transactions The interest which will be reported includes deferred interest on H/HH bonds as well as interest earned on E/EE bonds from the issue date until the date of reissue.

4   _____ is/are the trustee/co-trustees of the trust.

5   The trust was created on _____
   (Month/Day/Year)

6   _____ , whose Social Security Account number is ☐☐☐ – ☐☐ – ☐☐☐☐
   (Name of coowner)

   is the principal coowner of any bonds registered in coownership form submitted herewith. He/she is responsible for any tax liability arising from the reissue transaction requested herein.   (A principal coowner is a coowner who (1) purchased the bonds with his or her own funds or (2) received them as a gift, inheritance or legacy, or as a result of judicial proceedings, and has them reissued in coownership form, provided her or she has received no contribution in money or money's worth for designating the other person as coowner on the bonds. Both registrants are considered to be coowners when bonds are registered in the form "A" or "B")

7. Form in which bonds _____
    are to be reissued.
    (Inscription: include name(s) of trustee(s) of creator(s) or trustor(s) and date of trust's creation.)

    _____
    (Address)

(Taxpayer identifying
number Assigned to
Trust)

☐☐ – ☐☐☐☐☐☐   ☐☐☐ – ☐☐ – ☐☐☐☐
(Employer Identification Number)   (Social Security Account Number)

If the new bonds are not to be
delivered to address shown
thereon deliver them to:

_____
(Name)

_____
(Street Address)

_____
(City or town)   (State)   (ZIP Code)

OWNER AND OTHER REGISTRANTS MUST SIGN AND HAVE THEIR SIGNATURE CERTIFIED ON PAGE 2

SEE INSTRUCTIONS FOR PRIVACY ACT AND PAPERWORK REDUCTION ACT NOTICE

Figure 13.3 Reissue Form PD F 1455

PD F 1455
Department of the Treasury
Bureau of the Public Debt
(Revised February 1994)

**REQUEST BY FIDUCIARY FOR REISSUE
OF UNITED STATES SAVINGS BONDS/NOTES**

OMB No. 1535-0012

**"BONDS" AS REFERRED TO
BELOW INCLUDES SAVINGS
NOTES WHEN APPROPRIATE.**

IMPORTANT: Follow instructions in filling out this form. You should be aware that the making of any false, fictitious or fraudulent claim to the United States is a crime punishable by imprisonment of not more than five years or a fine up to $250,000, or both, under 18 U.S.C. 287 and 18 U.S.C. 3571. Additionally, 31 U.S.C. 3729 provides for civil penalties for the maker of a false or fraudulent claim to the United States of an amount not less than $5,000 and not more than $10,000, plus treble the amount of the Government's damages as an additional sanction.
PRINT IN INK OR TYPE ALL INFORMATION

TO: Federal Reserve Bank.
The following-described United States Savings Bonds totaling $ _____ (face amount), are surrendered for reissue as indicated below:

ISSUE DATE	DENOMINATION (FACE AMOUNT)	SERIAL NUMBER	INSCRIPTION (Please type or print names, including middle names or initials, social security account number, if any, and addresses as inscribed on the bonds.)

(If space is insufficient, describe additional bonds on back of this form.)

I/We hereby request that the above-described bonds, to the extent $ _____ (face amount), be reissued in the following form

☐ Mr. ☐ Mrs. ☐ Miss ☐ Ms _____

(See instructions 2. and 3.)

Address _____

(Number and street or rural route)   (City or town)   (State)   (ZIP Code)

Taxpayer Identifying No.
(See Instruction 4.)   ☐☐☐ – ☐☐ – ☐☐☐☐   **OR**   ☐☐ ☐☐☐☐☐☐☐

(Social Security Account Number)   (Employee Identification Number)

NOTE: If the transaction involves Series H/HH bonds, the new owner must complete I.R.S. Form W-9, unless he/she executes a request on a September 1983 or later revision of PD F 4000, and the applicable form must be submitted with this request. (See instructions 2. and 4. (e).) and request that the new bonds be delivered to: _____

Address _____

(Number and street or rural route)

_____

(City or town)   (State)   (ZIP Code)

I/We certify that the person in whose name reissue is requested (in his/her own right or in a fiduciary capacity) is lawfully entitled thereto by reason of _____ and has agreed to such reissue.

(See instruction 5.)

Sign here _____   (___) ___ – ___

(Daytime Telephone Number)

See "TAX LIABILITY" in Instructions as reissue may result in a Federal tax liability.

(Show fiduciary capacity and include reference to estate or trust. See instruction 6.)

_____

I certify that the above-named person, whose identity is well-known or proved to me, personally appeared before me on the _____ day of _____, 19 _____ at _____ and signed the above request, acknowledging the same to be a free act and deed (and the free act and deed of said corporation).

(OFFICIAL STAMP OR SEAL)

_____
(Signature and official designation of certifying officer)

_____
(Address)

SEE INSTRUCTIONS FOR PRIVACY ACT AND PAPERWORK REDUCTION ACT NOTICE

Chapter 14

PURCHASING U.S. SAVINGS BONDS

▶ *Which Bonds Are Currently Available?*
▶ *When Is the Best Time to Purchase Bonds?*
▶ *Where and How Can Bonds be Purchased?*
▶ *Who Can Buy U.S. Savings Bonds?*
▶ *Purchase Limitations*
▶ *How Should Bonds Be Registered?*
▶ *Purchasing for Special Occasions*
▶ *Bond Investment Growth with Systematic Purchase*
▶ *Quick Tips on Purchasing*

Although sales have slowed significantly since 1992, more than $7 billion of savings bonds were sold in 1995 and over $5 billion in 1996 and 1997. Of the many Americans who purchase each year, approximately 7 million do so through payroll deduction, a systematic purchase strategy.

This chapter will describe the purchase process. The discussion of interest rates and timing issues is limited to new issues of U.S. Savings Bonds. (See Chapters 3 and 4 for details on older bonds).

Which Bonds Are Currently Available?

There are three types of bonds available today: Series EE, I, and HH. Each series has a very different purpose.

- **The Series EE bond is an interest accrual bond.** The interest it earns becomes part of the value of the bond. At redemption, you receive the purchase price plus all the interest earned.

- **The Series I bond (Inflation Protection Bond)** is also an interest accrual bond. The interest it earns becomes part of the value of the bond. At redemption, you receive the purchase price plus all the interest earned.

- **The Series HH bond** is a current income bond. As the name suggests, the investor receives an interest payment every six months. The HH bond will always be worth the face value at redemption.

The greatest distinction between the three is that only Series EE and Series I bonds can be bought for cash. HH bonds are obtained by exchanging Series E or EE bonds or Savings Notes or by reinvesting eligible H bonds. For this reason, the bulk of this chapter will deal with the Series EE and I bond. Additional information on HH bonds is provided in Chapter 12 and a more detailed analysis of the I bond is included in Chapter 18.

In an effort to help you determine whether the EE or I bond is a wise investment for you, the following information will include the characteristics and the pros and cons of each bond. Determining which bond, if either, is right for you, will ultimately be based on your personal financial goals and objectives.

Series EE Bond Characteristics

- It is purchased at half the face value: A $100 bond costs $50.

- It is guaranteed to reach face value in seventeen years or less.

- The original maturity period is fixed at seventeen years.

- If a bond is cashed within the first five years, three months of interest is forfeited. This penalty is new to the bond program and was introduced in May 1997.

- A new market rate will be assigned to the bond at each six-month compounding period. The first rate assigned to a bond, if purchased between May 1, 1998 and October 31, 1998 is 5.06%. For current rate information for new purchases of Series EE bonds, call 1-800-4USBOND.

- The bond will earn interest for a total of thirty years from the date of purchase.

- It is an interest accrual security. This means interest is added to the value of the bond periodically. The bond will increase in value monthly and interest is compounded semi-annually.

- The interest earned is tax-deferred. A bond owner may elect to report interest annually; however, most holders do not report interest until they redeem the bonds. (See Chapter 10 for more tax information.)

- Interest earned is subject to federal tax, but exempt from state and local taxes. A 1099-INT is provided to the party redeeming the bond by the agency that cashes the bond.

- When specific guidelines are met, the bonds may be tax-free for qualified educational expenses. (See Chapter 16.)

- The following denominations are available: $50, $75, $100, $200, $500, $1,000, $5,000, and $10,000. If you purchase bonds through payroll deduction, the minimum denomination you may buy is $100.

- The purchase limit is $15,000 ($30,000 face value) per person, per calendar year. (See "Purchase Limitations," page 175.)

The Pros and Cons of Purchasing Series EE Bonds

Pros

1. No-load to purchase or redeem (no fees to buy or sell bonds).
2. You can start with as little as $25.
3. The first new market rate for May 1, 1998 to October 31, 1998 is 5.06%. Current rates may beat savings accounts and are generally competitive with CDs or money market funds, although not as liquid for the first six months. Call 1-800-4USBOND for interest rate information.
4. They are fully guaranteed by the United States government.
5. There is no penalty for redemption before maturity if held at least five years.
6. The interest is exempt from state and local taxes.
7. The principal is secure (though the interest income is modest).

Cons

1. Bonds must be held for six months (no liquidity for six months; some exceptions in extreme emergencies do apply).
2. Purchase limitations of $15,000 per person per year apply, although this can be exceeded by adding co-owners. (Read about purchase limitations later in this chapter.)

3. The market interest rate may be much lower than your expectations or needs.

4. It may take twelve to eighteen years to reach face value at current market rates. If the average of the market rates is 6% during the original maturity period, then the bonds would reach face value in approximately twelve years.

5. Interest is subject to federal tax.

6. The real rate of return (after taxes) may not meet your investment objectives. Consider an investor in the 28% tax bracket who buys a Series EE bond that has an average interest rate of 5% for a time period where inflation averages 2.5%. They would realize a real rate of return of about 1% after taxes.

Series I Bond Characteristics

- The bond is purchased at face value: A $100 bond costs $100.

- If it is cashed within the first five years, three months of interest is forfeited. This penalty is the same as the EE bond penalty enacted for purchases May 1997 and after.

- A fixed interest rate will be assigned to the bond at purchase. An inflation adjusted rate is added to the fixed rate every six months to create the earnings rate for that six-month period. Thus the earnings rate is comprised of two parts. The new fixed rates and the inflation adjusted rate will be announced each May and November. The inflation adjusted rate is based on the CPI-U (Consumer Price Index-Urban Consumers) for a six-month period. The first fixed rate assigned to a bond, if purchased between September 1, 1998 through October 31, 1998 is 3.4%. When combined with the inflation adjusted rate, this results in an initial earnings rate of 4.66%. For current rate information for new purchases of Series I bonds, call 1-800-4USBOND.

- The bond will earn interest for a total of thirty years from the date of purchase.

- The I bond is an interest accrual security. This means interest is added to the value of the bond periodically. At redemption you receive your purchase price plus the interest. Interest is added to the bond monthly and compounded semi-annually.

- The interest you earn is tax-deferred. A bond owner may elect to report interest annually; however, most bond owners do not report interest until they redeem the bonds. (See Chapter 10 for more tax information.)

- Interest earned is subject to federal tax, but exempt from state and local taxes. A 1099-INT is provided to the party redeeming the bond by the agency that cashes the bond.

- When specific guidelines are met, the bonds may be tax-free for qualified educational expenses. (See Chapter 16.)

- You may purchase the following denominations: $50, $75, $100, $200, $500, $1,000, $5,000, and $10,000. The $200 and $10,000 bonds will not be available until May 1999.

- The purchase limit is $30,000 (twice that of the EE bond) per person per calendar year. (See "Purchase Limitations," page 175.)

The Pros and Cons of Purchasing Series I Bonds

Pros

1. No-load to purchase or redeem (no fees to buy or sell bonds).

2. You can start with as little as $50.

3. The first new interest rate for September and October 1998 is 4.66%. Current rates may beat savings accounts and will always exceed the inflation rate. Call 1-800-4USBOND for interest rate information for new purchases.

4. They are fully guaranteed by the United States government.

5. There is no penalty for redemption before maturity if held at least five years.

6. The interest is exempt from state and local taxes.

7. The principal is secure (though the interest income is modest).

Cons

1. Bonds must be held for six months (no liquidity for six months; some exceptions in extreme emergencies do apply).

2. The interest rate may be much lower than your expectations or needs.

3. It may take twelve to twenty years for the bond to double in value at current interest rates. If the interest rate (combination of fixed and CPI-U index) averages 5%, then the bonds would double in approximately fourteen years.

4. Interest is subject to federal tax.

5. The real rate of return (after taxes) may not meet your investment objectives. Consider an investor in the 39% tax bracket who buys a series I bond that has an average interest rate of 7% (made up of a fixed rate of 3.4% and an inflation rate of 3.6%). In a time period where inflation averages 3.6%, they would realize a real rate of return of less than 0.75% after taxes when cashing their bonds.

If, after a detailed look at each of the bonds, along with their strengths and weaknesses, you have decided to move ahead with your purchase, the following information will guide you in the "how tos."

When Is the Best Time to Purchase Bonds?

The best time to buy bonds is late in the month. Why? Whenever a person buys a bond, they begin to earn interest the first day of the month in which it was purchased. This means that a bond owner can use his or her money elsewhere until late in the month, then invest in the EE bond and be credited with interest as of the first day of the month.

Caution: If you buy late in the month, the funds must be readily available to the bank. Cash, a cashier's check, or a check drawn on the bank that you are purchasing through will qualify. A check from an out-of-state money market account will not work because it may require a hold period. So, if a bond is purchased on the last day of the month with an out-of-state check, the bond owner will likely receive an issue date of the following month.

Where and How Can Bonds Be Purchased?

U.S. Savings Bonds can be applied for in-person or through the mail by several different means:

- Most commercial banks
- Some savings & loans
- Some credit unions
- All Federal Reserve Banks (FRBs)
- Many companies via the Payroll Savings Plan
- Via the Internet (go to www.savingsbonds.gov to download the purchase application)
- The EasySaver Program (see page 178)

Banks, Savings & Loans, Credit Unions, and Federal Reserve Banks

While the Series I and EE savings bonds can be applied for in-person at thousands of institutions around the country, it is best to call first. Some banks in certain areas of the country no longer sell or service U.S. Savings Bonds.

You may also call or write to a FRB for a bond purchase application. Via mail, send a completed application, with a check, to the FRB in your region. (A listing of FRBs appears in Chapter 19.) If a personal check is sent, the bond will be mailed after the check clears.

The institutions that sell bonds provide a Purchase Application for Series I and EE bonds (Figure 14.1, page 179). The following information will be needed:

- Name or names to appear on bond
- Social Security number of the first person named on bond
- Mailing address
- Number of bonds to be purchased

Upon receiving an application, the bank or institution forwards it to a regional FRB for processing. The bond should be mailed within one to two weeks.

Important note: In the past, investors received their bond the day it was purchased. During the early 1990s, the government converted to a Regional Delivery System. This means that local banks no longer have the actual bond in stock. They simply take an application and forward it to the FRB for processing. When buying a birthday or holiday gift, be aware that it takes up to three weeks for delivery. In lieu of the bond, most banks offer a gift certificate which indicates that a bond has been purchased and is "on the way" (Figure 14.2).

Figure 14.2   Gift Certificate

Payroll Savings Plan

Millions of Americans buy U.S. Savings Bonds through payroll deduction. If this method of purchase interests you, check with the human resources, personnel, or payroll departments of your company to see if they participate. If the company has a program in place, they will have the necessary forms.

Who Can Buy U.S. Savings Bonds?

The information in the following section has been taken, and in some cases adapted for your convenience, from "The Book on U.S. Savings Bonds." Persons eligible to buy and hold bonds inscribed in their names include:

- Residents of the United States, its territories and possessions, and the Commonwealth of Puerto Rico
- Citizens of the United States residing abroad
- Civilian employees of the United States, or members of its Armed Services, regardless of residence or citizenship, provided they have a Social Security number
- Residents of Canada or Mexico who work in the United States, but only if the bonds are purchased on a payroll deduction plan and the owner provides a Social Security account number

A person who is not previously listed may, nevertheless, be designated as co-owner or beneficiary of a bond "whether original issue or reissue," unless that person is a resident of an area where the Treasury restricts or regulates the delivery of checks drawn on U.S. funds. Contact your FRB for current information. Such persons who become entitled to bonds by right of inheritance or otherwise will not have the right to reissue, under Treasury regulations. But they may hold the bonds without change of registration with the right to redeem them when their area of residence changes or current restrictions are lifted. For full details see Treasury Circular, PD Series 3-80, Section 353.6

Series EE bonds may be bought by individuals, corporations, associations, public or private organizations, fiduciaries, and other investors in their own right. Bonds purchased by a public or private organization cannot have a co-owner or beneficiary listed on the bond. Likewise an individual bond owner cannot list an organization of any type on a savings bond as their co-owner or beneficiary.

Author's note: This means that you cannot list a charity, church, pet cemetery, or any other organization on a bond as co-owner or beneficiary.

An Intriguing Exception: Gifts to the United States

Some people buy bonds with the intent that upon their death the bonds will become a gift to the United States. This may be done by designating the United States Treasury as either the co-owner or beneficiary. Note: These bonds may not be reissued to change such designation, unless they are Series EE or HH bonds and the Treasury has been designated as beneficiary.

Author's note: Let's review the math on this one. Based on the fact that the outstanding debt of our nation is over $5.5 trillion (1998 figures, I always have to increase the number from previous editions of the book), and the total of outstanding bonds is approximately $180 billion, if all bond owners gift their bonds to Uncle Sam, and we all die tomorrow (in which case we won't care about the debt), we will have covered less than 3.3% of the national debt.

Purchase Limitations

The maximum purchase allowed for Series EE bonds is $15,000 per person per calendar year ($30,000 face value). This means that an investor can buy $15,000 on December 30th and another $15,000 on January 2nd. This would use the limitations for each year in which Series EE bonds were bought. However, if a couple purchase in one spouse's name with the "or" being the other spouse, they may buy double that amount—$30,000 ($60,000 face value) per year. (They are combining their individual limitations of $15,000.) Want to invest another $15,000? An investor can buy with his son or daughter as a co-owner and use his or her $15,000 limitation.

The maximum purchase allowed for Series I bonds is $30,000 per person per calendar year.

Caution: Remember that anyone named as a co-owner on a bond can cash that bond. Give careful consideration to whom you name as co-owner on any bonds.

Why are there limitations on the amount of EE bonds you can purchase? Originally, the intent was to keep the bond program directed toward the individual investor. Limitations keep large blocks of money from one entity from entering and exiting the bond program. For instance, a company cannot buy $10 million of U.S. Savings Bonds. It is strange that the limits have not been raised since 1980. It would seem logical that they be adjusted upward every five to ten years, especially since the government, from all indications, could use the extra money (or has used the extra money).

How Should Bonds Be Registered?

U.S. Savings Bonds are registered securities. This means that the name of the person or entity entitled to the bonds is printed on the face of the bond.

The three most common forms of registration are single ownership, co-ownership, and owner with beneficiary.

Single Ownership

As the name implies, only one person is listed on the bond as owner.

> S.S. # 123-45-6789
> John S. Anybody
> 123 Bond Ave.
> Interest, NY 11001

Co-ownership

Two persons are listed on the bond as co-owners. Either party can cash the bond without the other party's consent. Co-ownership means equal ownership. Upon the death of one co-owner, the remaining co-owner becomes the sole owner of the bond. The bonds can be reissued to remove the deceased party's name and to add a new co-owner or beneficiary.

> S.S. # 123-45-6789
> John S. Anybody
> 123 Bond Ave.
> Interest, NY 11001
>
> OR Mary B. Anybody

Beneficiary

This form of ownership allows for one owner and one beneficiary to be listed on the bonds. The owner may cash the bond at any time (after the first six months). The beneficiary may cash the bonds only after providing a death certificate of the owner. The beneficiary is listed as the "POD" (Pay on Death). This does not mean that the bond must be cashed upon the death of the owner; however, the bond cannot be negotiated by the person named as POD until the owner is deceased. The registration appears as follows:

> S.S. # 123-45-6789
> John S. Anybody
> 123 Bond Ave.
> Interest, NY 11001
>
> POD Mary B. Anybody

The maximum number of names on a bond is two, regardless of the form of registration. You cannot have two co-owners and a beneficiary.

Purchasing for Special Occasions

Bonds may take up to three weeks to be delivered. Therefore, plan ahead when buying for special occasions (birthdays, holidays, graduations). If you do get stuck purchasing a bond a few days before the important event, the bank will provide a gift certificate, indicating that a bond is on the way (see Figure 14.2).

The purchase application will ask for the Social Security number of the first-named party on the bond. If that number is not known, the purchaser may use his or her own number. However, this means that the purchaser's number will appear on the bond. This does not create any tax liability for the purchaser, since the person who redeems the bond is required to supply their Social Security number at the time of redemption. The person redeeming the bond is supposed to get the 1099-INT. However, the fact that the purchaser's Social Security number is on the bond may lead some bank tellers to incorrectly assign the 1099-INT to that number. The best bet is to call the recipient's family and obtain the correct Social Security number.

The purchase application also asks for a "mail to" address. If when buying a gift, a purchaser lists her name and address under "mail to," then her name and address will appear on the bond. (Bonds are mailed in window envelopes.) Thus, although there will be three names on the bond, only the first-named party and the designated co-owner or beneficiary are entitled to it. The "mail to" person is not entitled. This will inevitably cause some confusion down the road, but it is unavoidable under the present system.

Note: If you list the bank as the "mail to" address, the bank name and address will appear on the bond.

Bond Investment Growth with Systematic Purchase

As previous stated, millions of Americans have used bonds to build or supplement their savings. Table 14.1 (page 180) illustrates what can be expected under several different scenarios. The table outlines projected savings at interest rates of 4%, 5%, 6%, and 7%. The 4% interest rate is the guaranteed minimum for eighteen years on Series EE bonds issued from March 1993 to April 1995. The 6% interest rate is the guaranteed minimum for twelve years on Series EE bonds issued from November 1986 to February 1993. Current issues of Series EE bonds do not have a guaranteed rate, and the market rates in the 1990s have ranged from 4.25% to 7.19%.

Quick Tips on Purchasing

- There are three bonds available today: Series I, EE , and HH.

- Only Series I and EE can be bought; Series HH must be exchanged for.

- The best time to purchase bonds is late in the month.

- Savings bonds can be applied for in-person or through the mail by several different means: most banks, some savings & loans, some credit unions, all FRBs, and through a Payroll Savings Plan.

- To fill out the Purchase Application, you will need: name or names to appear on the bond, Social Security number of the first person named on the bond (if available), mailing address, and number of bonds to be purchased.

- The purchase limitation for Series EE bonds is $15,000 per person per calendar year ($30,000 face value). The purchase limitation for Series I bonds is $30,000.

- The three most common forms of registration are single ownership, co-ownership, and owner with beneficiary.

A recent change offers an additional purchase option (see page 172):

EasySaver Program

In the fall of 1998, the government introduced EasySaver, a new option for systematic savings. Now bond owners can sign up for the automatic purchase of Series EE or I bonds through an automatic withdrawal from their checking or savings account. For applications, call 1-877-811-SAVE or visit the government web site at www.easysaver.gov.

Figure 14.1 Purchase Application for Series EE Bonds

☆ U.S. GOVERNMENT PRINTING OFFICE: 1989—238-673

PD F 5263
Dept of the Treasury
Bur of the Public Debt
(Rev June1 1989)

ORDER FOR SERIES EE U.S. SAVINGS BONDS

OMB No. 1535-0084
Expires 8-31-90

PLEASE FOLLOW THE INSTRUCTIONS ON THE BACK WHEN COMPLETING THIS PURCHASE ORDER.

1. **OWNER OR FIRST-NAMED COOWNER (Bonds registered to)**

   Name

   Soc. Sec. No.

2. **BONDS TO BE DELIVERED "CARE OF"** (Do not complete this section unless name is different from the owner or first-named coowner in section 1 above.)

   Mail to:

3. **ADDRESS WHERE BONDS ARE TO BE DELIVERED**

   (NUMBER AND STREET OR RURAL ROUTE)

   (CITY OR TOWN)   (STATE)   (ZIP CODE)

4. **COOWNER OR BENEFICIARY** Coownership will be assumed if neither block is checked (See #4 on back)
   The following person is to be named as   coowner   beneficiary:

   Name

5. **BONDS ORDERED**

Denom.	Quantity	Issue Price	Total Issue Price	FOR AGENT USE ONLY
$ 50		X $ 25.00	= $	
$ 75		X $ 37.50	= $	
$ 100		X $ 50.00	= $	
$ 200		X $ 100.00	= $	
$ 500		X $ 250.00	= $	
$ 1,000		X $ 500.00	= $	
$ 5,000		X $ 2,500.00	= $	
$ 10,000		X $ 5,000.00	= $	
TOTAL ISSUE PRICE OF PURCHASE			$	AFFIXED AGENT STAMP CERTIFIES THAT TOTAL AMOUNT OF PURCHASE IS CORRECT

6. **DATE PURCHASE ORDER AND PAYMENT PRESENTED TO AGENT**

   (MO)   (DAY)   (YR)

7. **SIGNATURE**

   PURCHASER'S SIGNATURE

   (   )

   PURCHASER'S NAME, IF OTHER THAN OWNER OR FIRST-NAMED COOWNER (Please print)   DAYTIME TELEPHONE NUMBER

   STREET ADDRESS (If not shown above)   CITY   STATE   ZIP CODE

NBD 571 Rev. 9/90   **FRB COPY**

Table 14.1 Systematic Purchase Pattern

Estimated Value of Saving Bond Investment at the End of . . .									
	Five Years		Ten Years		Twenty Years		Thirty Years		
	4%	5%	4%	5%	4%	5%	4%	5%
Save $25/mo., purchase $150 of EE bonds every 6 months	$1,642	$1,680	$3,644	$3,831	$9.060	$10,110	$17,107	$20,398
Save $50/mo., purchase $300 of EE bonds every 6 months	$3,284	$3,361	$7,289	$7,663	$18,120	$20,220	$34,215	$40,797
Save $100/mo., purchase $600 of EE bonds every 6 months	$6,569	$6,722	$14,578	$15,326	$36,241	$40,441	$68,430	$81,595
Save $200/mo., purchase $1,200 of EE bonds every 6 months	$13,139	$13,444	$29,156	$30,653	$72,482	$80,883	$136,861	$163,189
Save $500/mo., purchase $3,000 of EE bonds every 6 months	$32,849	$33,610	$72,892	$76,633	$181,205	$202,207	$342,154	$407,974

Estimated Value of Saving Bond Investment at the End of . . .

	Five Years		Ten Years		Twenty Years		Thirty Years	
	6%	7%	6%	7%	6%	7%	6%	7%
Save $25/mo., purchase $150 of EE bonds every 6 months	$1,720	$1,760	$4,031	$4,242	$11,310	$12,682	$24,458	$29,478
Save $50/mo., purchase $300 of EE bonds every 6 months	$3,439	$3,519	$8,061	$8,484	$22,620	$25,365	$48,916	$58,955
Save $100/mo., purchase $600 of EE bonds every 6 months	$6,878	$7,038	$16,122	$16,968	$45,241	$50,730	$97,832	$117,910
Save $200/mo., purchase $1,200 of EE bonds every 6 months	$13,756	$14,076	$32,244	$33,936	$90,482	$101,460	$195,664	$235,820
Save $500/mo., purchase $3,000 of EE bonds every 6 months	$34,392	$35,194	$80,611	$84,839	$226,203	$253,650	$489,160	$589,550

©1995 The Savings Bond Informer, Inc. All Rights Reserved.

The calculations in the above table are based on the following assumptions.

1. The bond purchaser will save money at an even monthly rate and will purchase bonds twice a year. A monthly purchase pattern will result in a slightly higher final value.
2. That the interest rates used to calculate future values will be consistent over the time period the calculations were made.
3. The money invested is the purchase price of the bonds. Thus the term purchase of $300 of bonds every six months means $300 purchase price, $600 face value for EE bonds and $300 face value for I bonds.
4. There is no guaranteed rate for Series EE bonds purchased after April 30, 1995. Call 1-800-USBONDS for rate information on current purchases of Series EE or I bond.

Note: This table does not guarantee a specific return on any investment you make. Market conditions and rules governing the savings bond program may change without notice. Obtain current rate information and complete details before making any investment.

Chapter 15

REDEEMING U.S. SAVINGS BONDS

► *Where Can Bonds Be Cashed?*
► *Who Is Eligible to Cash a Particular Bond?*
► *Help, It's My Bond, But the Bank Won't Cash It!*
► *What Are the Tax Consequences?*
► *What Should Be Considered Prior to Redemption?*
► *Watch Out for These Errors*
► *Quick Tips on Redemption*

"What's the big deal?" many bond owners ask. "I'll just cash my bonds whenever I need the money." Many bond owners have held their savings bonds for a long period of time. It does not make sense to collect bonds for twenty years and then suddenly cash them all on the same day without careful analysis. In addition to knowing how and when to cash, being aware of which bonds to redeem, and the resulting tax consequences will enable you to get the maximum return on your investment and avoid costly mistakes. After reading these two true stories, you will understand what the "big deal" is.

A Sad Story

John was a blue-collar worker who purchased bonds through the Payroll Savings Plan. His family knew he was buying bonds, but they never realized how many he had until after his death. They were surprised to find 180 *savings bonds. Those advising John's wife suggested that she cash the bonds. She did just that. Late in November she redeemed 180 bonds, worth a total of almost $60,000. What she was not told, and what she did not realize, was that 30 of the bonds were due to increase December 1st. Thus, by holding the bonds only a few more days, she could have pocketed an additional $300 to $375. Not only that, holding another specific group of 30 bonds until January 1st would have netted her another $300 to $375. As with most bond owners, she did not realize how important it is to time the redemption of savings bonds.*

A Happier Story

Betty works for a local school district. She saved her money, much of it in savings bonds, and she planned to purchase a condominium. She had only eight bonds, but each had a face value of $10,000! In June, Betty found a condominium she liked; she signed a purchase agreement and the closing was set for September. She was not sure whether to cash her bonds immediately or wait until nearer the closing date. To address her question, she chose to have her bonds analyzed. She discovered that six of the bonds, with a redemption value of $50,000, were due to increase September 1st. By waiting until September to cash the bonds, she would receive $1,500 more than if she cashed them in June. She also discovered that the remaining two bonds had increased in value June 1st, and would not increase again until December. She cashed those last two bonds immediately and put the money into an interest-bearing account.

Betty was thrilled to have the extra $1,500. Before learning about her bonds, she had planned on just cashing them all during June or July.

As you can see, careful planning can be very advantageous in the redemption of U.S. Savings Bonds. This chapter is devoted to covering all the issues you need to consider.

Where Can Bonds Be Cashed?

All Federal Reserve Banks (FRB) can redeem savings bonds, although the Bureau of the Public Debt (BPD) may handle some cases that require legal rulings. Bonds may be redeemed at thousands of commercial banks across America and at some savings & loans and credit unions, as well.

The easiest place to start is with your local bank, but call first. If your bank does not redeem bonds, try another bank.

Remember: The bank's role is to give you the money that you are due when you present the bond for redemption. They are not required to advise you on timing issues, nor are they particularly good at it. (For a full explanation, see Chapter 2, "Banks and Bonds.") It is ultimately the responsibility of the bond owner to choose the moment to submit a bond for redemption.

Who Is Eligible to Cash a Particular Bond?

A person cashing a bond needs to have valid identification. At least one piece of the following identification is necessary for redemptions of under $1,000 at a bank where you are not known.

General
- Current operator's license
- State identification card
- Employer identification card

Governmental
- Armed Forces identification card
- United States passport
- Federal employee identification card

Call before you go to see if your bank has additional requirements. Typically, the bank is the big loser if a person who is not entitled cashes bonds. For that reason, bank personnel are required to ensure that the person redeeming a bond is entitled to the funds.

In Chapter 14, various options for registering a bond were presented. The registration choice made when the bond was purchased determines who is eligible to redeem the bond.

If the bond is in one name only, and that person is living, he or she is the only one who can cash the bond. (Some exceptions may apply in power of attorney cases. However, a local bank will not redeem in power of attorney cases; those bonds must be forwarded to the BPD for a ruling.)

If the bond is in co-ownership form, either co-owner may cash it without the other's consent. The person cashing the bond will supply his or her Social Security number and will receive a 1099-INT for interest earned.

If the bond is registered in one name with another person listed as the beneficiary, then only the first-named party may cash the bond. Upon the death of the first-named party, the beneficiary may cash the bond. A death certificate for the first-named party is required for a beneficiary to cash a bond. For rulings regarding personal representatives of an estate, call your regional FRB.

The person submitting bonds for redemption is required to sign the back of each bond. When there are numerous bonds and it would be difficult for the bond owner to negotiate numerous signatures, PD F 1522 (Figure 15.2, page

192) may be used to list all the bonds; the bond owner need sign only once. Read the instructions thoroughly before attempting to use this form.

Help, It's My Bond, But the Bank Won't Cash It!

There are two cases for which a bank may not cash your bond:

- First, some banks do not participate in the savings bond program. They may not be an authorized paying agent for the government, so they will refuse to handle any savings bond transactions, redemption or otherwise.

- Second, a bank can limit what they cash for non-customers. Consider the following letter from John who lives in Florida, which illustrates a frequent complaint of bond owners:

  I live in Florida and have trouble cashing bonds over $1,000. Banks in this area will not do so unless we have a bank account with them. Is there a simple way or an easier way to cash bonds over the $1,000 range? Is there a Federal Reserve Bank in my area?

Unfortunately, cashing large sums of bonds can be quite a pain for non-bank customers, or customers whose bank does not provide savings bond service. The bank can limit non-customers to $1,000 redemption value per person per day. This is a real problem if your bond is worth more than $1,000 (as many are). If your bank will not cash a bond over $1,000, your only option is to submit the bond to a FRB. The FRB that serves your area is listed in Chapter 19. Call first to get the complete instructions before sending the bond(s).

What Are the Tax Consequences?

For Series E and EE bonds and Savings Notes, redemption is when you receive the interest that has accrued. The interest income earned is deferred until the bond is cashed or until the bond reaches final maturity, whichever comes first. In most cases, owners of Series E and EE bonds and SNs have not reported interest earnings prior to redemption. Thus, when the bond is redeemed, the owner creates a taxable event. The one exception is when a person has chosen to report interest earned on an annual basis. (See Chapter 10, "Taxation Issues for U.S. Savings Bonds," page 110, for more information on that option.)

The bank that redeems the bond has two basic responsibilities related to the 1099-INT. First, they must provide a copy of the 1099-INT to the person who redeemed the bond. Some banks do this on the spot; others mail all 1099-

INT forms at the end of the year (only interest payments totaling more than $10 need to be reported). Second, they must report the interest earned, name, and Social Security number for each transaction to the IRS. This is normally done in one file at the end of the year.

When a Series E or EE bond or SN is redeemed, the bank will require that the person redeeming the bond supply his or her Social Security number. The bank will not (or should not) automatically use the number printed on the bond.

Conflicting Government Rules

Regarding interest responsibility, the rules outlined in IRS and Treasury Department literature and what really happens when banks report interest income are not exactly "in sync." The Treasury Department publication "Legal Aspects of U.S. Savings Bonds" (1993, p.4) states that "the principal owner" (defined as "the person whose funds were used to purchase the bonds") bears the tax liability. However, the data collection and reporting systems are not set up to support this statement. In reality, the person who redeems the bonds receives the 1099-INT. Thus, if John Q. Public bought a bond with his son as the co-owner and the son redeems the bond, the bank will ask for the son's Social Security number and will issue the 1099-INT to the son. The IRS has no idea whose funds were used to purchase the bonds; they expect the son to report the interest that the bank reported under his Social Security number. The IRS rules state that the person receiving the 1099-INT should then issue a 1099 to the principal owner and to the IRS. However, in the years that the author has worked with bonds, he has never met one bond owner who was aware of this IRS rule. (This topic is covered in more detail in Chapter 10.)

Important: Make a note of the interest earned on your bond at the time of redemption. Put this note (or the 1099-INT, if the bank supplied one) with your tax papers for that calendar year. Many bond owners cash bonds early in the year and forget that they have interest income to report. The bond owner may lose, misfile, or not remember having received a 1099-INT, and fail to report the interest on their annual tax return. But guess who makes a habit of making sure you remember—that's right, your friends at the IRS. The bank supplies them with a copy of the same 1099-INT information that you receive. The IRS does a simple computer check to see if the amount you reported matches the amount they think you should have reported. If the numbers don't match, you are a likely candidate for some communication from the IRS.

Interest earned on bonds is subject to federal tax, but is exempt from state and local tax. In some cases, if the bond qualifies for the education feature, the interest might be tax-free. (Refer to the educational feature guidelines in Chapter 16.)

What Should Be Considered Prior to Redemption?

Selective Redemption

Now is the time to study your alternatives. Do not wait until your back is against the wall and you must liquidate your bonds immediately. Those situations do happen, so advance planning can be a great benefit.

In the next few pages, we will examine a practice called "Selective Redemption." It is built upon a simple premise: *At a given point in time it may make more sense to cash one particular bond than another.*

The concept of selective redemption was first presented in Chapter 12 as an alternative to exchanging for HH bonds. In this chapter, selective redemption is applied to a typical redemption situation.

Selective redemption is an alternative to randomly redeeming large groups of U.S. Savings Bonds. If you randomly redeem your bonds, it is unlikely that you will maximize your savings bond potential. Chapters 3 and 4 (on interest rates and timing issues) explain that each bond carries a unique set of information. Tracking the bonds, whether you do it yourself or secure the services of a reputable reporting service, such as The Savings Bond Informer (see Figure 15.1), enables you to analyze the data for each bond. It provides a means for comparing the data and determining which bonds to redeem at any given point in time. (If you have a completed bond statement, you may want to refer to it during this discussion or see Figure 15.1.)

In evaluating your bonds, you should consider several factors.

1. What rate of interest applies to each bond?
2. When does each of my bonds increase in value?
3. What is the accrued interest on each bond?
4. What is the value of each bond?
5. How much interest-earning life is left in each bond?

It is important to note that each bond owner may place a different priority on the above questions. For one investor, minimizing the amount of interest income that will have to be reported may be highest objective (#3). For another, keeping bonds that have the longest life left may be most important (#5). For yet another, the priority may be in keeping the bonds that are paying the highest rates of interest and redeeming the lower-paying ones (#1).

The Best Time of the Month to Cash Bonds

Always cash bonds early in the month. If your bond is due to increase in July and you redeem it July 1, you will be credited with the July increase. If you hold that same bond until July 30, you will receive the same amount as you would have on July 1.

The Best Time of Year to Cash Bonds

If you are thinking of redeeming bonds toward the end of a calendar year, you may want to consider waiting until after January 1. That way you will have one additional year before you must report the interest. In certain cases it makes sense to redeem some bonds at the end of one year and more bonds at the beginning of the next. This will spread the tax liability over two years.

A Penalty for Cashing Savings Bonds?

Any series EE or I bond purchased May 1997 or after is subject to a three-month interest penalty if the bond is cashed before it is five years old. There is no penalty for cashing once the bond is five years old. There is no penalty for cashing bonds purchased prior to May 1997.

Watch Out for These Errors

The author talks with clients of The Savings Bond Informer, Inc. on a daily basis. The following is a summary of bond owner experiences resulting in two key areas to watch out for when redeeming bonds.

1. Banks do occasionally provide incorrect redemption values. This can happen when a teller reads the wrong number on a chart or takes the wrong issue date to value the bond. How do you know you got the right amount? Double-check their work. Chapter 7 outlines some of your options for obtaining detailed redemption information.

2. Tellers sometimes tell a bond owner that bonds are still earning interest when they are not. This has become more prevalent with the thirty-year bonds that have stopped earning interest. Two types of mistakes have been reported. In the first, a teller assumes that all Series E bonds are good for forty years. If that were true, no bond issued in the 1960s would have stopped earning interest. Second, and more common, tellers do not properly read the tables and date ranges for thirty-year bonds. Thus they arrive at an inaccurate conclusion, not because the government table is wrong, but rather their interpretation of the table is wrong. Any Series E bond purchased December 1965 and after will stop earning interest thirty years from the date of purchase.

Allow time to analyze the options before redemption. Knowing your options will help you get the maximum return from your savings bond investment.

Quick Tips on Redemption

- Savings bonds can be redeemed at many commercial banks, some savings & loans and credit unions, and all FRBs listed in Chapter 19.

- You will need proper identification if you are going to cash a bond.

- If your bank will not cash a bond worth over $1,000, your only option is to submit the bond to a FRB.

- If you cash a bond, your bank will issue a 1099-INT. This normally results in a taxable event.

- Before redeeming them, take time to analyze your bonds, so you understand the interest rates, timing issues, and maturities for each.

- If you randomly cash bonds, it is unlikely that you will maximize each bond's potential.

- Always cash bonds early in the month.

- Make sure you double-check the amount you should receive when redeeming your bonds.

Figure 15.1 Example of a TSBI Bond Statement

The Savings Bond Informer, Inc.
Account #: CS000000106

Savings Bond Statment For:
NAME OF BOND OWNER
August 1998

P.O. Box 9249
Detroit, MI 48209
Phone: (313) 843-1910
Fax: (313) 843-1912

Statement Summary:

Number of Bonds on this Statement:	3
Total Purchase Price:	$2,656.25
Total Interest Accumulated on Bonds:	$3,718.42
Total Redemption Value of Bonds:	$6,374.67
Interest Earned Year-to-Date:	$261.34

Consumer Notice: This statement reflects the rates, values and rating system in effect as of the date of this statement. The government can change the bond program at any time and TSBI, Inc. makes no guarantee of any future returns. The "Bond Statement Explanation Sheet" (enclosed with your order) provides a detailed description of each column including the exclusive Savings Bond Informer Rating System (columns G and H). Thank you for using our service.

Detail Listing of Savings Bonds:

A	B	C	D	E	F	G	H	I	J	K	L	M	N
Line Number & Series	Issue Date	Face Value	Guaranteed Rate	Guar. Rate Until	Current Yield	2-Year Rating	5-Year Rating	Increase Dates	Last 12-Month Yield	Current Value	Interest Accumulated to Date	Bond Stops Earning Interest	Notes
1 E	NOV 1960	$75	4.00 %	NOV 2000	4.00 %	D	NR	AUG & FEB	6.09 %	$540.03	$483.78	NOV 2000	
2 EE	JUL 1986	$5,000	4.00 %	JUL 2006	3.96 %	D	D	JUL & JAN	4.05 %	$5,654.00	$3,154.00	JUL 2016	
3 EE	AUG 1988	$200	6.00 %	AUG 2000	6.02 %	A	C	AUG & FEB	6.06 %	$180.64	$80.64	AUG 2018	
									Page Totals:	$6,374.67	$3,718.42		

To order a savings bond statement, see the last page of this book.

© The Saving Bond Informer, Inc. 1998   Sort Order: Bond Order   Page: 1

Figure 15.2 Request for Payment PD F 1522

PD F 1522
Department of the Treasury
Bureau of the Public Debt
(Revised August 1996)

FOR FEDERAL RESERVE BANK USE ONLY
TRANSFER MONTH & YEAR _____ / _____
FISCAL AGENT CODE _____

**SPECIAL FORM OF REQUEST FOR PAYMENT OF
UNITED STATES SAVINGS AND RETIREMENT SECURITIES
WHERE USE OF A DETACHED REQUEST IS AUTHORIZED**

OMB No. 1535-0004

IMPORTANT: Follow instructions in filling out this form. You should be aware that the making of any false, fictitious or fraudulent claim to the United States is a crime punishable by imprisonment of not more than five years or a fine up to $250,000, or both, under 18 U.S.C. 287 and 18 U.S.C. 3571. Additionally, 31 U.S.C. 3729 provides for civil penalties for the maker of a false or fraudulent claim to the United States of an amount not less than $5,000 and not more than $10,000, plus treble the amount of the Government's damages as an additional sanction.
PRINT IN INK OR TYPE ALL INFORMATION

I am the owner or person entitled to payment of the following-described securities which bear the name(s)
of _____ and hereby request payment.

(This line for use in case of partial redemption only. See paragraph 4 of Instructions.)

ISSUE DATE	SERIAL NUMBER	ISSUE DATE	SERIAL NUMBER	ISSUE DATE	SERIAL NUMBER

(If space is insufficient, use continuation sheet, sign it, and refer to it above. PD F 3500 may be used for this purpose.)

OR

Social Security Account Number of Payee   Employer Identification Number for Payee

**Sign in ink in presence
of certifying officer:** _____

Daytime Telephone Number: _____
Address
(For delivery of check) _____

(Number and street or rural route)   (City or town)   (State)   (ZIP Code)

I CERTIFY that the above-named person, whose identity is well-known or proved to me, personally appeared before me
this _____ day of _____, _____, at _____

(City)   (State)

and signed the above request, acknowledging the same to be his/her free act and deed.

**(OFFICIAL STAMP
OR SEAL)**

_____
(Signature and title of certifying officer)

_____
(Address)

(SEE INSTRUCTIONS ON REVERSE)

SEE INSTRUCTIONS FOR PRIVACY ACT AND PAPERWORK REDUCTION ACT NOTICE

Chapter 16

THE EDUCATIONAL FEATURE OF SERIES EE AND I BONDS

▶ *Common Misconceptions*
▶ *What the Advertising Didn't Tell You*
▶ *Conditions for Qualifying for the Tax-Free Status*
▶ *Record Keeping for the Educational Feature*
▶ *Will the Current Interest Rates Be Enough?*
▶ *Pros and Cons of the Educational Feature*
▶ *An Alternative for Reducing the Tax Burden*
▶ *Two Ways Bond Owners Lose Out
   on the Tax-Free Feature*
▶ *Quick Tips on the Educational Feature*

What you have heard is true: The largest single expenditure you will ever make, other than buying a home, will most likely be your child's college tuition. By the first decade of the twenty-first century, if recent inflation rates hold, four years at an in-state public institution will cost at least $86,000, and four years at a private college will total about $163,000.

—Janet Bamford,"The Class of 2013,"
Sesame Street Parents
(September 1994), pp. 52–55

With educational costs skyrocketing, many parents are paying increased attention to investment options to pay their children's future tuition. This is certainly true in the author's state, whose public universities have announced tuition hikes of 5 to 10%. The educational feature of the Series EE bond (and now the I bond also) has received a lot of media attention. A closer examination will enable you to assess whether it is right for you. In addition, if you have already purchased bonds with the assumption that you will be able to use them "tax free" for education, you will want to take a close look at the qualifying conditions of this feature, an alternative for shifting the tax burden, and how unsuspecting bond owners sometimes lose out on this option.

Common Misconceptions

"Tax-Free for Education." In the early 1990s, you probably heard the radio advertisements pitch the sale of EE bonds for the purpose of saving for a college education. Here are the most common misunderstandings.

Misconception #1: *All bonds are now tax-free if used for education.*
No. There is an abundance of misinformation on this point. All Series I bonds and only Series EE bonds purchased as of January 1, 1990, are eligible, and then only if *seven* other conditions have been met. A complete list of the conditions is presented later in this chapter.

Misconception #2: *I must buy the bonds in my child's name so I can use them tax-free for education.*
No. But buying bonds in your child's name is not necessarily a bad idea, as you will see later in this chapter. However, if you do buy a bond in your child's name, you have just eliminated that bond from being eligible for the tax-free educational feature. If you have already registered your bonds this way because someone gave you inaccurate information, you can retitle the bond. Call your regional Federal Reserve Bank (see Chapter 19, "U.S. Savings Bond Resources"), explain the situation, and ask for the appropriate reissue form. The transaction may be forwarded to the Bureau of the Public Debt (BPD) for approval and processing. They should honor your request because many people were given wrong information about how the bonds should be registered.

Misconception #3: *I'm buying bonds in the name of my grandchildren so they can use the tax-free educational feature.*
No. Grandparents have to purchase the bonds in the name of the *parents* of their grandchildren to qualify the bonds for the tax-free educational feature.

This could be risky business in some families: The parents may not honor the wishes of the grandparents concerning the intent of the bonds. Since they are named on the bonds, the parents are free to negotiate the bonds at their own discretion. However, if properly used by all involved, this can be a way for grandparents to contribute to their grandchildren's education.

Misconception #4: *At the time of purchase, I have to declare that the bonds will be used for education.*
No. You do not have to declare your intent with any bond purchase. You can buy the bonds with the intent of using them for education and then change your mind. Cashing them for another purpose means you forfeit the opportunity for the bonds to be "tax-free for education," but there are no additional penalties or hidden fees (unless purchased after April 1997 and cashed within the first five years).

What the Advertising Didn't Tell You

Most of the misconceptions that bond owners have about the educational feature of bonds were the result of brief media announcements or advertisements. Regardless of the cause, many who bought bonds because "they are now tax-free for education" were unhappy to learn that they did not know "the rest of the story." And they are not alone.

What is the "rest of the story"? For starters you need to know the conditions that must be met to qualify for the tax-free status.

Conditions for Qualifying for the Tax-Free Status

There are eight conditions which must be met in order to qualify for the tax-free feature of EE bonds and I bonds (yes, I bonds are also eligible for the tax-free status if all the same conditions are met). The conditions, as given in the government publication, "U.S. Savings Bonds: Now Tax-Free for Education," are (these are modified and updated to include 1998 income levels and the new I bond):

1. Only EE and I bonds purchased after December 31, 1989, qualify.

2. The bonds must be registered in the name of either one or both of the parents. The child cannot be listed on the bond as owner or co-owner. However, the child can be listed on the bond as the POD (Pay on Death) recipient.

3. The parents must be at least twenty-four years of age when purchasing the bonds. (**Author's note:** Let's see . . . sixteen years old to drive, eigh-

teen years old to vote, and twenty-four years old to buy bonds tax-free. . . . I love this country.)

4. The income of the parents *in the year the bond is cashed* will determine whether the bond is exempt from federal tax. (U.S. Saving Bonds are always exempt from state and local taxes.) In 1990, this was set at $60,000 for a married couple filing jointly and $40,000 for a single parent. A partial tax break was available (up to $90,000) for a married couple filing jointly. These income limits are indexed to inflation each year. The 1998 income limits are set at $78,350 for a married couple filing jointly and $52,250 for a single parent. A partial tax break is available (up to $108,350 for a married couple filing jointly or up to $67,250 for a single parent). Contact the BPD for the income limits in future years. (See Chapter 19 for the address and phone number.)

5. Bonds must be redeemed the same year that the bond owner pays his, her, or their child's educational expenses to an eligible institution.

6. The only expenses to which bonds can be applied are tuition and fees. Room, board, and books do not qualify.

7. Educational institutions that are eligible include colleges, universities, technical institutes, and vocational schools located in the United States.

8. The interest on bonds that qualify for the educational feature can be excluded from federal income tax only if the redemption proceeds (interest and principal) are less than or equal to the qualifying tuition and fees paid during the year. If the value of the bonds cashed is greater than the eligible tuition and fees, a proportional amount of the bond interest is exempt. That is, if the tuition and fees total $5,000, yet you redeem $20,000 of eligible bonds, only 25% of the interest income can be excluded from federal income tax. This can have chilling effects on the "tax-free" status that you thought you would enjoy. See the case study at the end of the chapter for an illustration.

Additional rule for married couples: Couples who wish to use the educational feature tax exclusion must file a joint return.

Author's note: Prepaid tuition plans can qualify for the tax-free feature due to a 1997 tax law change.

Record Keeping for the Educational Feature

According to the BPD, bond owners should keep records on EE bonds that qualify for the educational feature. For each bond you should have the following:

✓ Social Security number
✓ Serial number
✓ Face value
✓ Issue date
✓ Date of redemption
✓ Total proceeds received (principal and interest)

In addition, you will need to document:

✓ The name of the educational institution that received payment
✓ The date the expenses were paid
✓ The amount of qualified expenses

Forms 8815 and 8818 are both appropriate IRS forms for recording your transaction. Figures 16.1 and 16.2 (pages 203 and 204) provide copies of these forms. You may order the forms from the IRS by calling (800) 829-3676.

To avoid duplication in record keeping, please note that several of the items mentioned above are already a part of your bond records—if you followed the suggestions in Chapter 5, "Organizing Your Bonds." (Additional information is presented in Chapter 7, "Tracking Your Investment.")

Will the Current Interest Rates Be Enough?

Good question. And here is where the debate really heats up. The author is neither a financial planner nor a financial advisor, but he has heard plenty of views on whether interest rates on bonds will "cut the mustard."

The guaranteed rate for bonds purchased between March 1993 and April 1995 is 4%. At 4%, it will take a bond eighteen years to reach face value (that is, to double). So if Junior was born yesterday and somehow makes it through high school by eighteen, the bonds purchased at his birth will be worth double their purchase price by the time he starts college. Not exactly bowled over yet?

There is an upside potential. If the average market rate on the bonds exceeds 4% and the bonds are held for at least five years, then this higher rate will be realized. For example, if the average market rate is 6% after the first twelve years of the bond's life, then the bond will reach face value (or double) in only twelve years. That may be better, but is it good enough?

Remember, though, that interest rates will not be constant under the new rules. The rates will fluctuate, tied to five-year Treasury yields (if you buy EE bonds) or the CPI-U (if you buy I bonds). If the rates average 6%, your money will double in twelve years. If the rates average 4%, your money will double in eighteen years. If the rates average 7%, your money will double in a little over ten years.

Table 16.1 Time Period to Double Investment

Constant Interest Rate Compounded Semi-Annually	Approximate Number of Years for Investment to Double
3%	24 years
4%	18 years
5%	14.4 years
6%	12 years
7%	10.3 years
8%	9 years
9%	8 years

Table 16.2 (page 205) shows how much you can expect to save for college by using savings bonds in a systematic savings program. Please note that on line one, projections at 4% were guaranteed as a minimum for bonds purchased March 1993 to April 1995. As you can see in the last column, it will take a savings of $250 a month for eighteen years at an interest rate of 5% to reach the $86,000 cost projected for four years of college in-state in the first decade of the next century.

Pros and Cons of the Educational Feature

Pros

1. Bonds can be used for the educational expenses of a husband, wife, or children. They are not limited to children only.

2. If not used for education, there is no additional penalty; you simply are not eligible for federal tax exemption.

3. Bonds can be used at the eligible school of your choice, in-state or out-of-state.

4. There is no set window or time frame for enrollment—any time after December 31, 1989.

5. You can invest as little as $25 or as much as $15,000 per person per year for the EE bonds and as little as $50 or as much as $30,000 per person on the I bonds. You can buy the limit of both in the same year.

6. The bonds are backed by the full faith and credit of the United States government.

7. The bonds are no-load; there are no commissions or fees for entry or exit.

8. The bonds are easily purchased through payroll deduction (at participating companies) or from most local banks.

Cons

1. The interest rate may be unattractive to you.

2. The unknown factor of having your tax-free status determined by your income in the year the bond is redeemed may be too risky. This is especially true if your income is already near the established level and you expect it to outpace inflation.

3. Record keeping is the responsibility of the bond owner.

An Alternative for Reducing the Tax Burden

There is an alternative to using bonds for education with a reduced tax burden. In fact, it may prove to be more of a guarantee than waiting fifteen years to see if your income allows you to qualify for the tax-free status.

You can shift the tax liability to your children by buying the bonds in their name. The parent can appear as a beneficiary on the bond, but not as a co-owner. If you register the bond this way, however, it will not be eligible for the educational feature described earlier.

In choosing this alternative, you must annually report the interest income of the bonds. If the child's total income is under $650 (this is the limit for 1997; check with IRS for annual adjustments), the child pays no taxes on the interest earned. And because the interest is reported annually, most of it will have been reported by the time the bonds are redeemed.

To use the annual reporting method, you must file a return the first year to show intent to use this method. You must also file a return any year the child's income exceeds the limit set by the IRS. Many tax laws change every year, so consult with your accountant before you take action.

Note: If you choose to report interest annually, make sure you clearly understand how to avoid double taxation. When cashing the bonds, a 1099-INT will be issued for all the interest dating back to the date of purchase. The amount previously reported can be deducted from the 1099-INT amount on the tax return. Failure to deduct the amount previously reported will result in double taxation of some of the interest.

Two Ways Bond Owners Lose Out on the Tax-Free Feature

Illustration #1: *Income Outpaces Indexed Income Numbers*

Bob and Vicki have two children, ages four and six. Bob works for a car company and Vicki works without pay as a stay-at-home mom. Savings bonds look like a potential option for college savings, especially the tax-free part. Because their income is $68,000 in 1997—below the limits established for qualifying for the tax-free feature at that time—they move ahead with their plans.

Over the years they invest more than $120,000 in savings bonds resulting in over $70,000 in accrued interest by the time their eldest is ready for her first year of college. In the meantime, the income guidelines have been adjusted about 2% each year.

In the year 2002, Vicki goes back to her former career as a public relations director and the family income doubles. By the time their eldest goes to college, they are earning over $150,000 annually—too much to qualify for the tax-free feature. Not only do they not qualify for the tax-free feature, but all the interest they earned (if the bonds were cashed and used for education) will be taxed at a bracket even higher than the bracket they were in when the bonds were purchased.

The tax bill amounted to over $20,000 for this family—taxes that they thought would not have to be paid on "tax-free" savings bonds.

Illustration #2: *Misunderstanding How the Calculations are Done*

Lisa is in a 28% tax bracket. She thinks the tax-free feature of EE bonds will provide significant savings for her child's education. However, she gets started a little late and has only three years to save before Junior heads to college.

For three years she invests $30,000 a year into savings bonds receiving an average return of 5% that results in a total value approximately $99,200. Since Junior goes to college at the end of the third year, Lisa cashes all the bonds with the expectation that since his tuition and fees are $10,000 and the total interest earned on the bonds is only $9,200, that the interest will all be tax-free (assume there is no three-month penalty for cashing prior to five years).

However, the actual calculations prove to be quite painful because she is unaware of two things: (1) investors are required to report the total redemption value on their IRS forms, and (2) this value is compared to the actual tuition and fees. Should the total redemption value exceed tuition and fees (as it does in this case) only a portion of the interest earned will be tax-free.

Let's examine the calculations.

Abbreviated version IRS form 8815 (tax year 1998)

Line 2.	Tuition and fees	$10,000
Line 3.	Minus non-taxable scholarships or grants	0
Line 4.	Subtract line 3 from line 2	$10,000
Line 5.	Total proceeds from all eligible bonds cashed	$99,200
	(**Author's comment:** using total proceeds hurts the bond owner)	
Line 6.	Interest from eligible bonds cashed	$ 9,200
Line 7.	Is line 4 less than line 5? If yes, divide line 4 by line 5, enter result as a decimal (round to second place)	.10
Line 8.	Multiply line 6 by line 7	$ 920.00
	(**Author's comment:** this is where the bond owner is getting shafted)	
Line 9.	Enter modified adjusted gross income	$65,000
Line 10.	Enter $78,250 if filing jointly	$78,250
Line 11.	Subtract line 10 from line 9, if zero or less, skip line 12, enter "0" on line 13, and go to line 14.	
Line 12.		Skip
Line 13.		0
Line 14.	Subtract line 13 from line 8. Enter result.	$ 920.00

Instead of receiving $9,200 tax-free, the actual amount that can be deducted from income is only $920.00—about 10% of what she thought they would receive. The unexpected tax bill comes to:

Interest she thought would be tax-free	$ 9,200
Actual interest that is tax-free	$ 927.42
Interest that will be taxed at 28% (or higher)	$ 8,272.58
Unexpected tax due	$ 2,316.32

Lisa lost more than $2,300 because she did not understand how the tax calculation would be done. Furthermore her "tax-free" investment proved to be hardly that, with barely 10% of the interest gains actually receiving the "tax-free" status.

In Lisa's case, if she cashed in one-quarter of her holdings each year (over four years), then approximately $920 a year or $3,680 total could be "tax-free." This only allowed 40% of the interest to be "tax-free." The unexpected tax bill for the income that is not eligible ($5,520) is still $1,546.

Tip: The closer you can get to making the total amount of bonds cashed equal to or less than the amount of tuition, the higher the percentage of interest that may be excluded from being taxed.

Quick Tips on the Educational Feature

- You may be under the mistaken impression that all the bonds you have purchased are tax-free for education.

- You must meet eight conditions to qualify for the tax-free status (see page 195).

- Bonds that have been incorrectly registered and therefore do not qualify the investor for tax-free status may be retitled by petitioning the BPD.

- Record keeping is the responsibility of the bond owner.

- An alternative for reducing the tax burden is to shift the liability to the children by purchasing bonds in their names and having them report the income annually.

- If you chose to report interest annually, proper records should be kept on how to avoid double taxation.

- Two ways that bond owners can lose out on the tax-free feature is (1) when income outpaces indexed income numbers, and (2) when they purchase without considering how the calculations will be done at redemption.

Figure 16.1 IRS Form 8815

Form **8815**	**Exclusion of Interest From Series EE**	OMB No. 1545-1173
Department of the Treasury Internal Revenue Service	**U.S. Savings Bonds Issued After 1989** (For Filers With Qualified Higher Education Expenses) ▶ Attach to Form 1040 or Form 1040A.	**1997** Attachment Sequence No. **57**

Caution: *If your filing status is married filing separately, **do not** file this form. You **cannot** take the exclusion even if you paid qualified higher education expenses in 1997.*

Name(s) shown on return | Your social security number

1

(a) Name of person (you, your spouse, or your dependent) who was enrolled at or attended an eligible educational institution	**(b)** Name and address of eligible educational institution

If you need more space, attach additional sheets.

2 Enter the total qualified higher education expenses you paid in 1997 for the persons listed in column (a) of line 1. See the instructions to find out which expenses qualify	**2**	
3 Enter the total of any nontaxable educational benefits (such as nontaxable scholarship or fellowship grants) received for 1997 for the persons listed in column (a) of line 1. See instructions	**3**	
4 Subtract line 3 from line 2. If zero or less, **stop.** You **cannot** take the exclusion	**4**	
5 Enter the total proceeds (principal and interest) from all series EE U.S. savings bonds **issued after 1989** that you **cashed during 1997**	**5**	
6 Enter the interest included on line 5. See instructions	**6**	
7 Is line 4 **less than** line 5? **No.** Enter "1.00." **Yes.** Divide line 4 by line 5. Enter the result as a decimal (rounded to two places)	**7**	× .
8 Multiply line 6 by line 7	**8**	
9 Enter your modified adjusted gross income. See instructions . . . **9** **Note:** *If line 9 is $65,850 or more ($106,250 or more if married filing jointly or qualifying widow(er)),* **stop.** *You **cannot** take the exclusion.*		
10 Enter $50,850 ($76,250 if married filing jointly or qualifying widow(er)) **10**		
11 Subtract line 10 from line 9. If zero or less, skip line 12, enter -0- on line 13, and go to line 14 . . . . **11**		
12 Divide line 11 by $15,000 (by $30,000 if married filing jointly or qualifying widow(er)). Enter the result as a decimal (rounded to two places)	**12**	× .
13 Multiply line 8 by line 12	**13**	
14 **Excludable savings bond interest.** Subtract line 13 from line 8. Enter the result here and on Schedule B (Form 1040), line 3, or Schedule 1 (Form 1040A), line 3, whichever applies . . ▶	**14**	

General Instructions

Section references are to the Internal Revenue Code.

Purpose of Form

If you cashed series EE U.S. savings bonds in 1997 that were issued after 1989, you may be able to exclude from your income part or all of the interest on those bonds. Use Form 8815 to figure the amount of any interest you may exclude.

Who May Take the Exclusion

You may take the exclusion if **all four** of the following apply:

1. You cashed qualified U.S. savings bonds in 1997 that were issued after 1989.

2. You paid qualified higher education expenses in 1997 for yourself, your spouse, or your dependents.

3. Your filing status is any status **except** married filing separately.

4. Your modified AGI (adjusted gross income) is less than $65,850 (less than $106,250 if married filing jointly or qualifying widow(er)). See the line 9 instructions to figure your modified AGI.

U.S. Savings Bonds That Qualify for Exclusion

To qualify for the exclusion, the bonds must be series EE U.S. savings bonds issued after 1989 in your name, or, if you are married, they may be issued in your name and your spouse's name. Also, you must have been age 24 or older before the bonds were issued. A bond bought by a parent and issued in the name of his or her child under age 24 does not qualify for the exclusion by the parent or child. **Bond information may be verified with Department of the Treasury records.**

For Paperwork Reduction Act Notice, see back of form. Cat. No. 10822S Form **8815** (1997)

Figure 16.2 IRS Form 8818

Form **8818** (Rev. March 1995) Department of the Treasury Internal Revenue Service	**Optional Form To Record Redemption of Series EE U.S. Savings Bonds Issued After 1989** (For Individuals With Qualified Higher Education Expenses) ▶ Keep for your records. **Do not send to the IRS.** ▶ **See instructions on back.**	OMB No. 1545-1151

Name		Date cashed

1	(a) Serial number	(b) Issue date (must be after 1989)	(c) Face value

2	Add the amounts in column (c) of line 1	2	
3	Total redemption proceeds from bonds listed above that were issued after 1989. Be sure to get this figure from the teller when you cash the bonds	3	
4	Multiply line 2 above by 50% (.50). This is your cost	4	
5	Subtract line 4 from line 3. This is the interest on the bonds	5	

For Paperwork Reduction Act Notice, see back of form.   Cat. No. 10097L   Form **8818** (Rev. 3-95)

Table 16.2
Using Savings Bonds to Save for Education Expenses

Assumed Interest Rate	Save $50/month to purchase $300 of bonds every six months. Value after 10 years	Save $50/month to purchase $300 of bonds every six months. Value after 18 years	Save $100/month to purchase $600 of bonds every six months. Value after 10 years	Save $100/month to purchase $600 of bonds every six months. Value after 18 years	Save $250/month to purchase $1,500 of bonds every six months. Value after 10 years	Save $250/month to purchase $1,500 of bonds every six months. Value after 18 years
4%	$7,289	$15,598	$14,578	$31,196	$36,446	$77,991
5%	$7,663	$17,190	$15,326	$34,380	$38,316	$85,952
6%	$8,061	$18,982	$16,122	$37,965	$40,305	$94,913
7%	$8,484	$21,002	$16,968	$42,005	$42,420	$105,011

The calculations in the above table are based on the following assumptions.

1. The bond purchaser will save money at an even monthly rate and will purchase bonds twice a year. A monthly purchase pattern will result in a slightly higher final value.

2. That the interest rates used to calculate future values will be consistent over the time period the calculations were made.

3. The money invested is the purchase price of the bonds, not the face value. Thus, the phrase "purchase $300 of bonds every six months" means $300 purchase price, $600 face value. (Remember EE bonds are purchased for one-half the face value.)

4. There is no guaranteed interest rate for Series EE bonds purchased after April 1995. Series EE bonds purchased May 1998 to October 1998 receive an interest rate of 5.06% for the first six months. Call 1-800-USBONDS for interest rate information on new purchases.

Note: This table does not guarantee a specific return on any investment you make. Market conditions and rules governing the savings bond program may change without notice. Obtain current rate information and complete details before making any investment.

Chapter 17

ESPECIALLY FOR GRANDPARENTS AND OTHER GIFT GIVERS

▶ *Savings Bonds and Relationships*
▶ *Do Savings Bonds Make a Good Gift?*
▶ *Registration Consequences for Gifts, Inheritances, and Charities*
▶ *How Can You Be Sure that the Money Is Used as Intended?*
▶ *Who Gets the Money When You Are Gone?*
▶ *Records for Your Heirs*
▶ *Quick Tips for Gift Givers*

This chapter is especially for grandparents, but it will also be of interest to parents, aunts and uncles, brothers and sisters, and those others who play a significant role in a child's life.

Through a combination of phone consultations and seminars, the author finds that gift givers have a variety of savings bond questions that require special attention. Many want to know if bonds are a good gift and how to leave bonds as an inheritance to children and grandchildren. The issues surrounding these answers, such as tax consequences and registration of a bond, can make a considerable difference as to whether your wishes are carried out or not.

Savings Bonds and Relationships

Many people have used savings bonds as a tangible expression of their care for other family members. Marian of Virginia recently sent this example in a letter:

> *My husband and I maintained a small collection of Series E bonds that had accumulated from a "pay as you go" plan while I was working as a secretary. Each month we received a "little gem" and tucked it away.*
>
> *Three days before Christmas 1995, Bill succumbed to a fast moving cancer, surviving less than three weeks after the initial diagnosis. And because of the usual extra activities most families incur during the holiday season, we were, as a family, inundated with things that had to somehow just get done. We didn't think "bonds." We were busy notifying relatives, making funeral arrangements . . . and all the while wrapping grandchildren's packages to put under the tree. We preferred to stay busy; that way there was less time for tears.*
>
> *However, the tears did come later in the Christmas of 1996 after I had the time to review the bonds that Bill and I had accumulated. Can you imagine my initial surprise when I found three $5,000 bonds, one made out to each of our daughters, neatly tucked away with the rest of the stack? Bill had bought them and said nothing. It meant that even though their Dad had passed away, he and I (and I emphasize "he" for his astuteness) were able to give each daughter a substantial Christmas gift.*
>
> *When Christmas morning arrived, the surprise came like a bomb/bond and the long delayed tears followed. The full impact came even later when each daughter realized the bonds would gather interest and "gift" them each Christmas.*
>
> *Even though I don't have those bonds in my possession, I include them each year when I call for my analysis. That way, each daughter receives a Christmas update remembrance from Dad by way of The Savings Bond Informer, Inc.*

The author has heard of hundreds of children, grandchildren, nieces, and nephews who reflect fondly upon a loved one as a result of a savings bond gift. It isn't about the money, it is about the relationship and remembrance. That little piece of paper has a way of bringing back memories of a special someone who cared for us.

Do Savings Bonds Make a Good Gift?

Without fail, during every radio interview, someone asks the question, "Are savings bonds a good investment?" Often the caller wants to buy bonds for a family member, but the opinions of others have caused him or her to question whether savings bonds are a wise choice as a monetary gift. Several variables impact this question and are worthy of consideration. And, as previously presented, not all of these variables are monetary. Looking at the pros and cons may help you decide. (See Chapter 14, "Purchasing U.S. Savings Bonds," page 169, for an expanded list.)

Pros

Savings bonds are a safe investment.
Several years from now, what you give today will be worth what you paid for it plus the interest that has accumulated. It cannot be worth less than the purchase price; there is no risk of lost principal.

> *The week that I was working on this chapter, the stock market dropped almost 600 points (over 6%). An article in the* Wall Street Journal *highlighted a man who had over $200,000 in mutual funds and cashed it all because in my words, "He couldn't take it anymore." He had done very well, but now he wanted less risk. With savings bonds, you'll sleep at night.*

Savings bonds can serve as a remembrance.
They represent a token of love that has often meant more than their actual monetary value.

Savings bonds are easy to buy.
You can walk into most banks and fill out an application, and the bond will be delivered to the address you have chosen. There are no fees or commissions. In addition, there is no pressure to buy more or less than what you want.

Savings bonds compete well with other conservative investments.
While you will not see spectacular yields, savings bond interest rates are comparable to CDs and money market funds and beat savings accounts. A bond bought in mid-1998 received an interest rate of 5.06% for the first six months.

Cons

Savings bonds provide conservative returns.
While bonds have earned rates generally between 4% and 6%, the stock market has enjoyed an average of a double-digit gain over the last decade. They will not make the nightly news as the best paying investment in the marketplace.

Savings bonds are a complex investment.
Rule changes have affected the interest rates, timing issues, and maturity dates of savings bonds. With the new I bond we now have a two-part interest rate, while the EE bond has an interest rate that changes every six months. If a per-

son has purchased bonds over the last five years there are several sets of interest rates and rules to digest. That can make it more difficult to track a savings bond investment.

Savings bonds no longer carry a guaranteed rate.
How long does it take a bond to reach face value? Due to rule changes implemented in May 1995 and May 1997, the exact length of time will depend on the interest rates assigned during the life of a bond. These will change every six months. When you buy a bond there will be no way to know exactly what rate will be in effect in the future. The higher the rate, the quicker a bond will reach face value. A Series EE bond will always pay a rate equal to 90% of the five-year Treasury yields. Here are the most recent rates:

May 1997	5.68%
November 1997	5.59%
May 1998	5.06%

If interest rates continue to be in this range over the next ten to fifteen years (a big"if,"I know), a bond purchased today will reach face value in about thirteen years.

You might be asking, "Well I remember when bonds used to reach face value in seven years, what happened?" The last time bonds reached face value in seven years was back in the 1970s. The reason they reached face value so quickly was largely because you paid 75% of the face value when you purchased the bond (not 50% as you do today for the EE bond).

Registration Consequences for Gifts, Inheritances, and Charities

How to Title New Bonds as Gifts for Your Grandchildren

If you buy bonds on a regular basis (every birthday and holiday), giving consideration to how the bonds are titled is important. How you register a bond will determine who is eligible to cash the bonds.

In most cases, the author is in support of putting bonds in the name of the grandchild with either you or a parent listed as a co-owner or beneficiary. Although this inscription will not qualify the bonds for the tax-free feature if used for a college education, it will probably provide the most flexibility to the intended recipient of the gift. (See Chapter 16, page 195, for registration guidelines needed to qualify for the educational feature.)

Note: When you register bonds with co-owners, either co-owner can redeem the bond *without* the consent of the other. If you are concerned about a parent cashing your grandchild's bond, you can put the bond in the name of a grandchild alone. Then there is less likelihood that the child's parent will cash the bonds—but no guarantee, because parents can cash on behalf of a minor, even if they are not listed on the bond. The reason there is less likelihood is that most parents are unaware of this possibility. In most families this type of registration will not present a problem, but here are some suggestions for grandparents who are concerned that the parents may cash their children's bonds.

Option 1: Hold the bonds until you feel your grandchild is old enough to receive them. In addition, give instructions to someone you trust: Should something happen to you, that person will know what is to be done with the bonds and when they are to be given.

Option 2: List yourself on the bond as a co-owner. This would protect against the bonds being claimed and replaced as lost bonds because this cannot be done without your signature. Once again, this option gives you the control to decide when to hand the bonds over.

Note: If your estate is subject to estate tax, the value of the bonds must be included in the estate should you die before the bonds are cashed. However, if your estate (including savings bonds) is under $625,000, don't worry about it.

How to Title Bonds that are Being Passed on to Heirs

Many grandparents determine that they do not need the bonds they own and decide to give them to a grandchild, other family member, friend, or charity. Although a warm gesture, this can cause tax consequences and, in some cases, even create double taxation.

Note: If you are the first-named, principal co-owner and decide to have your name removed from the bonds, you will receive a 1099-INT for all the interest earned up to the point of transfer, even though no money will be received. The amount of tax you have to pay will be based on the tax bracket that you are in at the time of transfer. Even worse, if you choose to have the bonds retitled into the name of the intended recipient, guess what he or she will again receive at the time of redemption? A 1099-INT for all the interest back to the date of purchase. True, they can deduct the amount previously reported, but what if they don't know that you reported it? In many cases, unsuspecting family members report the full amount and so a portion of the bonds' value has been taxed twice.

There is an alternative: If the bonds are titled in your name alone, you can add a co-owner of your choice (people only, you cannot add an organization as co-owner). Then, the recipient who cashes the bonds will supply his or her social security number and *that person* will receive the 1099-INT. This alternative is presented in full in the tax chapter and involves a discrepancy between the IRS rules and the reporting system.

Reminder: If the bonds remain in your name with the recipient as a co-owner, the value of the bonds must be included in the value of your estate if you die before the bonds are cashed.

Gifting Bonds to a Charity or Charitable Remainder Trust

The same basic rule that applies to retitling bonds for heirs applies here. If you gift bonds to a charity or charitable remainder trust while you are living, your name will need to be removed from the bond, which creates a taxable event for you. However, since a tax-exempt charity is not subject to tax, there is no danger of double taxation. See Chapter 11, page 129 for more information on gifting bonds to a charity.

How Can You Be Sure that the Money Is Used as Intended?

Here is where trust replaces control. Once you title a bond in someone else's name, they are the rightful owner and you have no control over how the money is used. Here is a strategy for wielding some influence.

One savvy grandpa bought bonds in the name of his grandchildren with himself listed as a co-owner. He let them know that when they turned a certain age, if they were not involved in various activities (i.e., drugs, destructive lifestyles, etc.), he would give them the bonds. He was very excited at his 75th birthday to hand bonds over to each of his grandchildren. (**Remember:** If a grandparent buys bonds and lists himself as the co-owner, he is considered the principal co-owner and the value of the bonds should be included in the value of his estate should he die before the bonds are cashed.)

Who Gets the Money When You Are Gone?

Proper registration cannot be stressed enough. Titling a bond is the single most important element in determining who will receive the bonds. If you have a co-owner or beneficiary listed on your bond and something happens to you, that person becomes the rightful owner. In the absence of a co-owner or beneficiary, your legal will directs who will receive your bonds. Therefore, beware of this situation:

John and his family had cared for his Aunt Esther for over 15 years. She loved her nephew and his family and had named John as the co-owner on her most valuable possession; $50,000 of U.S. Savings Bonds. Sadly, John died and although she lived for several years afterward, Aunt Esther did not realize that she should have had her bonds retitled. You see Aunt Esther intended for the bonds to go to John's family. However, since John predeceased her, the bonds became a part of her estate upon her death. In her will she had left everything else to other relatives. Since John's family was not named in the will, his family had no entitlement to the bonds.

It was bad enough that Aunt Esther did not receive her wishes, but in some cases, a lack of planning can lead to family fighting and broken relationships. Make sure your bonds are titled as you have chosen. And while you are at it, if you haven't done so already, make a will that reflects your current wishes.

If your estate is over $650,000, have a competent estate planner review your financial affairs. You don't have to take the advice offered, but a professional may save you and your family a bundle.

An Afterthought

Your heirs will not receive a stepped-up cost basis if they inherit your bonds. You could spend all of the savings you have in bonds and leave assets that will receive a stepped-up cost basis to your family.

Records for Your Heirs

Millions of bond owners have failed to keep a record of their savings bond holdings. The result, when they pass on, is that their heirs do not know that the bonds existed. In Chapter 5, "Organizing Your Bonds," you will find a list of the data that should be recorded for each bond you own and a worksheet.

Quick Tips for Gift Givers

- Savings bonds can be a visible reminder of your care for the recipient.

- When giving bonds as a gift or for an inheritance, study your titling options; how a bond is registered has bearing on who is eligible to cash it.

- Gifting bonds to a charity while you are living creates a taxable event.

- If a co-owner on your bond is deceased, retitle the bonds according to your wishes to ensure that your intentions for the money are realized.

- If you do not keep records of your bond holdings for your heirs, your savings may unintentionally become a gift to Uncle Sam.

- You might want to consider redeeming some of your bonds in retirement, since your heirs will not get a stepped-up-basis on them once inherited.

The New I Bond

Who says big government never changes? For the first time in eighteen years it has launched a new savings bond—the I bond. Much of the attention at the initial press conference was devoted to whose pictures would be on the bonds. And although this is a nice feature, with all due respect I'd rather have a $100 dollar bill than a $1 dollar bill, regardless of whose picture is on it. Thus, this chapter goes into more detail about what type of investment the I bond is. That is, is it good, bad, or still to be determined?

The initial unveiling of this bond was like a car company showing us the exterior of a car. Now that we've kicked the tires and seen the paint job, we'll examine what is under the hood.

What Is an I Bond?

The I bond is a new savings bond issued by the Treasury that is designed to offer protection from inflation. By linking the return of the bond to an inflation index, the bond is always guaranteed to earn a fixed rate above the inflation rate. It is sort of a hybrid between the Treasury Inflation Indexed Bonds (which are issued as marketable securities and available through the Treasury Direct System or for purchase on the secondary market) and the EE bond. As you will see later in this chapter, the I bond contains elements of both.

This bond represents another way for the government to borrow money to finance the debt. Since the debt stands at over $5.5 trillion one can understand the launch of some additional financing options. The trick for the Treasury is to offer a product that is attractive enough to gain investors' confidence and money, yet not offer more than they have to, in order to keep the cost of financing the debt as low as possible. If the entire debt were financed at 5%, the interest expense alone would be $275 billion a year. A 1% savings in the cost of borrowing represents a savings of over $55 billion a year in interest expense.

The I bonds were made available September 1, 1998. They can be purchased at banks where EE bonds are sold. You will also be able to purchase them through payroll deduction (although not immediately; ask your payroll or human resources department about availability through your company).

The Window Dressing

Each I bond features an outstanding American—someone who has made significant contributions to our society. The following is a list of these people and the denomination of the bond on which their likeness appears (as quoted from a press release the government used to introduce the new bonds):

- *$50 I bond:* Helen Keller, a noted author and advocate for individuals with disabilities. Ms. Keller is also responsible for Braille becoming the standard for printed communication with the blind.

- *$75 I bond:* Dr. Hector Garcia, a leading advocate for Mexican-American veterans rights, an activist in the Latino civil rights movement, and the founder of the American GI forum.

- *$100 I bond:* Dr. Martin Luther King, Jr., one of the nation's most prominent civil rights leaders. Dr. King was also a minister and Nobel Peace Prize recipient.

- *$200 I bond:* Chief Joseph-Nez Percé Chief, one of the greatest Native American leaders.

- *$500 I bond:* General George Marshall, U.S. Army Chief of Staff during World War II, Secretary of State and Defense, author of the Marshall plan, and Nobel Peace Prize recipient.

- *$1,000 I bond:* Albert Einstein, a physicist and creator of the theory of relativity. Einstein was also a Nobel Prize recipient for Physics.

- *$5,000 I bond:* Marian Anderson, a world-renowned vocalist and the first African-American to sing with the Metropolitan Opera.

- *$10,000 I bond:* Spark Matsunaga, a former U.S. Senator and Congressman and a World War II hero.

How Does It Work?

The I bond is an accrual bond. At redemption, the bond owner will receive the purchase price plus the gain in interest that has been added to the value of the bond. Here are the details.

Purchase price: All I bonds will be purchased at face value. A $100 I bond will be purchased for $100. This eliminates the confusion about when a bond will reach face value. In other words, you purchase at face value and interest is added to the bond to increase the value of the bond.

Minimum and maximum purchase: You can purchase up to $30,000 per person per year. This is double the limit for EE bonds. You can purchase the limit of both EE bonds and I bonds in the same year. And, by adding co-owners, you can increase the amount you may purchase in a year. (See "Purchasing the I Bond" later in this chapter for registration options.) The minimum purchase is $50.

Denominations: The I bond is available in the following denominations: $50, $75, $100, $200, $500, $1,000, $5,000, and $10,000.

Where to buy: You can buy I bonds at any financial institution (bank, savings & loan, credit union) that sells EE bonds. Not all financial institutions participate in the bond program, so call before you go. You can also buy directly through a FRB (see Chapter 19 for the one closest to you). The purchase application can be downloaded from the government web site at www.publicdebt.treas.gov.

Where to redeem: You must hold an I bond for six months before selling it. You can cash them at any financial institution that handles savings bonds. If you are not a customer of that institution, they may limit your redemption to $1,000 per person per day. You can also cash at many FRBs. (See Chapter 19 for the one closest to you and call for instructions before preceding with the transaction.)

Penalties: If you cash your I bond before it turns five years old, you forfeit three months of earnings. That means if you redeem a bond that is four-years, six months old you will receive four-years, three months' worth of interest.

Tax issues: Interest earned on I bonds is treated as interest income and is reported in the year the bond is redeemed or reaches final maturity (30 years), whichever comes first. A bond owner can elect to report interest annually (see Chapter 10 for the same conditions that apply to series E and EE bonds). Interest is subject to federal tax, but exempt from state and local taxes.

Maturity: The I bond will earn interest for 30 years. Since you buy at face value, you don't need to be concerned about how long it will take to reach face value. Unlike the older E and EE bonds, the I bond does not have an original and an extended maturity period.

Interest rates: There are two components to the I bond interest rate: the fixed rate and the semi-annual inflation rate.

> **The fixed rate** is assigned at purchase and remains with the bond for its life. The first fixed rate is 3.4%. This is the fixed rate for bonds purchased in September and October 1998. Although a new fixed rate can be announced each May and November (for new issues of I bonds), don't look for the announcements to provide much change. Future fixed rates that will govern future purchases of the I bond will probably be the same as or close to the first fixed rate published September 1998.

> **The semi-annual inflation rate**, as the name suggests, is the portion of the bonds earnings that is tied to the inflation rate. The CPI-U (consumer price index-urban consumers) is the measuring stick used to determine this rate. This rate is published every May and November and is based on a time period that starts two months back from the publishing date and then measures the preceding six months for change in the CPI-U.

> For instance: The initial fixed rate is 3.4%. The initial semi-annual inflation rate is based on measuring the CPI-U from October 1997 to March 1998. The CPI-U increased 62 basis points. When annualized with the fixed rate of 3.4%, that provides an earnings rate of 4.66% for the first six-month period. A $1,000 I bond would be worth about $1,023.30. However, if you cash the bond before five years, you forfeit three months of interest, so the redemption table will show the value of this bond after six months as being only $1,011.65.

When do the increases occur?: The I bond will increase in value monthly and interest is compounded semi-annually (at six-month intervals from the issue date). At every semi-annual period your values and rates are "locked" in. This means that the government cannot use a retroactive feature or any other gimmick to "take away" previous rates as was possible under the old EE bond rules.

How Will It Perform?

The CPI-U has increased at an annual average of 3.425% over the last sixteen years; 3.4% over the last ten years; 2.58% over the last five years; only time there was no inflation in the last sixteen years was a six-month period of 10/82 to 3/83.

The inflation rate at the time the I bond was introduced is one of the lowest we have seen since 1980. The first CPI-U number that will be used is based on an annual rate of about 1.25%. Had the I bond been available in the mid-1980s it would have averaged an annual return of about 6.8% (based on the fixed rate of 3.4% and an average increase in the CPI-U of 3.4%).

How Does the I Bond Compare to the EE Bond?

Now that two savings bonds are available for purchase at the same time, which one should you buy and how do they compare?

Similarities

As mentioned earlier in the chapter, the new I bond is a hybrid of the EE bond and the Treasury Inflation Indexed Notes/Bonds. Here are the features that the EE and I bonds share:

- They earn interest for thirty years.
- They are interest accrual bonds. That is, interest is added to the value of the bond and does not have to be reported as income until the bond is cashed or reaches final maturity, whichever comes first.
- They increase in value monthly, and the interest is compounded semi-annually.
- If you don't hold them five years, you forfeit three months of interest.
- You must hold them at least six months before cashing.
- Rates that impact the bond are published each May and November.
- You can purchase them at a bank or through payroll deduction.
- They can be used "tax free" for education if all the conditions are met. (See Chapter 16 for a list of the conditions.)

Differences

- Interest on EE bonds is based on 90% of five-year Treasury yields and the rate is reset every six months. Interest on I bonds has two parts: a fixed rate assigned at purchase that remains for the life of the bond and an inflation indexed rate that is adjusted every six months based on changes in the CPI-U.

- The purchase price for EE bonds is one-half the face value; you pay $50 for a $100 face value. Purchase price for I bonds is face value; you pay $100 for a $100 bond.

- The purchase limitation on EE bonds is $15,000 purchase price per person per year. The I bond limitation is $30,000 purchase price per person per year.

- EE bonds can be exchanged for HH bonds. The I bond cannot be exchanged for HH bonds.

Analyzing the I Bond's Potential

While the I bond is new, how would it perform if we examined it in a historical context? The following analysis covers data back to 1982—the year that the bond program introduced the market rate program. For the purposes of our discussion, we will assume that we could buy both the EE bond and the I bond under their current rules throughout the last sixteen years. Which one would have been the better deal?

Here is what was discovered: The grid shows a comparison of the bonds over a five-, ten-, and sixteen-year period. Because the fixed rate component of the I bond is critical to its performance, the grid reflects three assumed rates—3%, 3.25%, and 3.5%. (The first fixed rate published for the I bond is 3.4%.)

Table 18.1 Average Annual Earnings Rate Comparison of I Bonds and EE Bonds

	I Bond 3.0% fixed rate	I Bond 3.25% fixed rate	I Bond 3.5% fixed rate	EE Bond, 90% of 5-yr. Treas.
Last 5 years	5.23%	5.48%	5.74%	5.52%
Last 10 years	6.10%	6.35%	6.60%	6.18%
Last 16 years	6.21%	6.47%	6.74%	7.20%

Here is the difference represented in basis points.

Table 18.2 Average Annual Basis Point Comparison
+/- comparison of I Bonds and EE Bonds (May 1997 rules)
Positive number, EE is greater than I; negative number, I is greater than EE

	I Bond 3.0% fixed rate	I Bond 3.25% fixed rate	I Bond 3.5% fixed rate	EE Bond, 90% of 5-yr. Treas.
Last 5 years	29	4	-22	5.52%
Last 10 years	8	-17	-42	6.18%
Last 16 years	99	73	46	7.20%

When measuring the performance of each bond over the last sixteen years, the EE bond would have done better in comparison to the I bond's assumed rates. In fact, it would have taken a fixed rate of 4% for the I bond to equal the performance of the EE bond. However, when looking at the last five or ten years, it would have taken a fixed rate of only 3.25% to equal the performance of the EE bond.

If we compare the last five- and ten-year periods of the five-year Treasury yields to the CPI, we see that the bonds would have performed about the same if the I bond fixed rate had been 3.25% (basis point differential of 4 and –17). Consequently, anything less than 3.25% and the consumer would have been better off purchasing the EE bond. Anything at 3.25% or over, and the I bond would have been more attractive.

At the present rates of inflation, it will take a fixed rate of about 3.75% to equal the EE bond rate of 5.06%.

Summary of comparison: The key to determining which bond is the best buy, is the fixed rate on the I bond. A fixed rate of 3.25% or better would make the I bond a pretty good bet under conditions where inflation is a moderate 2% to 4% and interest rates are low. During periods where interest rates are high (9% to 12% on five-year Treasury yields), the EE bond would have performed better.

Hey, Where's the Protection?

Although the I bond is dubbed as protection against inflation—meaning our purchasing power is not eroded by inflation—the I bond does not take into account another arm of government that may wipe out the very protection that we thought we had.

In some cases, the tax that you pay on your I bond income may eliminate your inflation protection. This is true if the percentage of your earnings that is funded by the fixed rate component of the I bond is less than your tax rate.

Consider this scenario: Suppose you are in a 36% tax bracket and you purchase the I bond. Assume the I bond has a fixed rate of 3% and we are experiencing an inflation rate of 6%. Your fixed rate represents 33% of your total earnings. (To illustrate this for a one-year period, assume there is no three-month penalty when cashing prior to five years.)

At the end of the year, you have earned 9% on a $1,000 I bond. You cash the bond and receive $1,090. The interest ($90) is subject to federal tax at your rate of 36%. Your tax bill comes to $32.40. That means your net return after taxes was $57.60. With an inflation rate of 6%, you needed $60.00 just to keep pace with inflation. Not all investors will get the protection they thought they would.

Although this example would be a considerable change from the economy at the time of writing, we know that it is historically possible. **Remember:** if your tax bracket is greater than the percentage of your return covered by the fixed rate, you will be in jeopardy of losing your protection.

I Bond Sales Predictions

Since the news broke that the I bond would go on sale, bond owners and investors have been asking the question "Should I buy the I?" Ultimately we will see what they have decided as we watch the sales figures over the next twelve to eighteen months. The author expects a slow start for three reasons:

1. Those that are interested in the I bond are still unfamiliar with this new product. They will want to learn more about it and watch its performance before they buy.

2. Inflation is at one of the lowest points it has been in the last fifteen years. The idea of protection from something that, at the time of writing, does not seem threatening will deter some would-be buyers.

3. The backbone of savings bond sales is the payroll deduction. Since many companies will not offer the I bond right away, it may not be possible for those who want to purchase through their company to do so.

However, if inflation starts to rise, this is a product that will be positioned to capture dollars that will be exiting from investments that are negatively affected by inflation. Also a turbulent stock market may cause queasy stomachs for many investors who would prefer a safer haven for their money.

Should I Buy the I?

Here are four reasons why the I bond might be compatible with some of your investment goals.

- You own a lot of Series E and EE bonds and you would like to diversify a bit, but would like to remain very conservative. The I bond represents another conservative investment choice.

- You think inflation is abnormally low right now and you fear the impact of inflation on other investments you have. Buying the I bond will offer you a measure of protection on this portion of your investment portfolio.

- You have money parked in a savings account at 2%. Even without the inflation adjustment you will do better with the I bond.

- The initial investment is very low ($50). Therefore you can participate without any risk to your overall investment goals.

If you decide to invest in I bonds, you may want to start small and watch what happens. If you like what you see, you can buy more. If it isn't your cup of tea, you can get out any time after six months (with a three-month penalty) and any time after five years without penalty.

Purchasing the I Bond

The following points will provide guidance on buying the I bond:

- You will buy the bond for its face value.

- When choosing how to register the bonds, you have three options:

  Single Ownership: Purchase in one name alone

  Co-Ownership: Two names are listed on the bond with the word "or" between them. Either co-owner can cash without the other's consent. The first named is generally considered the principal owner.

  Single Owner with Beneficiary: One owner is named on the bond and one beneficiary. The word "POD" will precede the beneficiary's name. "POD" means "Pay on Death." The beneficiary can only cash the bond with a valid death certificate for the first-named owner.

- Be ready with the proper spelling of the name, social security number, and address of each party that you want named on the bonds.

- Buy late in the month. The bond actually begins to earn interest as of the first day of the month of purchase.

- If you buy one as a gift, ask for a gift certificate for the recipient. The bond will be mailed to the address you direct. The certificate lets them know that it came from you.

- If you purchase through a bank, make sure the bank teller understands that you want to buy the I bond, not the EE bond.

- If you don't receive your new bond within four weeks, contact the organization where you purchased the bond.

- If you want to buy the limit ($30,000 per person, per year) each year, remember that the limit is reset every January 1st. Example: You can purchase your 1998 limit in December 1998 and then purchase your 1999 limit in January 1999.

Quick Tips on the I Bond

- The new I bond was first issued September 1, 1998, and is a Treasury product designed to offer protection from inflation.

- The pictures are nice, but check the interest rates before you buy.

- The interest rate has two parts: a fixed rate that remains with your bond for life, and an inflation adjusted rate that will change every six months.

- If we are in a period of high inflation, and you are in a high tax bracket, you may not get the inflation protection you thought.

- The I bond is purchased at face value. It will always be worth at least face value.

- Interest is deferred until you cash the bond or until the bond reaches final maturity, whichever comes first.

- Interest earned is subject to federal tax, but exempt from state and local taxes.

Chapter 19

U.S. SAVINGS BOND RESOURCES

▶ *Organizations that Perform Savings Bond Services*
▶ *Common Savings Bond Activities: Who Do You Call?*
▶ *Forms, Publications, Tables, and How to Get Them*

Doesn't anybody know anything about U.S. Savings Bonds?
It seems like I have called all over and every person gives me
a different answer!
—A frustrated bond owner

Every week the author's office receives calls that echo these sentiments. Bond owners are often frustrated, angry, and perplexed as to why they cannot get answers to their questions.

There is good news for those people: Many government agencies and a few private companies work exclusively with U.S. Savings Bonds. If you look in the right places, you will find people who do know bonds and who can answer your questions.

This chapter is intended to guide you to the most established and reliable sources of savings bond information. The resources listed range from information tables for the do-it-yourselfer to full-service companies that will analyze your bond holdings for you. The first section lists the organizations, what they do, and how to contact them. The next section lists savings bond activities and assigns the appropriate resource(s) to each. Finally, a listing of savings bond publications is given, with ordering information.

Organizations that Perform Savings Bond Services

Government

The Bureau of the Public Debt (BPD)

There are two major offices within the BPD: the U.S. Savings Bond Marketing Office and the U.S. Savings Bond Operations Office.

> **U.S. Savings Bond Marketing Office**
> Department of the Treasury
> Bureau of the Public Debt
> U.S. Savings Bond Marketing Office
> Washington, DC 20226
> www.savingsbonds.gov

The purpose of this office is to promote the sale and retention of U.S. Savings Bonds. Formerly known as "The Savings Bond Division," this office handles government responsibilities for the annual savings bond drive campaign activities. It also handles many of the press releases and media contacts for changes in the bond program.

> **U.S. Savings Bond Operations Office**
> Bureau of the Public Debt
> U.S. Savings Bond Operations Office
> P.O. Box 1328
> Parkersburg, WV 26106-1328
> (304) 480-6112
> www.savingsbonds.gov

At the operations center, hundreds of activities critical to the bond program are maintained and performed. The Bureau has several "bond consultants" staffing phones each day from 8:00 a.m. to 4:30 p.m. Eastern Standard Time, Monday through Friday. The bond consultants are well-versed in a variety of savings bond issues and can answer questions or, at least, point you in the right direction. Unfortunately, they do not have an 800 number for the general public. The phone number listed will put you into their automated answering system.

This is one government agency that the author has used extensively. They are taxed with thousands of calls each month, so it can be difficult to get through. Be persistent, though—the staff is knowledgeable and helpful.

The Savings Bond Wizard

The Savings Bond Wizard is a software program developed and distributed by the Treasury Department. The features of the program include redemption values and accrued interest. You input the issue date, series, denomination, and serial number. You can download current values every six months.

The Wizard provides a quick way to determine the bond's value; it helps you keep an inventory of bond information; and the updates are offered at no charge. However, don't be mislead into thinking that it provides all you need to know about your savings bond investment. Note that the program does not provide a complete analysis, which should include interest rates, increase dates, dates bonds enter into extended maturities, date bonds stop earning interest, and a rating of projected future performance.

If you decide to use the Wizard, use it in conjunction with the information in Chapter 7 to build a complete analysis of your bond holdings. If you prefer to have a complete analysis done for you, along with a rating of your bonds, see the last page of this book.

To obtain the program either buy it on 3.5" disk from the government for $17 or download it for free from www.publicdebt.treas.gov

Federal Reserve Banks (FRB):

> As fiscal agents of the United States, Federal Reserve Banks and Branches (FRB) perform a number of activities in support of the Savings Bond program, including issuing, redeeming, and reissuing Savings Bonds and Notes. In recent years, both the Bureau of the Public Debt and Federal Reserve Offices have recognized that there would be benefits associated with consolidating certain Saving Bond activities. . . . .
>
> —Department of Treasury, BPD, Part 353, 3-80,
> 6th Amendment (3-4-94)

To help point you to the correct FRB, here is the list of consolidated sites as explained in the above publication:

Federal Reserve Bank of New York
Buffalo Branch
Attn: Savings Bond Examinations
P.O. Box 961
Buffalo, NY 14240-0961
(716) 849-5165

This office serves the reserve districts of New York and Boston. The geographic region served includes the following states or portions of states and/or territories: CT, MA, ME, NH, NJ (northern half), NY (city & state), RI, VT, Puerto Rico, and Virgin Islands.

Federal Reserve Bank of Kansas City
P.O. Box 419440
Kansas City, MO 64141-6440
(816) 881-2919
This number will also service Spanish-speaking customers.

This office serves the reserve districts of Dallas, San Francisco, Kansas City, and St. Louis. The geographic region served includes the following states or portions of states and/or territories: AK, AR, AZ, CA, CO, HI, ID, IL (southern half), IN (southern half), KS, KY (western half), LA (northern half), MO, MS, NE, NM, NV, OK, OR, TN (western half), TX, WA, WY, UT, and GU (Guam).

Federal Reserve Bank of Minneapolis
P.O. Box 214
Minneapolis, MN 55480
(612) 204-7000

This office serves the reserve districts of Minneapolis and Chicago. The geographic region served includes the following states or portions of states: IA, IL (northern half), IN (northern half), MI, MN, MT, ND, SD, and WI.

Federal Reserve Bank
Pittsburgh Branch
P.O. Box 299
Pittsburgh, PA 15230-0299
(412) 261-7900

This office serves the reserve districts of Cleveland and Philadelphia. The geographic region served includes the following states or portions of states: DE, KY (eastern half), NJ (southern half), OH, PA, and WV (northern panhandle).

Federal Reserve Bank of Richmond
P.O. Box 85053
Richmond, VA 23285-5053
(804) 697-8370

This office serves the reserve districts of Richmond and Atlanta. The geographic region served includes the following states or portions of states: AL, DC, FL, GA, LA (southern half), MD, MS (southern half), NC, SC, TN (eastern half), VA, and WV (except northern panhandle).

Non-Government

The Savings Bond Informer, Inc.

The Savings Bond Informer, Inc.
P.O. Box 9249
Detroit, MI 48209
(800) 927-1901 for brochure and description of services
www.bondinformer.com

This fee-based company was founded by the author in 1990 to service bond owners and financial professionals whose clients own U.S. Savings Bonds.

Products and Services

- The book for investors—*Savings Bonds: When to Hold, When to Fold and Everything In-Between*

- The book for professionals—*U.S. Savings Bonds: The Definitive Guide for Financial Professionals*

- Savings Bond Statement—Customized analysis of your bond holdings including an exclusive rating system, interest rates, increase dates, values, and maturity dates

- Paperwork completion for reissue and exchange transactions

- Consultations and analysis

- Seminars for bond owners and financial professionals

The primary service of this organization is to create a bond statement of your savings bond holdings (an alternative to the do-it-yourself tracking described in Chapter 7). An example of the bond statement is found on page 79. An order form and price list can be found on the last page of this book.

Important note: Consultations without ordering a bond statement are available for a fee of $35 per fifteen-minute segment (minimum billing $35). Credit card payment is required at the time of call.

National Bond & Trust, Co. (NBT)

National Bond & Trust, Co.
P.O. Box 846
Crown Point, IN 46307
(800) 426-9314 (For business inquiries only)
www.nbtco.com

NBT supplies a full range of support services to companies that would like to start a payroll deduction program or that would like to consider service alternatives to the program they already have. They essentially do what the government does in terms of conducting a bond drive. However, as a private company, they add additional elements of service and product to the mix.

In many companies, accounting, payroll, or human resources staff handles savings bond activities. Having an outside firm handle the administrative aspects of the program reduces a company's cost of having a bond program.

NBT also offers a unique insurance component to participants of the bond program. This component is not mandatory for the bond owner.

Commercial Banks

A thorough description of the bank's relationship to the bond program is discussed in Chapter 2, "Banks and Bonds: The Untold Story." Here is a summary of the highlights:

- ✓ U.S. Savings Bonds are not a bank product.

- ✓ Surveys indicate that banks are not a reliable source of information for questions that involve analyzing bonds, such as interest rates and timing issues.

- ✓ While many banks assist bond owners with processing paperwork when seeking to reissue or exchange savings bonds, fees can be as high as $5 per bond on a reissue transaction.

When you obtain savings bond information from a bank, get it in writing.

Other Financial Professionals

This next category is very difficult to characterize. There are hundreds of specialty areas within each profession. Although a financial professional may be highly trained, often that training has not included a study of U.S. Savings Bonds. This section is neither an endorsement nor an indictment of any particular group of financial professionals, but an attempt to give you some bond-related background for each.

Accountants: Accountants may be very helpful in evaluating tax issues related to your bond holdings. If you want an accountant to evaluate your bonds, determine a cost for the service ahead of time. A bond owner in Ohio was surprised to discover that because of the time-consuming nature of tracking a bond investment, an accountant charged over $1,000 to value her bonds. Before you engage the services of an accountant, (1) find out if he or she has had previous experience with bond-related work, (2) and establish a fee before proceeding.

Accountant, Professional Counsel: Brent Dawes is a C.P.A. who specializes in tax questions, research, and counsel on savings bond issues. He is also a contributor to this book (see Chapter 10). His fee is $35 per fifteen minutes, minimum fee $35 (charged to Visa or Mastercard at the time of call). This may be helpful to other financial professionals or bond owners who have a particular situation that calls for tax advice. The firm is American Express Tax and Business Services, Inc; their number is (800) 851-2324. Tell them that you are calling for tax counsel regarding U.S. Savings Bonds.

Attorneys: Many attorneys handle savings bond transactions, most commonly for estate settlement or trust purposes. Many law offices use the services of The Savings Bond Informer, Inc. to value bonds, others calculate the data themselves. Fees vary depending on the complexity of the case and the pricing structure of the individual office.

Financial Planners: It is the author's assessment that a good financial planner will take the time to understand your financial situation and evaluate your status before they offer counsel. Related to savings bonds, a planner should be able to provide you with written details about your investment. The written analysis will allow you to compare your holdings to other options and will contribute to an accurate net worth statement.

A helpful resource in this area is *Smart Questions to Ask Your Financial Advisers* by Lynn Brenner, Bloomberg Press, $19.95.

Common Savings Bond Activities: Who Do You Call?

The following is a list of common bond activities. Listed after each activity are the organizations or institutions to contact regarding that particular activity. The address and phone number for many of the organizations can be found in the preceding pages of this chapter.

Buying Bonds

Financial Institutions: Most commercial banks still sell U.S. Savings Bonds, but call before you go. In our phone survey of banks, we discovered several banks that no longer sell bonds. (Some savings & loans and credit unions also sell U.S. Savings Bonds.) The commercial bank will take your application and money and forward it to a regional FRB site for processing.

Federal Reserve Banks: You can mail your application to purchase U.S. Savings Bonds directly to any FRB. Make your check payable to "The Federal Reserve Bank." Be sure to include your purchase application, completed in full. Also include your telephone number so they can reach you if there are any questions.

Payroll Deduction: To buy bonds through payroll deduction, your company must have a Payroll Savings Plan in place. Printing and mailing the bonds is handled at a regional FRB, another qualified issuing agent, or through another party such as National Bond & Trust. (Typically, no fees are charged to deal with the organizations; however, the level and type of service they offer may differ.)

Redeeming Bonds and Exchanging Bonds

Financial Institutions: Most commercial banks will redeem and exchange U.S. Savings Bonds, but, again, call before you go. In our phone survey of banks, we discovered several no longer provide these services. Some savings & loans and credit unions redeem U.S. Savings Bonds. The commercial bank has a specific set of guidelines to follow. Cases that they are unable to process will be forwarded to the FRB or the BPD. H and HH bonds are forwarded to the FRB. If you are redeeming less than $1,000 in E or EE bonds and have proper identification, you should receive your money the same day.

Federal Reserve Banks: FRBs will act as a redemption site for bond owners, though the request may be forwarded to another FRB for processing. Expect to wait three to five business days for payment. Call for specific instructions from the FRB you intend to use.

Determining the Value of Your Bonds

Author's note: If you have 50 bonds or more, none of the free services listed below will read the redemption values to you over the phone or in person. They will mail you a redemption table and expect you to value the bonds yourself. Why? Consider it from a bank's perspective. It's Friday afternoon, hundreds of customers are cashing payroll checks, and your needs will consume at least one hour of a teller's time—for which the bank will not make any money. Savvy banks will send you to the customer service area so that their financial representative can pitch the bank's own products in exchange for their time. Remember that bank information on savings bond interest rates and timing issues is often inaccurate (see Chapter 2).

Commercial Banks (no fee): The level of service here may vary, depending on your customer status. Most banks will provide values for a reasonable number of bonds without any qualms. Larger numbers of bonds may not be serviced for reasons noted above.

Federal Reserve Bank (no fee): FRBs will mail a redemption table to you and may price a couple of bonds over the phone.

Bureau of the Public Debt (no fee): BPD will mail a redemption table to you. The best free information is the Savings Bond Wizard, a program available on the government web site that can be used to provide the value of your bonds at no cost.

The Savings Bond Informer, Inc. (fee). TSBI will produce a statement of your savings bond holdings, which includes values as well as interest rates, timing issues, explanation of maturity dates, accrued interest, and a rating for each bond. You supply the month/year of purchase (issue date), face value, and series. Refer to the last page of this book for prices.

Tables for Analyzing Bonds On Your Own

There are several current government tables you will need to analyze the details of your bonds. There is no charge for these tables.

✓ Table of Redemption Values for Series E and EE bonds and SN
✓ Guaranteed Minimum Rates Table
✓ Interest Accrual Dates

Examples of these can be found in Chapter 7, Tables 7.1 through 7.7. Chapter 7 also provides a thorough step-by-step explanation of how to analyze your bonds and create a bond statement.

The FRB will mail most of the items; the BPD will mail any or all of the items. Contact:

Bureau of the Public Debt
P.O. Box 1328
Parkersburg, WV 26106-1328
(304) 480-6112
www.savingsbonds.gov

Additional note: The Tables of Redemption Values provides values for the lowest denomination of bonds, but you must multiply that value by the correct multiple for your bond. An expanded redemption table which lists the values for all denominations and does not require calculations on the part of the reader is available from:

> **Superintendent of Documents**
> P.O. Box 371954
> Pittsburgh, PA 15250-7954

An annual subscription is $5.00 (price subject to change). For Series E, ask for TRVE; for Series EE ask for TRVEE. (TRV stands for Table of Redemption Values; E or EE indicates the series.)

Reissuing Bonds

Federal Reserve Bank: FRB regional sites accept all reissue transactions. Customer service representatives will answer questions related to reissue transactions. Some cases are forwarded to the BPD.

Commercial Banks: Banks may have the forms needed to complete reissue transactions. Some will help you complete the forms, but there may be a fee involved, as much as $5 a bond.

Bureau of the Public Debt: (304) 480-6112. Bond consultants staff phones from 8:00 a.m. to 4:30 p.m. EST. All reissue forms may be ordered from the BPD. Many forms can be downloaded from the web site at www.savingsbonds.gov.

Legal Questions

Bureau of the Public Debt: See address listing.

Attorneys: You may also want to consult with an attorney for estate, probate, custody issues, and other legal concerns.

Educational Feature of Bonds

Ask for both the "Questions and Answers" publication on the educational feature of EE bonds and the brochure that outlines the guidelines, available from:

- Bureau of the Public Debt
  P.O. Box 1328
  Parkersburg, WV 26106-1328
- Federal Reserve Bank Regional Sites
- Some commercial banks

Lost, Stolen, or Destroyed Bond

Ask for form PD F 1048, available from:

- Bureau of the Public Debt (download it at www.savingsbonds.gov)
- Federal Reserve Bank regional sites
- Some commercial banks

Forms, Publications, Tables, and How To Get Them

The following forms and regulations are available from the BPD, Savings Bond Operations Office. FRBs will also have most, if not all, of them. Many banks stock the forms used most often. Table 19.1 and the following lists are from "The Book on U.S. Savings Bonds" and "U.S. Savings Bonds, Buyers Guide 1993-94."

Table 19.1 Treasury Circulars

Subject	CFR Part	Treasury Circular
Offering of Series E Bonds	316	No. 653
Offering of Series EE Bonds	351	No. I-80
Offering of Savings Notes	342	No. 3-67
Offering of Series H Bonds	332	No. 905
Offering of Series HH Bonds	352	No. 2-80
Regulations Governing Series E and H Bonds	315	No. 530
Regulations Governing Series EE and HH Bonds	353	No. 3-80
Regulations Governing Exchange Transactions	352	No. 2-80

Adapted from "The Book on U.S. Savings Bonds," p. 1.

The following is a list of PD forms pertinent to U.S. Savings Bonds and Notes. The government often revises forms to accommodate changes that have occurred in the bond program. When ordering a form, explain why you need it. That way, if there have been any changes, you will get the most recent, and appropriate, form. If you use the governments web site, here is the exact page you need: www.savingsbonds.gov/sav/savforms.htm

PD F 1048
Application for Relief on Account of Loss, Theft, or Destruction of United States Savings and Retirement Securities

PD F 1455
Request by Fiduciary for Reissue of United States Savings Bonds/Notes

PD F 1522
Special Form of Request for Payment of United States Savings Bonds/Notes and Retirement Securities Where Use of a Detached Request is Authorized

PD F 1849
Disclaimer of Consent With Respect to United States Savings Bonds/Notes

PD F 1851
Request for Reissue of United States Savings Bond/Notes in Name of Trustee of Personal Trust Estate

PD F 1938
Request for Reissue of United States Savings Bond/Notes During the Lives of Both Co-owners

PD F 1980
Description of United States Savings Bonds Series H/HH

PD F 1993
Request for Purchase of United States Savings Bonds With Proceeds of Payment of Matured Savings Bonds

PD F 2216
Application by Preferred Creditor for Disposition Without Administration Where Deceased Owner's Estate Includes United States Registered Securities and/or Related Checks in Amount not Exceeding $500

PD F 2458

Certificate of Entitlement—United States Savings and Retirement Securities and Checks After Administration of Decedent's Estate

PD F 2488-1

Certificate by Legal Representative(s) of Decedent's Estate, During Administration, of Authority to Act and of Distribution Where Estate Holds No More Than $1,000 (Face Amount) United States Savings Bonds/Notes, Excluding Checks Representing Interest

PD F 2513

Application by Voluntary Guardian of Incompetent Owner of United States Savings Bonds

PD F 2966

Special Bond of Indemnity to the United States of America

PD F 3062

Claim for Relief on Account of Inscribed United States Savings Bonds Lost, Stolen or Destroyed Prior to Receipt by Owner, Co-owner, or Beneficiary

PD F 3253

Exchange Subscription for United States Savings Bonds or Series HH

PD F 3360

Request for Reissue of United States Savings Bond/Notes in the Name of a Person or Persons Other Than the Owner (Including Legal Guardian, Custodian for a Minor Under a Statute, etc.)

PD F 4000

Request by Owner for Reissue of United States Savings Bonds/Notes to Add Beneficiary or Co-owner, Eliminate Beneficiary or Decedent, Show Change of Name, and/or Correct Error in Registration

PD F 4881

Application for Payment of United States Savings Bonds of Series EE or HH and/or Related Checks in an Amount Not Exceeding $1,000 by the Survivor of a Deceased Owner Whose Estate is Not Being Administered

PD F 5263

Order for Series EE U.S. Savings Bonds (RDS)

PD F 5336
Application for Disposition of United States Savings Bonds/Notes and/or Related Checks Owned by Decedent Whose Estate is Being Settled Without Administration

> This resource section should provide you with an organization to contact for virtually any question that was not addressed in this book. Since change is ongoing within the bond program, you may want to contact the publisher for revised copies of this book in future years.

JUST THE BASICS, PLEASE!

▶ *The Difference between Savings Bonds*
   and Treasury Bonds
▶ *Series I Bonds*
▶ *Series EE Bonds*
▶ *Series E Bonds*
▶ *Savings Notes/Freedom Shares*
▶ *Series HH Bonds*
▶ *Series H Bonds*

This appendix has been added to the fourth edition to provide a backdrop for the more technical information that is presented in other chapters. If you are not familiar with bonds, or just want to verify that you have the basics down, this is the place to start. If you are already well-versed in savings bonds, briefly review this information and then dive into the meatier and more surprising information found in Chapter 3, "Understanding Interest Rates," and Chapter 4, "Timing Issues and Maturity Periods."

The Difference between Savings Bonds and Treasury Bonds

Though both are instruments issued by the Treasury to borrow money, a Treasury bond is much different from a U.S. Savings Bond. When you hear the term "bond market" or "the long-term bond" on radio or television, it is in reference to Treasury bonds, not U.S. Savings Bonds. The terms should not be used interchangeably. Technically, however, savings bonds are considered a product of the Treasury Department.

Savings bonds are non-marketable. That is, they have no secondary market for resale or trading. And because of this, there is far less written and reported on them. As a financial instrument they follow other instruments rather than lead. Consequently, the media does not closely track them.

Other Treasury securities (Treasury notes and Treasury bonds) can be bought and sold in a secondary market after they have been issued and before they reach maturity. Their value is directly affected by market conditions. If interest rates go up after your purchase, the value of your Treasury security goes down; thus if you have to sell, you would be selling at a discount (less than face value). If interest rates go down after your purchase, the value of your Treasury note goes up and you are able to sell for a premium (more than face value).

Types of Bonds—The Preliminaries

Only three series of U.S. Savings Bonds are currently being issued; Series I, EE, and HH. Only the Series I and EE can be purchased for cash.

Series I Bonds

The I bond is a new savings bond issued by the Treasury designed to offer protection from inflation. By linking the return of the bond to an inflation index, the bond is always guaranteed to earn a fixed rate above the inflation rate. The first I bonds were issued September 1,1998. See Chapter 18 for a complete description of the interest rate features of this new bond.

Purchase Price: Purchased for face value. For example, a bond with a face value of $100 is purchased for $100.

Denominations: $50, $75, $100, $200, $500, $1,000, $5,000, $10,000

Date of Issue: September 1, 1998 to present

Tax Features: Subject to federal tax, but exempt from state and local taxes. Reporting of interest is usually deferred until the bond is cashed or reaches final maturity. Exceptions include:

1. interest that is reported annually (see Chapter 10, page 110),

2. certain reissue transactions create a taxable event even though no money is received by the bond owner (see Chapter 10, page 114),

Interest may also be exempt from federal tax if the bond qualifies for the educational feature. (See the complete guidelines for the educational feature of I bond, Chapter 16, page 195.)

Final Maturity: Thirty years from the date of purchase. The first I bond will stop earning interest in the year 2028.

When it can be cashed: Anytime after the first six months. A three-month interest penalty is invoked if the bond is cashed before it is five years old.

Who can cash it: Persons listed on the bond as owner or co-owner. A person listed as POD (Pay on Death) can cash the bond if they have a valid death certificate for the owner of the bond.

When it can be exchanged: Cannot be exchanged for HH bonds.

How it should be registered (inscribed): Registration options are presented in Chapter 14. The exact registration option may vary based on your intent, that is, who you wish to be able to redeem the bonds.

Series EE Bonds

Series EE bonds bonds represent more than 62% of the $180 billion plus (based on current value) in outstanding redemption value.

Purchase Price: Purchased for one-half the face value. For example, a bond with a face value of $100 is purchased for $50.

Denominations: $50, $75, $100, $200, $500, $1,000, $5,000, $10,000

Date of Issue: January 1980 to present

Tax Features: Subject to federal tax, but exempt from state and local taxes. Reporting of interest is usually deferred until the bond is cashed or reaches final maturity. Exceptions include:

1. interest that is reported annually (see Chapter 10, page 110),
2. certain reissue transactions create a taxable event even though no money is received by the bond owner (see Chapter 10, page 114),
3. a bond owner can elect to report accrued interest at the time of exchange even though no money has been received.

Interest may also be exempt from federal tax if the bond qualifies for the educational feature. (See the complete guidelines for the educational feature of EE bond, Chapter 16, page 195.)

Original Maturity: Eight to eighteen years to original maturity, depending on the exact date of issue. The interest rate in effect for a given bond determines the length of the original maturity period. For example, from November 1982 to October 1986, bonds had a guaranteed rate of 7.5% for the original maturity period. Those bonds took ten years to reach original maturity. (See Chapter 4, page 49, for the "Guide to Extended and Final Maturity Periods.")

Final Maturity: Reaches final maturity thirty years from the date of purchase. The first EE bond will stop earning interest in the year 2010.

When it can be cashed: Anytime after the first six months. A three-month interest penalty is invoked if the bond is purchased after April 1997 and cashed prior to five years.

Who can cash it: Persons listed on the bond as owner or co-owner. A person listed as POD (Pay on Death) can cash the bond if they have a valid death certificate for the owner of the bond.

When it can be exchanged: From six months after purchase up to one year past final maturity date.

How it should be registered (inscribed): Registration options are presented in Chapter 14. The exact registration option may vary based on intent, that is, who will to be able to redeem the bonds.

Series E Bonds

Often referred to as the "war bond," the Series E bond was first issued during World War II. It is no longer available for purchase. Over 30% of the bonds outstanding (based on current value) are E bonds.

Purchase Price: Purchased for 75% of the face value. For example, an E bond with a face value of $100 was purchased for $75.

Denominations: $25, $50, $75, $100, $200, $500, $1,000, $5,000, $10,000

Date of Issue: May 1941 to June 1980

Tax Features: Subject to federal tax, but exempt from state and local taxes. Reporting of interest is usually deferred until the bond is cashed, or reaches final maturity. Exceptions include:

1. interest that is reported annually (see Chapter 10, page 110),
2. certain reissue transactions create a taxable event even though no money is received by the bond owner (see Chapter 10, page 114),

3. a bond owner can elect to report accrued interest at the time of exchange even though no money has been received.

These bonds are *not* eligible for the tax-free educational feature.

Original Maturity: From five years to nine years and eight months, depending on exact issue date. The interest rate in effect for a given bond determines the length of the original maturity period. Since E bonds were purchased for 75% of face value, they generally reach face value quicker than Series EE bonds. (See Chapter 4, page 49, "Guide to Extended and Final Maturity Periods.")

Final Maturity: Forty years for bonds issued prior to December 1965; thirty years for bonds issued after November 1965.

When it can be cashed: All E bonds are past six months old and so can be cashed at anytime. Keep in mind the timing issues for redemption. They are outlined in Tables 7.5 and 7.6 on pages 84 and 85.

Who can cash it: Persons listed on the bond as owner or co-owner. The person listed as POD (Pay on Death) can cash the bond if they have a valid death certificate for the owner of the bond.

When it can be exchanged: Any E bond that is currently earning interest can be exchanged. E bonds that have stopped earning interest must be exchanged within one year of final maturity.

How it should be registered (inscribed): All E bonds have been previously registered. If the bonds need to be retitled, consult Chapter 13 regarding options.

Savings Notes/Freedom Shares

Savings Notes and Freedom Shares (SN/FS) are different names for the same security. They were issued for only three and one-half years during the Vietnam War era and so are not as common as Series E and EE bonds. The SN/FS accrues interest like Series E and EE bonds.

Purchase Price: All FS/SN were purchased for 81% of the face value. For example, a FS with a $100 face value was purchased for $81.

Denominations: $25, $50, $75, $100, $200, $500, $1,000, $5,000, $10,000

Date of Issue: May 1967 to October 1970

Tax Features: Subject to federal tax, but exempt from state and local taxes. Reporting of interest is usually deferred until the bond is cashed, or reaches final maturity. Exceptions include:

1. interest that is reported annually (see Chapter 10, page 110),

2. certain reissue transactions create a taxable event even though no money is received by the bond owner (see Chapter 10, page 114),

3. a bond owner can elect to report accrued interest at the time of exchange even though no money has been received.

These bonds are *not* eligible for the tax-free educational feature.

Original Maturity: Four years and six months. Since these bonds were purchased for 81% of face value, they reached face value much quicker than Series EE bonds. (See Chapter 4, page 49, "Guide to Extended and Final Maturity Periods.")

Final Maturity: Thirty years from date of issue. The first FS/SN stopped earning interest in May 1997 (thirty years after the issue date of May 1967). All FS/SN will stop earning interest by October 2000.

When it can be cashed: All FS/SN are past six months old and can be cashed at anytime.

Who can cash it: Persons listed on the bond as owner or co-owner. The person listed as POD (Pay on Death) can cash the bond if they have a valid death certificate for the owner of the bond.

When it can be exchanged: Any FS/SN that is currently earning interest can be exchanged for HH bonds up to one year beyond final maturity.

How it should be registered (inscribed): All FS/SN bonds have been previously registered. If the bonds need to be retitled, consult Chapter 13.

Series HH Bonds

HH bonds are also called current income bonds because the holder receives an interest payment every six months from the date of issue. The most significant advantage of HH bonds is that interest income from old E, EE, or FS/SN can be deferred for up to twenty additional years.

HH bonds cannot be purchased for cash. You must either exchange E, EE, FS/SN, or reinvest matured H bonds. The interest rate that you receive when you exchange is fixed for the first ten years that you hold the bond.

Purchase Price: Exchanged at face value. A bond with a face value of $500 was "purchased" for $500 of E, EE, FS/SN, or matured H bonds.

Denominations: $500, $1,000, $5,000, $10,000

Date of Issue: January 1980 to present

Tax Features: Interest that is paid semi-annually is subject to federal tax, but exempt from state and local taxes. Reporting interest that was rolled over from E, EE, or FS/SN must be done when the HH bond is cashed or reaches final maturity, whichever comes first. Exceptions include:

1. interest can be reported for E, EE, and/or FS/SN at the time of exchange,

2. certain reissue transactions create a taxable event even though no money is received by the bond owner (see Chapter 10, page 114).

These bonds are *not* eligible for the tax-free educational feature.

Original Maturity: Ten years. When you exchange for an HH bond, the interest rate is locked in for the first ten years (4% at the time of writing). This is a fixed rate as there is no market rate on HH bonds. After the first ten years, these bonds will automatically enter a ten-year extension and will assume the new guaranteed rate in effect at the time.

Final Maturity: Twenty years from date of issue

When it can be cashed: Anytime after six months

Who can cash it: Persons listed on the bond as owner or co-owner. The person listed as POD (Pay on Death) can cash the bond if they have a valid death certificate for the owner of the bond.

Series H Bonds

H bonds are also referred to as current income bonds because owners receive an interest payment every six months from date of issue. These bonds are no longer being issued, although many of them are still paying interest. At one time, early in the life of H bonds, they could be purchased for cash. However, most H bonds were obtained by exchanging E bonds or FS/SN.

The interest rate on H bonds is fixed for a ten-year period and then changes every ten years. A significant advantage of H bonds was that interest income from old E bonds or FS/SNs could be deferred for up to thirty additional years.

Purchase Price: Purchased at face value. An H bond with a face value of $500 was purchased for $500 or the equivalent of $500 redemption value from E bonds or FS/SN.

Denominations: $500, $1,000, $5,000, $10,000

Date of Issue: 1952 to December 1979

Tax Features: Interest that is paid semi-annually is subject to federal tax, but exempt from state and local taxes. Reporting interest that was rolled over from

E bonds or FS/SNs must be done when the H bond is cashed or reaches final maturity, whichever comes first. Exceptions include:

1. interest can be reported from an E, EE, and/or FS/SN at the time of exchange,

2. certain reissue transactions create a taxable event even though no money is received by the bond owner (see Chapter 10, page 114).

Note: These bonds are *not* eligible for the tax-free educational feature.

Original Maturity: Ten years. When an H bond was obtained, the interest rate was locked in for the first ten years (there were some cases where the government adjusted this rate upward in the middle of a maturity period). This rate is fixed; there is no market rate on H bonds. After the first ten years, the bond automatically enters a ten-year extension and assumes the new guaranteed rate in effect at the time. A final extension of ten years gives the H bond a total life of thirty years.

Final Maturity: Thirty years from date of issue

When it can be cashed: Anytime after six months from issue date

Who can cash it: Persons listed on the bond as owner or co-owner. The person listed as POD (Pay on Death) can cash the bond if they have a valid death certificate for the owner of the bond.

The government has introduced several changes to the bond program in the 1990s. When significant changes are made, future editions of this publication will examine the benefits and limitations of each new change.

COMMON QUESTIONS
BOND OWNERS ASK

The Savings Bond Informer, Inc. has assisted thousands of savings bond owners throughout the nation over the last eight years. The following questions
reflect some of their greatest needs and concerns.

1. What is the interest rate of bonds purchased today (September 1998)?
For Series EE bonds: 5.06%. New rates are published every May and November.
For Series HH bonds: 4%. New rates are published at the discretion of the Treasury.
For Series I bonds: 4.66%. New rates are published every May and November.
Call 1-800-USBONDS for the current rates.

2. What do you think of the government's web site?
The ability to obtain forms and get answers to many questions is very helpful to
investors. The Savings Bond Wizard is a good tool for valuing bonds and record
keeping. (Remember, however, you need more than just the values to make
wise decisions about your bonds.) It also saves the government money by providing an alternative to answering phone calls and sending printed materials.
(Now if we can get them to use some of the savings to pay down the debt,
rather than spending it elsewhere, we'll be in business.)

3. How long does it take a new EE bond to reach face value?
The time it will take a bond to reach face value is determined by the interest
rates assigned to that bond. A Series EE bond purchased today is guaranteed to

reach face value in seventeen years or less. If the market rates assigned to a bond average 5%, then that bond will reach face value in about fourteen years. If the market rates average 6%, the bond will reach face value in about twelve years. (For older bonds, see Chapter 4, "Timing Issues and Maturity Periods.")

4. Do you have to redeem a bond when it matures?

There is a difference between original and final maturity. If you mean original maturity, the answer is no. A Series EE bond purchased today is guaranteed to reach original maturity in seventeen years. However, Series EE bonds will earn interest for thirty years from the date of purchase. After thirty years they stop earning interest: This is final maturity. When bonds stop earning interest, you may either redeem them or exchange them for HH bonds.

There is good reason not to hold your bonds past final maturity. First, they have stopped earning interest. Second, IRS rules require you to report the interest income on bonds when they reach final maturity (unless you exchange them for HH bonds).

5. I have EE bonds with my mother as beneficiary. May I take her name off and put my wife on instead?

Yes, with EE bonds the owner may remove the beneficiary's name without the beneficiary's consent. You may then add your wife as a co-owner or beneficiary.

The rules are different for Series E bonds. For them, a living beneficiary must consent to having his or her name removed.

6. Should I exchange all my E and EE bonds for HH bonds? I am retired and would like the income.

If your E bonds have not reached final maturity, you would generally receive a higher overall yield by selectively redeeming some E and EE bonds instead of exchanging them all for HH bonds. (This is being written when HH bonds are guaranteed 4%. When you exchange, the current rate is locked in for the first ten years.) See Chapter 12 for a complete explanation of selective redemption.

7. Banks seem to be offering fewer and fewer savings bond services. Is it just my bank or is this a trend?

This is a very common complaint. Many banks have decreased the level of their savings bond service. For instance, recent complaints have centered on the exchange process: either banks refuse to help people who want to exchange or they are so uninformed of the process that the customer has little confidence in the accuracy.

The government is taking steps to have more direct contact with bond owners. Selling bonds on-line (in the near future) and servicing bond owners through the government web site are examples. Perhaps one of the most significant changes is the 1-800-USBONDS government telephone line. For over ten years, a recording has told bond owners to ask their financial institution for interest rates on older bonds, which, as you know from the chapter on banks and bonds, will likely result in inaccuracies and frustration. In August 1998 the recorded line was changed and investors are no longer referred to banks for that information. Banks will have a decreasing roll as the middleman.

8. Is there a penalty for redeeming a bond if you have held it for less than five years?

For EE bonds purchased May 1997 and after, and for Series I bonds, you forfeit three months of interest if you cash before the bond turns five years old.

9. I should be buying bonds every chance I get because they are all tax-free for education, right?

Not exactly. You must meet the guidelines that apply to this program in order to be eligible. See Chapter 16.

10. I'm buying bonds to use for my daughter's college education. I meet the guidelines for the tax-free feature, but if I use the bonds for her, can I still claim her as a dependent?

If you buy Series EE bonds as of January 1, 1990, you may qualify for the educational tax-free status. Taking advantage of the tax-free aspect of EE bonds when used for college does not affect your right to claim your child as a dependent.

11. Can a financial institution charge a fee to issue, redeem, or reissue a savings bond?

No, no, and yes. The Treasury Department pays financial institutions for issuing and redeeming bonds. However, banks do not receive payment for completing reissue forms. Each bank has its own policy regarding the fees they charge for reissue transactions, but it is legal for a bank to charge a fee to process your reissue request. See Chapter 13, "Reissuing U.S. Savings Bonds," for additional information.

12. Over the last twenty years, I have purchased hundreds of bonds through payroll deduction. I want to trade them all for a few larger denominations. Can I do this?

There are a couple of considerations here. If you want to exchange for HH bonds, you can do it with all or a few of your bonds. However, that may not be the best thing to do considering that HH bonds are paying only 4% (at the time of writing) and some of your E and EE bonds are paying a much higher rate.

If you were hoping to exchange or reinvest into EE bonds of a larger denomination, the answer is a little more complicated. You cannot exchange E or EE bonds for other EE bonds. The process would be a redemption (cash in your old bonds) and a purchase (buy new EE bonds). Since you have a number of bonds, get them analyzed to determine the worst performers. If some of the bonds are languishing at 4%, you could do much better even with the current EE bond. However, redeeming and repurchasing creates a taxable event. Consult Chapter 9, "Comparing Your Bonds to Other Investment Options," before you take action.

13. I am going to buy a used car. I have $4,000 (face value) of Series E savings bonds. In order to get the loan, I am going to leave my bonds with the car dealership as collateral. Are there any problems with this?

If the dealer takes your bonds, there is a problem that he does not see. Bonds cannot be transferred or used as collateral, so they are totally worthless to the dealer. Also, keep in mind that depending on the issue date, those E bonds are worth between two to six times their face value—somewhere between $8,000 and $24,000. Forget that used car dealer and head over to the new car lot. But first get an accurate value of your bonds and don't forget the timing issues. Chapter 19 provides a list of resources that will help you to do this.

14. I purchased Series EE bonds in the 1980s and was planning to exchange them for HH bonds. Now that the guaranteed rate has been lowered and I will only be receiving 4% interest, I am not so sure that I want to do this. My bonds have not matured. Why do bonds have to be held to maturity before they can be exchanged?

They don't. Series EE bonds may be exchanged for HH bonds any time after they are six months old. Sorry, but you missed the boat on this one. If you had exchanged prior to March 1, 1993, you would have locked in at the old 6% rate. The most probable reason for this misconception is that the two alternatives presented at final maturity are redemption or exchange. The exchange option, which is rarely explained, exists from the time the bonds are six months old until one year past final maturity.

15. My uncle and aunt were listed on their bonds as co-owners. My uncle died first and then my aunt. Who is entitled to the bonds?

The estate of the last deceased co-owner is entitled to the bonds.

16. My wife and I recently created a trust and we want to reissue our bonds into it. Will this create any tax consequences and what do I need to do?

If you are co-owners of the bonds and are also trustees of the trust, and the Social Security number that is on the bonds is also used for the trust, then you can have your bonds reissued into the trust without creating a taxable event. You need to complete form PD F 1851, available from your regional Federal

Reserve Bank (FRB). There are some cases in which reissuing bonds into a trust will create a taxable event. See Chapter 10 for more information on tax issues and Chapter 19 for the address and phone number of your regional FRB.

17. How long does it take to get a response from the Bureau of the Public Debt (BPD)?

If the request is for forms, they are usually mailed within one to three working days. The author has been very impressed with the quick response for recent orders. If the inquiry is for researching lost bonds, it can take up to a month or more depending on how thoroughly you completed the request form, that is, how much information you can provide. The BPD handles tens of thousands of requests from all over the country. It may take longer than you would like, but they will respond.

18. Are bond redemption tables free?

The basic version of the redemption table from the BPD is free. While this table provides values for the lowest denomination bonds, you must multiply that value by the correct multiple for your bond. Values can also be downloaded from the governments web site and obtained through the Savings Bond Wizard.

19. Are bonds a good short-term investment?

The penalty invoked on bond purchases May 1997 and afterward was specifically designed to discourage short-term investment. If you only hold a bond for one year, you will forfeit 25% of the earnings by losing three months of interest. Many of the short-term advantages have been eliminated with the introduction of the three-month penalty.

20. I received a $200 Series EE bond in 1994 when I bought an appliance. They advertised "buy this appliance and get a $200 bond." Is my bond worth $200?

Ah, advertising. All Series EE bonds are purchased for one-half of the face value. Your "$200" bond is worth the purchase price of $100, plus four years of interest—about $16 to $17. At the guaranteed rate of 4%, it will take eighteen years for your bond to reach the face value of $200. This is why many companies like to use bonds for promotions. Ask the merchant for the $200 instead of the $200 bond or better yet tell him you'll take the $200 I bond instead of the $200 EE bond (the I bond is worth face value immediately).

21. When will the guaranteed interest rate change again?

That is a good question. Although the new savings bond rules implemented on May 1, 1995, eliminated the guaranteed rate for new purchases of Series EE bonds, there is still a guaranteed interest rate on most older bonds and new issues of HH bonds. If the market rates stay relatively flat, do not expect to see the guaranteed rate change for a long time. Even if interest rates start to rise, historically the bond program has lagged behind in changing the guaranteed rate.

22. **If, due to mathematical errors, unexpected receipt of bonds as gifts after having purchased the maximum amount, ignorance about the maximum amount, confusion and/or disorganization, you find yourself in possession of more than the allowable maximum ($15,000 purchase price per person per year for Series EE bonds), what happens? What should you do, immediately cash the bonds held in excess (perhaps they will not pay interest on those bonds)? Hire a good lawyer and prepare to spend some time in federal prison? Make a run for the border to escape the firing squad?**

Save yourself the lawyer fees and don't pack the suitcase for that border run. Many bond owners purposefully or inadvertently hold more than the purchase limit for a given year. The BPD asks that you write informing them of your situation. They typically respond by asking you to remain within the guidelines for future purchases. There are no cases the author is aware of where they have failed to pay interest for the holding period, or asked the bond holder to cash in the bonds (let's face it, they need the money). So you can stop changing your name and address every two to three years.

Appendix C Tables of Redemption Values

FORM PD 3600
DEPT. OF THE TREASURY
BUR. OF THE PUBLIC DEBT
[REV. MAR 1999]

TABLES OF REDEMPTION VALUES

$50 SERIES I/EE BONDS $25 SERIES E BONDS/SAVINGS NOTES

FOR REDEMPTION MONTHS MARCH 1999 THROUGH AUGUST 1999

TABLES OF REDEMPTION VALUES FOR $50 SERIES I SAVINGS BONDS

ISSUE YEARS	MARCH 1999 ISSUE MONTHS	$50	APRIL 1999 ISSUE MONTHS	$50	MAY 1999 ISSUE MONTHS	$50	JUNE 1999 ISSUE MONTHS	$50	JULY 1999 ISSUE MONTHS	$50	AUGUST 1999 ISSUE MONTHS	$50	ISSUE YEARS
1999	Jan.-Mar.	*	Jan.-Apr.	*	Jan.-May	*	Jan.-June	*	Feb.-July	*	Mar.-Aug.	*	1999
									Jan.	50.62	Feb	50.62	
											Jan	50.84	
1998	Oct.-Dec.	*	Nov.-Dec.	*	Dec.	*	Dec	50.62	Dec.	50.84	Dec	51.04	1998
	Sep.	50.58	Oct.	50.58	Nov.	50.62	Nov.	50.84	Nov.	51.04	Nov	51.26	
			Sep.	50.78	Oct.	50.78	Oct	50.96	Oct	51.16	Oct	51.38	
					Sep.	50.96	Sep.	51.16	Sep	51.38	Sep	51.60	

TABLES OF REDEMPTION VALUES FOR $50 SERIES EE SAVINGS BONDS

ISSUE YEARS	MARCH 1999 ISSUE MONTHS	$50	APRIL 1999 ISSUE MONTHS	$50	MAY 1999 ISSUE MONTHS	$50	JUNE 1999 ISSUE MONTHS	$50	JULY 1999 ISSUE MONTHS	$50	AUGUST 1999 ISSUE MONTHS	$50	ISSUE YEARS
1999	Jan.-Mar.	*	Jan.-Apr.	*	Jan.-May	*	Jan.-June	*	Feb.-July	*	Mar.-Aug.	*	1999
									Jan.	25.28	Feb.	25.28	
											Jan.	25.38	
1998	Oct.-Dec.	*	Nov.-Dec.	*	Dec.	*	Dec.	25.28	Dec.	25.38	Dec.	25.48	1998
	Sep.	25.32	Oct.	25.32	Nov.	25.28	Nov.	25.38	Nov.	25.48	Nov.	25.58	
	Aug.	25.42	Sep.	25.42	Oct.	25.42	Oct.	25.52	Oct.	25.64	Oct.	25.74	
	July	25.52	Aug.	25.52	Sep.	25.52	Sep.	25.64	Sep.	25.74	Sep.	25.84	
	June	25.64	July	25.64	Aug.	25.64	Aug.	25.74	Aug.	25.84	Aug.	25.94	
	May	25.74	June	25.74	July	25.74	July	25.84	July	25.94	July	26.04	
	Apr.	25.92	May	25.84	June	25.84	June	25.94	June	26.04	June	26.14	
	Mar.	26.02	Apr.	26.02	May	25.94	May	26.04	May	26.14	May	26.22	
	Feb.	26.14	Mar.	26.14	Apr.	26.14	Apr.	26.24	Apr.	26.36	Apr.	26.46	
	Jan.	26.24	Feb.	26.24	Mar.	26.24	Mar.	26.36	Mar.	26.46	Mar.	26.56	
			Jan.	26.36	Feb.	26.36	Feb.	26.46	Feb.	26.56	Feb.	26.66	
					Jan.	26.46	Jan.	26.56	Jan.	26.66	Jan.	26.76	
1997	Dec.	26.36	Dec.	26.46	Dec.	26.56	Dec.	26.66	Dec.	26.76	Dec.	26.86	1997
	Nov.	26.46	Nov.	26.56	Nov.	26.66	Nov.	26.76	Nov.	26.86	Nov.	26.96	
	Oct.	26.66	Oct.	26.78	Oct.	26.88	Oct.	27.00	Oct.	27.10	Oct.	27.20	
	Sep.	26.78	Sep.	26.88	Sep.	27.00	Sep.	27.10	Sep.	27.20	Sep.	27.30	
	Aug.	26.88	Aug.	27.00	Aug.	27.10	Aug.	27.20	Aug.	27.30	Aug.	27.40	
	July	27.00	July	27.10	July	27.20	July	27.30	July	27.40	July	27.52	
	June	27.10	June	27.20	June	27.30	June	27.40	June	27.52	June	27.62	
	May	27.20	May	27.30	May	27.40	May	27.52	May	27.62	May	27.72	
	Apr.	26.78	Jan.-Apr.	27.38	Jan.-Apr.	27.38	Jan.-Apr.	27.38	Feb.-Apr.	27.38	Mar.-Apr.	27.38	
	Jan.-Mar.	27.38							Jan.	27.92	Jan.-Feb.	27.92	
1996	Nov.-Dec.	27.38	Nov.-Dec.	27.38	Dec.	27.38	Nov.-Dec.	27.92	Nov.-Dec.	27.92	Nov.-Dec.	27.92	1996
	Oct.	27.32	May-Oct.	27.94	Nov.	27.92	July-Oct.	27.94	Aug.-Oct.	27.94	Sep.-Oct.	27.94	
	May-Sep.	27.94	Jan.-Apr.	28.62	June-Oct.	27.94	May-June	28.50	May-July	28.50	May-Aug.	28.50	
	Apr.	28.00			May	28.50	Jan.-Apr.	28.62	Feb.-Apr.	28.62	Mar.-Apr.	28.62	
	Jan.-Mar.	28.62			Jan.-Apr.	28.62			Jan.	29.20	Jan.-Feb.	29.20	
1995	Nov.-Dec.	28.62	Nov.-Dec.	28.62	Dec.	28.62	Nov.-Dec.	29.20	Nov.-Dec.	29.20	Nov.-Dec.	29.20	1995
	Oct.	28.74	May-Oct.	29.38	Nov.	29.20	July-Oct.	29.38	Aug.-Oct.	29.38	Sep.-Oct.	29.38	
	May-Sep.	29.38	Apr.	29.30	June-Oct.	29.38	May-June	29.96	May-July	29.96	May-Aug.	29.96	
	Apr.	29.20	Mar.	29.40	May	29.96	Apr.	29.50	Apr.	29.60	Apr.	29.70	
	Mar.	29.30	Feb.	29.50	Apr.	29.40	Mar.	29.60	Mar.	29.70	Mar.	29.78	
	Feb.	29.40	Jan.	29.60	Mar.	29.50	Feb.	29.70	Feb.	29.78	Feb.	29.88	
	Jan.	29.50			Feb.	29.60	Jan.	29.78	Jan.	29.88	Jan.	29.98	
					Jan.	29.70							

* NOT ELIGIBLE FOR PAYMENT.

253

TABLES OF REDEMPTION VALUES FOR $50 SERIES EE SAVINGS BONDS

ISSUE YEARS	MARCH 1999 ISSUE MONTHS	$50	APRIL 1999 ISSUE MONTHS	$50	MAY 1999 ISSUE MONTHS	$50	JUNE 1999 ISSUE MONTHS	$50	JULY 1999 ISSUE MONTHS	$50	AUGUST 1999 ISSUE MONTHS	$50	ISSUE YEARS
1994	Dec.	29.60	Dec	29.70	Dec.	29.78	Dec	29.88	Dec.	29.98	Dec	30.08	1994
	Nov.	29.70	Nov	29.78	Nov.	29.88	Nov	29.98	Nov.	30.08	Nov.	30.18	
	Oct.	29.78	Oct	29.88	Oct	29.98	Oct	30.08	Oct	30.18	Oct	30.28	
	Sep.	29.88	Sep	29.98	Sep	30.08	Sep.	30.18	Sep	30.28	Sep	30.38	
	Aug.	29.98	Aug	30.08	Aug.	30.18	Aug	30.28	Aug	30.38	May-Aug.	32.36	
	July	30.08	July	30.18	July	30.28	July	30.38	May-July	32.36	Mar.-Apr.	32.34	
	June	30.18	June	30.28	June	30.38	May-June	32.36	Feb.-Apr.	32.34	Jan.-Feb.	33.04	
	May	30.28	May	30.38	May	32.36	Jan.-Apr.	32.34	Jan.	33.04			
	Apr.	30.38	Jan.-Apr.	32.34	Jan.-Apr.	32.34							
	Jan.-Mar.	32.34											
1993	Oct.-Dec.	32.34	Nov.-Dec.	32.34	Dec.	32.34	Nov.-Dec.	33.04	Nov.-Dec.	33.04	Nov.-Dec.	33.04	1993
	May-Sep.	33.12	May-Oct.	33.12	Nov.	33.04	July-Oct.	33.12	Aug.-Oct.	33.12	Sep.-Oct.	33.12	
	Apr.	33.16	Mar.-Apr.	33.94	June-Oct.	33.12	May-June	33.82	May-July	33.82	May-Aug.	33.82	
	Mar.	33.94	Jan.-Feb.	35.66	May	33.82	Mar.-Apr.	33.94	Mar.-Apr.	33.94	Mar.-Apr.	33.94	
	Jan.-Feb.	35.66			Mar.-Apr.	33.94	Jan.-Feb.	35.66	Feb.	35.66	Jan.-Feb.	36.72	
					Jan.-Feb.	35.66			Jan.	36.72			
1992	Oct.-Dec.	35.66	Nov.-Dec.	35.66	Dec.	35.66	July-Dec.	36.72	Aug.-Dec.	36.72	Sep.-Dec.	36.72	1992
	Apr.-Sep.	36.72	May-Oct.	36.72	June-Nov.	36.72	Jan.-June	37.82	Feb.-July	37.82	Mar.-Aug.	37.82	
	Jan.-Mar.	37.82	Jan.-Apr.	37.82	Jan.-May	37.82			Jan.	38.96	Jan.-Feb.	38.96	
1991	Oct.-Dec.	37.82	Nov.-Dec.	37.82	Dec.	37.82	July-Dec.	38.96	Aug.-Dec.	38.96	Sep.-Dec.	38.96	1991
	Apr.-Sep.	38.96	May-Oct.	38.96	June-Nov.	38.96	Jan.-June	40.12	Feb.-July	40.12	Mar.-Aug.	40.12	
	Jan.-Mar.	40.12	Jan.-Apr.	40.12	Jan.-May	40.12			Jan.	41.34	Jan.-Feb.	41.34	
1990	Oct.-Dec.	40.12	Nov.-Dec.	40.12	Dec.	40.12	July-Dec.	41.34	Aug.-Dec.	41.34	Sep.-Dec.	41.34	1990
	Apr.-Sep.	41.34	May-Oct.	41.34	June-Nov.	41.34	Jan.-June	42.58	Feb.-July	42.58	Mar.-Aug.	42.58	
	Jan.-Mar.	42.58	Jan.-Apr.	42.58	Jan.-May	42.58			Jan.	43.84	Jan.-Feb.	43.84	
1989	Oct.-Dec.	42.58	Nov.-Dec.	42.58	Dec.	42.58	July-Dec.	43.84	Aug.-Dec.	43.84	Sep.-Dec.	43.84	1989
	Apr.-Sep.	43.84	May-Oct.	43.84	June-Nov.	43.84	Jan.-June	45.16	Feb.-July	45.16	Mar.-Aug.	45.16	
	Jan.-Mar.	45.16	Jan.-Apr.	45.16	Jan.-May	45.16			Jan.	46.52	Jan.-Feb.	46.52	
1988	Oct.-Dec.	45.16	Nov.-Dec.	45.16	Dec	45.16	July-Dec.	46.52	Aug.-Dec.	46.52	Sep.-Dec.	46.52	1988
	Apr.-Sep.	46.52	May-Oct.	46.52	June-Nov.	46.52	Jan.-June	47.92	Feb.-July	47.92	Mar.-Aug.	47.92	
	Jan.-Mar.	47.92	Jan.-Apr.	47.92	Jan.-May	47.92			Jan.	49.34	Jan.-Feb.	49.34	
1987	Oct.-Dec.	47.92	Nov.-Dec.	47.92	Dec.	47.92	July-Dec.	49.34	Aug.-Dec.	49.34	Sep.-Dec.	49.34	1987
	Apr.-Sep.	49.34	May-Oct.	49.34	June-Nov.	49.34	Jan.-June	50.82	Feb.-July	50.82	Mar.-Aug.	50.82	
	Jan.-Mar.	50.82	Jan.-Apr.	50.82	Jan.-May	50.82			Jan.	51.84	Jan.-Feb.	51.84	
1986	Nov.-Dec.	50.82	Nov.-Dec.	50.82	Dec.	50.82	Nov.-Dec.	51.84	Nov.-Dec.	51.84	Nov.-Dec.	51.84	1986
	Oct.	56.54	May-Oct.	57.66	Nov.	51.84	July-Oct.	57.66	Aug.-Oct.	57.66	Sep.-Oct.	57.66	
	Apr.-Sep.	57.66	Jan.-Apr.	58.82	June-Oct.	57.66	Jan.-June	58.82	Feb.-July	58.82	Mar.-Aug.	58.82	
	Jan.-Mar.	58.82			Jan.-May	58.82			Jan.	60.00	Jan.-Feb.	60.00	
1985	Oct.-Dec.	58.82	Nov.-Dec.	58.82	Dec.	58.82	July-Dec.	60.00	Aug.-Dec.	60.00	Sep.-Dec.	60.00	1985
	Apr.-Sep.	60.00	May-Oct.	60.00	June-Nov.	60.00	Jan.-June	61.20	Feb.-July	61.20	Mar.-Aug.	61.20	
	Jan.-Mar.	61.20	Jan.-Apr.	61.20	Jan.-May	61.20			Jan.	62.42	Jan.-Feb.	62.42	
1984	Nov.-Dec.	61.20	Nov.-Dec.	61.20	Dec.	61.20	Nov.-Dec.	62.42	Nov.-Dec.	62.42	Nov.-Dec.	62.42	1984
	Oct.	61.72	May-Oct.	63.22	Nov.	62.42	July-Oct.	63.22	Aug.-Oct.	63.22	Sep.-Oct.	63.22	
	May-Sep.	63.22	Jan.-Apr.	66.22	June-Oct.	63.22	May-June	64.60	May-July	64.60	May-Aug.	64.60	
	Apr.	64.66			May	64.60	Jan.-Apr.	66.22	Feb.-Apr.	66.22	Mar.-Apr.	66.22	
	Jan.-Mar.	66.22			Jan.-Apr.	66.22			Jan.	67.70	Jan.-Feb.	67.70	
1983	Nov.-Dec.	66.22	Nov.-Dec.	66.22	Dec.	66.22	Nov.-Dec.	67.70	Nov.-Dec.	67.70	Nov.-Dec.	67.70	1983
	Oct.	67.48	May-Oct.	69.02	Nov.	67.70	July-Oct.	69.02	Aug.-Oct.	69.02	Sep.-Oct.	69.02	
	May-Sep.	69.02	Mar.-Apr.	72.88	June-Oct.	69.02	May-June	70.56	May-July	70.56	May-Aug.	70.56	
	Apr.	71.24	Jan.-Feb.	74.46	May	70.56	Mar.-Apr.	72.88	Mar.-Apr.	72.88	Mar.-Apr.	72.88	
	Mar.	72.88			Mar.-Apr.	72.88	Jan.-Feb.	74.46	Feb.	74.46	Jan.-Feb.	76.70	
	Jan.-Feb.	74.46			Jan.-Feb.	74.46			Jan.	76.70			
1982	Nov.-Dec.	74.46	Nov.-Dec.	74.46	Dec.	74.46	Nov.-Dec.	76.70	Nov.-Dec.	76.70	Nov.-Dec.	76.70	1982
	Oct.	81.14	May-Oct.	83.58	Nov.	76.70	July-Oct.	83.58	Aug.-Oct.	83.58	Sep.-Oct.	83.58	
	Apr.-Sep.	83.58	Jan.-Apr.	86.08	June-Oct.	83.58	Jan.-June	86.08	Feb.-July	86.08	Mar.-Aug.	86.08	
	Jan.-Mar.	86.08			Jan.-May	86.08			Jan.	88.66	Jan.-Feb.	88.66	

TABLES OF REDEMPTION VALUES FOR $50 SERIES EE SAVINGS BONDS

ISSUE YEARS	MARCH 1999		APRIL 1999		MAY 1999		JUNE 1999		JULY 1999		AUGUST 1999		ISSUE YEARS
	ISSUE MONTHS	$50	ISSUE MONTHS	$50	ISSUE MONTHS	$50	ISSUE MONTHS	$50	ISSUE MONTHS	$50	ISSUE MONTHS	$50	
1981	Oct.-Dec.	86.08	Nov.-Dec.	86.08	Dec.	86.08	July-Dec.	88.66	Aug.-Dec.	88.66	Sep.-Dec.	88.66	**1981**
	May-Sep.	88.66	May-Oct.	88.66	June-Nov.	88.66	May-June	91.32	May-July	91.32	May-Aug.	91.32	
	Apr.	90.82	Jan.-Apr.	93.54	May	91.32	Jan.-Apr.	93.54	Feb.-Apr.	93.54	Mar.-Apr.	93.54	
	Jan.-Mar.	93.54			Jan.-Apr.	93.54			Jan.	96.34	Jan.-Feb.	96.34	
1980	Nov.-Dec.	93.54	Nov.-Dec.	93.54	Dec.	93.54	Nov.-Dec.	96.34	Nov.-Dec.	96.34	Nov.-Dec.	96.34	**1980**
	Oct.	98.14	May-Oct.	101.10	Nov.	96.34	July-Oct.	101.10	Aug.-Oct.	101.10	Sep.-Oct.	101.10	
	May-Sep.	101.10	Jan.-Apr.	103.10	June-Oct.	101.10	May-June	104.12	May-July	104.12	May-Aug.	104.12	
	Apr.	100.10			May	104.12	Jan.-Apr.	103.10	Feb.-Apr.	103.10	Mar.-Apr.	103.10	
	Jan.-Mar.	103.10			Jan.-Apr.	103.10			Jan.	106.18	Jan.-Feb.	106.18	

TABLES OF REDEMPTION VALUES FOR $25 SERIES E SAVINGS BONDS

ISSUE YEARS	MARCH 1999 ISSUE MONTHS	$25	APRIL 1999 ISSUE MONTHS	$25	MAY 1999 ISSUE MONTHS	$25	JUNE 1999 ISSUE MONTHS	$25	JULY 1999 ISSUE MONTHS	$25	AUGUST 1999 ISSUE MONTHS	$25	ISSUE YEARS
1980	May-June	70.86	May-June	70.86	June	70.86	May-June	72.28	May-June	72.28	May-June	72.28	**1980**
	Apr.	70.15	Jan.-Apr	71.55	May	72.28	Jan.-Apr	71.55	Feb.-Apr.	71.55	Mar.-Apr	71.55	
	Jan.-Mar.	71.55			Jan.-Apr	71.55			Jan	72.98	Jan.-Feb	72.98	
1979	Nov.-Dec	71.55	Nov.-Dec	71.55	Dec	71.55	Nov.-Dec	72.98	Nov.-Dec	72.98	Nov.-Dec.	72.98	**1979**
	Oct.	70.89	June-Oct.	72.30	Nov	72.98	July-Oct.	72.30	Aug.-Oct.	72.30	Sep.-Oct.	72.30	
	June-Sep.	72.30	May	72.14	June-Oct.	72.30	June	73.75	June-July	73.75	June-Aug.	73.75	
	May	72.14	Jan.-Apr	72.87	May	73.58	May	73.58	May	73.58	May	73.58	
	Apr.	71.44			Jan.-Apr.	72.87	Jan.-Apr	72.87	Feb.-Apr.	72.87	Mar.-Apr.	72.87	
	Jan.-Mar.	72.87							Jan.	74.33	Jan.-Feb.	74.33	
1978	Dec.	72.86	Dec.	72.86	Dec	72.86	Dec.	74.32	Dec	74.32	Dec.	74.32	**1978**
	Nov.	72.66	Nov.	72.66	Nov	74.12	Nov.	74.12	Nov.	74.12	Nov.	74.12	
	Oct.	71.98	July-Oct.	73.42	July-Oct.	73.42	July-Oct.	73.42	Aug.-Oct.	73.42	Sep.-Oct.	73.42	
	July-Sep.	73.42	June	73.41	June	73.41	June	74.88	July	74.89	July-Aug	74.89	
	June	73.41	May	73.22	May	74.69	May	74.69	June	74.88	June	74.88	
	May	73.22	Mar.-Apr.	77.25	Mar.-Apr.	77.25	Mar.-Apr.	77.25	May	74.69	May	74.69	
	Apr.	75.50	Jan.-Feb.	83.18	Jan.-Feb.	83.18	Jan.-Feb.	83.18	Mar.-Apr.	77.25	Mar.-Apr.	77.25	
	Mar.	77.25							Feb.	83.18	Jan.-Feb.	85.67	
	Jan.-Feb.	83.18							Jan.	85.67			
1977	Dec.	83.18	Dec.	83.18	Dec.	83.18	Dec.	85.67	Dec.	85.67	Dec.	85.67	**1977**
	Nov.	82.95	Nov.	82.95	Nov.	85.44	Nov.	85.44	Nov.	85.44	Nov.	85.44	
	Oct.	90.45	July-Oct.	93.16	July-Oct.	93.16	July-Oct.	93.16	Aug.-Oct.	93.16	Sep.-Oct.	93.16	
	July-Sep.	93.16	June	93.18	June	93.18	June	95.97	July	95.96	July-Aug.	95.96	
	June	93.18	May	92.99	May	95.78	May	95.78	June	95.97	June	95.97	
	May	92.99	Jan.-Apr.	94.84	Jan.-Apr.	94.84	Jan.-Apr.	94.84	May	95.78	May	95.78	
	Apr.	92.08							Feb.-Apr.	94.84	Mar.-Apr.	94.84	
	Jan.-Mar.	94.84							Jan.	97.68	Jan.-Feb.	97.68	
1976	Dec.	94.84	Dec.	94.84	Dec.	94.84	Dec.	97.68	Dec.	97.68	Dec.	97.68	**1976**
	Nov.	94.57	Nov.	94.57	Nov.	97.40	Nov.	97.40	Nov.	97.40	Nov.	97.40	
	Oct.	93.66	July-Oct.	96.47	July-Oct.	96.47	July-Oct.	96.47	Aug.-Oct.	96.47	Sep.-Oct.	96.47	
	July-Sep.	96.47	June	96.48	June	96.48	June	99.38	July	99.36	July-Aug.	99.36	
	June	96.48	May	96.27	May	99.15	May	99.15	June	99.38	June	99.38	
	May	96.27	Jan.-Apr.	98.22	Jan.-Apr.	98.22	Jan.-Apr.	98.22	May	99.15	May	99.15	
	Apr.	95.36							Feb.-Apr.	98.22	Mar.-Apr.	98.22	
	Jan.-Mar.	98.22							Jan.	101.17	Jan.-Feb.	101.17	
1975	Dec.	98.21	Dec.	98.21	Dec.	98.21	Dec.	101.16	Dec.	101.16	Dec.	101.16	**1975**
	Nov.	98.00	Nov.	98.00	Nov.	100.94	Nov.	100.94	Nov.	100.94	Nov.	100.94	
	Oct.	97.05	June-Oct.	99.96	June-Oct.	99.96	July-Oct.	99.96	Aug.-Oct.	99.96	Sep.-Oct.	99.96	
	June-Sep.	99.96	May	99.73	May	102.72	June	102.96	June-July	102.96	June-Aug.	102.96	
	May	99.73	Jan.-Apr.	101.74	Jan.-Apr.	101.74	May	102.72	May	102.72	May	102.72	
	Apr.	98.78					Jan.-Apr.	101.74	Feb.-Apr.	101.74	Mar.-Apr.	101.74	
	Jan.-Mar.	101.74							Jan.	104.79	Jan.-Feb.	104.79	
1974	Dec.	101.75	Dec.	101.75	Dec.	101.75	Dec.	104.80	Dec.	104.80	Dec.	104.80	**1974**
	Nov.	101.50	Nov.	101.50	Nov.	104.55	Nov.	104.55	Nov.	104.55	Nov.	104.55	
	Oct.	100.54	July-Oct.	103.55	July-Oct.	103.55	July-Oct.	103.55	Aug.-Oct.	103.55	Sep.-Oct.	103.55	
	July-Sep.	103.55	June	103.56	June	103.56	June	106.66	June-July	106.66	June-Aug.	106.66	
	June	103.56	May	103.31	May	106.41	May	106.41	May	106.41	May	106.41	
	May	103.31	Jan.-Apr.	105.40	Jan.-Apr.	105.40	Jan.-Apr.	105.40	Feb.-Apr.	105.40	Mar.-Apr.	105.40	
	Apr.	102.33							Jan.	107.51	Jan.-Feb.	107.51	
	Jan.-Mar.	105.40											
1973	Dec.	105.40	Dec.	105.40	Dec.	105.40	Dec.	107.51	Dec.	107.51	Dec.	107.51	**1973**
	Sep.-Nov.	108.46	Sep.-Nov.	108.46	Sep.-Nov.	108.46	Sep.-Nov.	108.46	Oct.-Nov.	108.46	Nov.	108.46	
	Aug.	108.45	Aug.	108.45	Aug.	108.45	Aug.	111.70	Sep.	111.72	Sep.-Oct.	111.72	
	July	108.22	July	108.22	July	111.46	July	111.46	Aug.	111.70	Aug.	111.70	
	June	107.17	June	110.39	June	110.39	June	110.39	July	111.46	July	111.46	
	Feb.-May	110.13	Feb.-May	110.13	Feb.-May	110.13	Mar.-May	110.13	June	110.39	June	110.39	
	Jan.	109.85	Jan.	109.85	Jan.	112.05	Feb.	112.33	Apr.-May	110.13	May	110.13	
							Jan.	112.05	Feb.-Mar.	112.33	Feb.-Apr.	112.33	
									Jan.	112.05	Jan.	112.05	

TABLES OF REDEMPTION VALUES FOR $25 SERIES E SAVINGS BONDS

ISSUE YEARS	MARCH 1999 ISSUE MONTHS	$25	APRIL 1999 ISSUE MONTHS	$25	MAY 1999 ISSUE MONTHS	$25	JUNE 1999 ISSUE MONTHS	$25	JULY 1999 ISSUE MONTHS	$25	AUGUST 1999 ISSUE MONTHS	$25	ISSUE YEARS
1972	Dec.	108.81	Dec.	110.99	Dec.	110.99	Dec.	110.99	Dec.	110.99	Dec.	110.99	**1972**
	Aug.-Nov.	110.74	Aug.-Nov.	110.74	Aug.-Nov.	110.74	Sep.-Nov.	110.74	Oct.-Nov.	110.74	Nov.	110.74	
	July	110.50	July	110.50	July	112.71	Aug.	112.96	Aug.-Sep.	112.96	Aug.-Oct.	112.96	
	June	109.44	June	111.62	June	111.62	July	112.71	July	112.71	July	112.71	
	Mar.-May	111.31	Mar.-May	111.31	Mar.-May	111.31	June	111.62	June	111.62	June	111.62	
	Feb.	111.30	Feb.	111.30	Feb.	111.30	Mar.-May	111.31	Apr.-May	111.31	May	111.31	
	Jan.	111.04	Jan.	111.04	Jan.	113.26	Feb.	113.53	Mar.	113.54	Mar.-Apr.	113.54	
							Jan.	113.26	Feb.	113.53	Feb.	113.53	
									Jan.	113.26	Jan.	113.26	
1971	Dec.	109.98	Dec.	112.18	Dec.	112.18	Dec.	112.18	Dec.	112.18	Dec.	112.18	**1971**
	Aug.-Nov.	111.89	Aug.-Nov.	111.89	Aug.-Nov.	111.89	Sep.-Nov.	111.89	Oct.-Nov.	111.89	Nov.	111.89	
	July	111.69	July	111.69	July	113.93	Aug.	114.13	Aug.-Sep.	114.13	Aug.-Oct.	114.13	
	June	111.77	June	114.36	June	114.36	July	113.93	July	113.93	July	113.93	
	Feb.-May	114.04	Feb.-May	114.04	Feb.-May	114.04	June	114.36	June	114.36	June	114.36	
	Jan.	113.78	Jan.	113.78	Jan.	116.34	Mar.-May	114.04	Apr.-May	114.04	May	114.04	
							Feb.	116.61	Feb.-Mar.	116.61	Feb.-Apr.	116.61	
							Jan.	116.34	Jan.	116.34	Jan.	116.34	
1970	Dec.	128.50	Dec.	131.07	Dec.	131.07	Dec.	131.07	Dec.	131.07	Dec.	131.07	**1970**
	Aug.-Nov.	130.77	Aug.-Nov.	130.77	Aug.-Nov.	130.77	Sep.-Nov.	130.77	Oct.-Nov.	130.77	Nov.	130.77	
	July	130.46	July	130.46	July	133.07	Aug.	133.38	Aug.-Sep.	133.38	Aug.-Oct.	133.38	
	June	129.19	June	131.77	June	131.77	July	133.07	July	133.07	July	133.07	
	Mar.-May	131.15	Mar.-May	131.15	Mar.-May	131.15	June	131.77	June	131.77	June	131.77	
	Feb.	131.14	Feb.	131.14	Feb.	131.14	Mar.-May	131.15	Apr.-May	131.15	May	131.15	
	Jan.	130.82	Jan.	130.82	Jan.	133.43	Feb.	133.76	Mar.	133.78	Mar.-Apr.	133.78	
							Jan.	133.43	Feb.	133.76	Feb.	133.76	
									Jan.	133.43	Jan.	133.43	
1969	Dec.	129.59	Dec.	132.18	Dec.	132.18	Dec.	132.18	Dec.	132.18	Dec.	132.18	**1969**
	Sep.-Nov.	131.50	Sep.-Nov.	131.50	Sep.-Nov.	131.50	Sep.-Nov.	131.50	Oct.-Nov.	131.50	Nov.	131.50	
	Aug.	131.49	Aug.	131.49	Aug.	131.49	Aug.	134.12	Sep.	134.13	Sep.-Oct.	134.13	
	July	131.20	July	131.20	July	133.83	July	133.83	Aug.	134.12	Aug.*	135.01	
	June	129.94	June	132.54	June	132.54	June*	133.42	July*	134.71	July	134.71	
	May	135.88	May	135.88	May*	138.60	May	138.60	June	133.42	June	133.42	
	Apr.	134.58	Jan.-Apr.*	137.27	Jan.-Apr.	137.27	Jan.-Apr.	137.27	May	138.60	May	138.60	
	Jan.-Mar.*	137.27							Jan.-Apr.	137.27	Jan.-Apr.	137.27	
1968	Dec.	137.28	Dec.	137.28	Dec.	137.28	Dec.	137.28	Dec.	137.28	Dec.	137.28	**1968**
	Nov.	135.44	Nov.	135.44	Nov.	135.44	Nov.	135.44	Nov.	135.44	Nov.	135.44	
	July-Oct.	134.14	July-Oct.	134.14	July-Oct.	134.14	July-Oct.	134.14	July-Oct.	134.14	July-Oct.	134.14	
	June	134.16	June	134.16	June	134.16	June	134.16	June	134.16	June	134.16	
	May	132.57	May	132.57	May	132.57	May	132.57	May	132.57	May	132.57	
	Jan.-Apr.	131.28	Jan.-Apr.	131.28	Jan.-Apr.	131.28	Jan.-Apr.	131.28	Jan.-Apr.	131.28	Jan.-Apr.	131.28	
1967	Dec.	131.28	Dec.	131.28	Dec.	131.28	Dec.	131.28	Dec.	131.28	Dec.	131.28	**1967**
	Nov.	129.70	Nov.	129.70	Nov.	129.70	Nov.	129.70	Nov.	129.70	Nov.	129.70	
	July-Oct.	128.45	July-Oct.	128.45	July-Oct.	128.45	July-Oct.	128.45	July-Oct.	128.45	July-Oct.	128.45	
	June	128.46	June	128.46	June	128.46	June	128.46	June	128.46	June	128.46	
	May	127.06	May	127.06	May	127.06	May	127.06	May	127.06	May	127.06	
	Jan.-Apr.	125.86	Jan.-Apr.	125.86	Jan.-Apr.	125.86	Jan.-Apr.	125.86	Jan.-Apr.	125.86	Jan.-Apr.	125.86	
1966	Dec.	125.85	Dec.	125.85	Dec.	125.85	Dec.	125.85	Dec.	125.85	Dec.	125.85	**1966**
	Nov.	124.46	Nov.	124.46	Nov.	124.46	Nov.	124.46	Nov.	124.46	Nov.	124.46	
	July-Oct.	123.27	July-Oct.	123.27	July-Oct.	123.27	July-Oct.	123.27	July-Oct.	123.27	July-Oct.	123.27	
	June	123.28	June	123.28	June	123.28	June	123.28	June	123.28	June	123.28	
	May	122.02	May	122.02	May	122.02	May	122.02	May	122.02	May	122.02	
	Mar.-Apr.	121.94	Mar.-Apr.	121.94	Mar.-Apr.	121.94	Mar.-Apr.	121.94	Mar.-Apr.	121.94	Mar.-Apr.	121.94	
	Jan.-Feb.	128.13	Jan.-Feb.	128.13	Jan.-Feb.	128.13	Jan.-Feb.	128.13	Jan.-Feb.	128.13	Jan.-Feb.	128.13	

* BONDS ISSUED BETWEEN DECEMBER 1965 AND THIS DATE HAVE REACHED FINAL MATURITY AND WILL EARN NO ADDITIONAL INTEREST.

TABLES OF REDEMPTION VALUES FOR $25 SERIES E SAVINGS BONDS

ISSUE YEARS	MARCH 1999		APRIL 1999		MAY 1999		JUNE 1999		JULY 1999		AUGUST 1999		ISSUE YEARS
	ISSUE MONTHS	$25	ISSUE MONTHS	$25	ISSUE MONTHS	$25	ISSUE MONTHS	$25	ISSUE MONTHS	$25	ISSUE MONTHS	$25	
1965	Dec.	128.12	Dec.	128.12	Dec.	128.12	Dec.	128.12	Dec.	128.12	Dec.	128.12	**1965**
	Sep.-Nov.	141.65	Sep.-Nov.	141.65	Sep.-Nov.	141.65	Oct.-Nov.	141.65	Nov	141.65	Sep.-Nov.	144.83	
	Aug.	140.92	Aug.	140.92	Aug	144.09	Sep	144.83	Sep.-Oct.	144.83	Aug.	144.09	
	July	142.19	June-July	145.49	June-July	145.49	Aug.	144.09	Aug	144.09	June-July	145.49	
	June	145.49	Apr.-May	155.81	Apr.-May	155.81	June-July	145.49	June-July	145.49	Apr.-May	160.48	
	Apr.-May	155.81	Mar	155.82	Mar.	155.82	Apr.-May	155.81	May	155.81	Mar.	160.50	
	Mar.	155.82	Feb	155.07	Feb	159.72	Mar.	160.50	Apr	160.48	Feb.	159.72	
	Feb.	155.07	Jan.	174.12	Jan.	174.12	Feb.	159.72	Mar.	160.50	Jan.	174.12	
	Jan.	169.05					Jan.	174.12	Feb.	159.72			
									Jan.	174.12			
1964	Dec.	174.12	Dec.	174.12	Dec.	174.12	Dec.	174.12	Dec.	174.12	Dec.	174.12	**1964**
	Sep.-Nov.	173.01	Sep.-Nov.	173.01	Sep.-Nov.	173.01	Oct.-Nov.	173.01	Nov	173.01	Sep.-Nov.	178.20	
	Aug.	172.20	Aug.	172.20	Aug	177.37	Sep.	178.20	Sep.-Oct'	178.20	Aug	177.37	
	July	170.54	June-July	175.66	June-July	175.66	Aug.	177.37	Aug.	177.37	June-July	175.66	
	June	175.66	Apr.-May	174.49	Apr.-May	174.49	June-July	175.66	June-July	175.66	Apr.-May	179.73	
	Apr.-May	174.49	Mar.	174.51	Mar	174.51	Apr.-May	174.49	May	174.49	Mar	179.74	
	Mar.	174.51	Feb	173.68	Feb	178.89	Mar.	179.74	Apr.	179.73	Feb	178.89	
	Feb.	173.68	Jan.	177.19	Jan.	177.19	Feb.	178.89	Mar.	179.74	Jan.	177.19	
	Jan.	172.03					Jan.	177.19	Feb.	178.89			
									Jan.	177.19			
1963	Dec.	177.19	Dec.	177.19	Dec.	177.19	Dec.	177.19	Dec	177.19	Dec.	177.19	**1963**
	Sep.-Nov.	176.10	Sep.-Nov.	176.10	Sep.-Nov.	176.10	Oct.-Nov.	176.10	Nov.	176.10	Sep.-Nov.	181.38	
	Aug.	175.26	Aug.	175.26	Aug	180.51	Sep.	181.38	Sep.-Oct.	181.38	Aug.	180.51	
	July	173.56	June-July	178.76	June-July	178.76	Aug.	180.51	Aug.	180.51	June-July	178.76	
	June	178.76	Apr.-May	177.42	Apr.-May	177.42	June-July	178.76	June-July	178.76	Apr.-May	182.74	
	Apr.-May	177.42	Mar.	177.44	Mar	177.44	Apr.-May	177.42	May	177.42	Mar.	182.76	
	Mar.	177.44	Feb.	176.61	Feb.	181.91	Mar.	182.76	Apr.	182.74	Feb.	181.91	
	Feb.	176.61	Jan.	180.16	Jan.	180.16	Feb.	181.91	Mar.	182.76	Jan.	180.16	
	Jan.	174.91					Jan.	180.16	Feb.	181.91			
									Jan.	180.16			
1962	Dec.	180.16	Dec.	180.16	Dec.	180.16	Dec.	180.16	Dec.	180.16	Dec.	180.16	**1962**
	Sep.-Nov.	179.42	Sep.-Nov.	179.42	Sep.-Nov.	179.42	Oct.-Nov.	179.42	Nov.	179.42	Sep.-Nov.	184.80	
	Aug.	178.15	Aug.	178.15	Aug	183.50	Sep.	184.80	Sep.-Oct.	184.80	Aug.	183.50	
	July	176.46	June-July	181.75	June-July	181.75	Aug.	183.50	Aug.	183.50	June-July	181.75	
	June	181.75	Apr.-May	181.28	Apr.-May	181.28	June-July	181.75	June-July	181.75	Apr.-May	186.72	
	Apr.-May	181.28	Mar.	181.30	Mar	181.30	Apr.-May	181.28	May	181.28	Mar.	186.74	
	Mar.	181.30	Feb.	179.99	Feb.	185.39	Mar.	186.74	Apr.	186.72	Feb.	185.39	
	Feb.	179.99	Jan.	183.61	Jan.	183.61	Feb.	185.39	Mar.	186.74	Jan.	183.61	
	Jan.	178.26					Jan.	183.61	Feb.	185.39			
									Jan.	183.61			
1961	Dec.	183.61	Dec.	183.61	Dec.	183.61	Dec.	183.61	Dec.	183.61	Dec.	183.61	**1961**
	Oct.-Nov.	183.08	Oct.-Nov.	183.08	Oct.-Nov.	183.08	Oct.-Nov.	183.08	Nov.	183.08	Oct.-Nov.	188.57	
	Sep.	183.09	Sep.	183.09	Sep.	183.09	Sep.	188.59	Oct.	188.57	Sep.	188.59	
	Aug.	181.07	Aug.	181.07	Aug.	186.50	Aug.	186.50	Sep.	188.59	Aug.	186.50	
	July	179.35	June-July	184.73	June-July	184.73	June-July	184.73	Aug.	186.50	June-July	184.73	
	June	184.73	Apr.-May	184.19	Apr.-May	184.19	Apr.-May	184.19	June-July	184.73	Apr.-May	187.87	
	Apr.-May	184.19	Mar.	184.20	Mar.	184.20	Mar.	187.88	May	184.19	Mar.	187.88	
	Mar.	184.20	Feb	182.10	Feb	185.74	Feb.	185.74	Apr.	187.87	Feb.	185.74	
	Feb.	182.10	Jan.	183.98	Jan.	183.98	Jan.	183.98	Mar.	187.88	Jan.	183.98	
	Jan.	180.37							Feb.	185.74			
									Jan.	183.98			

TABLES OF REDEMPTION VALUES FOR $25 SERIES E SAVINGS BONDS

ISSUE YEARS	MARCH 1999		APRIL 1999		MAY 1999		JUNE 1999		JULY 1999		AUGUST 1999		ISSUE YEARS
	ISSUE MONTHS	$25	ISSUE MONTHS	$25	ISSUE MONTHS	$25	ISSUE MONTHS	$25	ISSUE MONTHS	$25	ISSUE MONTHS	$25	
1960	Dec.	183.98	Dec.	183.98	Dec.	183.98	Dec.	183.98	Dec.	183.98	Dec.	183.98	**1960**
	Oct.-Nov.	183.61	Oct.-Nov.	183.61	Oct.-Nov.	183.61	Oct.-Nov.	183.61	Nov.	183.61	Oct.-Nov.	187.28	
	Sep.	183.60	Sep.	183.60	Sep.	183.60	Sep.	187.27	Oct.	187.28	Sep.	187.27	
	Aug.	181.50	Aug.	181.50	Aug.	185.13	Aug.	185.13	Sep.	187.27	Aug.	185.13	
	July	179.79	June-July	183.38	June-July	183.38	June-July	183.38	Aug.	185.13	June-July	183.38	
	June	183.38	Mar.-May	183.07	Mar.-May	183.07	Apr.-May	183.07	June-July	183.38	Mar.-May	186.73	
	Mar.-May	183.07	Feb.	180.99	Feb.	184.61	Mar.	186.73	May	183.07	Feb.	184.61	
	Feb.	180.99	Jan.	182.85	Jan.	182.85	Feb.	184.61	Mar.-Apr.	186.73	Jan.	182.85	
	Jan.	179.26					Jan.	182.85	Feb.	184.61			
									Jan.	182.85			
1959	Dec.	182.85	Dec.	182.85	Dec.	182.85	Dec.	182.85	Dec.	182.85	Dec.	182.85	**1959**
	Oct.-Nov.	182.43	Oct.-Nov.	182.43	Oct.-Nov.	182.43	Oct.-Nov.	182.43	Nov.	182.43	Oct.-Nov.	186.08	
	Sep.	182.42	Sep.	182.42	Sep.	182.42	Sep.	186.07	Oct.	186.08	Sep.	186.07	
	Aug.	180.39	Aug.	180.39	Aug.	184.00	Aug.	184.00	Sep.	186.07	Aug.**	186.01	
	July	180.57	June-July	184.76	June-July	184.76	July	184.76	Aug.	184.00	June-July	187.88	
	June	184.76	May	190.90	Jan.-May**	191.53	June**	187.88	June-July**	187.88	Jan.-May	191.53	
	May	187.16	Jan.-Apr.**	191.53			Jan.-May	191.53	Jan.-May	191.53			
	Apr.	190.90											
	Jan.-Mar.**	191.53											

** BONDS WITH THIS AND PRIOR ISSUE DATES HAVE REACHED FINAL MATURITY AND WILL EARN NO ADDITIONAL INTEREST.

TABLES OF REDEMPTION VALUES FOR MATURED $25 SERIES E BONDS

All Bonds on this table have reached final maturity and will earn no additional interest.

ISSUE YEARS	MAR 99 - AUG 99		ISSUE YEARS	MAR 99 - AUG 99		ISSUE YEARS	MAR 99 - AUG 99		ISSUE YEARS	MAR 99 - AUG 99	
	ISSUE MONTHS	$25		ISSUE MONTHS	$25		ISSUE MONTHS	$25		ISSUE MONTHS	$25
1958	Dec.	189.34	**1954**	Dec.	177.53	**1950**	Dec.	154.26	**1945**	Dec.	117.28
	Aug.-Nov.	186.71		Nov.	177.17		Nov.	151.99		Nov.	114.43
	July	186.72		Oct.	177.16		June-Oct.	150.53		June-Oct.	113.33
	June	184.53		Sep.	174.81		May	148.48		May	111.54
	Jan.-May	183.12		June-Aug.	173.12		Jan.-Apr.	147.06		Jan.-Apr.	110.47
1957	Dec.	180.97		Apr.-May	172.69	**1949**	Dec.	147.06	**1944**	Dec.	110.47
	Aug.-Nov.	205.07		Mar.	170.51		Nov.	145.23		Nov.	108.75
	July	205.08		Jan.-Feb.	168.86		June-Oct.	143.83		June-Oct.	107.70
	June	202.72	**1953**	Dec.	168.86		May	138.02		May	106.11
	Feb.-May	199.90		Nov.	168.44		Jan.-Apr.	136.69		Jan.-Apr.	105.09
	Jan.	199.56		Oct.	168.43	**1948**	Dec.	136.69	**1943**	Dec.	105.09
1956	Dec.	199.56		Sep.	166.33		Nov.	134.51		Nov.	103.48
	Nov.	198.47		June-Aug.	165.81		June-Oct.	133.23		June-Oct.	102.48
	Oct.	198.48		Apr.-May	165.41		May	131.09		May	100.91
	Sep.	196.19		Mar.	163.38		Jan.-Apr.	131.41		Jan.-Apr.	99.95
	June-Aug.	194.29		Jan.-Feb.	178.14	**1947**	Dec.	131.41	**1942**	Dec.	99.95
	Apr.-May	193.83	**1952**	Dec.	178.14		Nov.	129.34		Nov.	98.40
	Mar.	188.59		Nov.	177.66		June-Oct.	126.57		June-Oct.	97.45
	Jan.-Feb.	186.79		Oct.	177.69		May	124.57		May	96.00
1955	Dec.	186.79		Sep.	175.46		Jan.-Apr.	123.38		Jan.-Apr.	94.35
	Oct.-Nov.	186.29		June-Aug.	173.78	**1946**	Dec.	123.38	**1941**	Dec.	94.35
	Sep.	183.82		May	173.38		Nov.	121.42		Nov.	92.86
	June-Aug.	182.05		Jan.-Apr.	170.66		June-Oct.	120.25		June-Oct.	91.96
	Apr.-May	181.57	**1951**	Dec.	170.65		May	118.41		May	90.59
	Mar.	179.26		Nov.	168.23		Jan.-Apr.	117.28			
	Jan.-Feb.	177.53		July-Oct.	166.60						
				June	166.61						
				May	164.16						
				Jan.-Apr.	162.60						

TABLES OF REDEMPTION VALUES FOR $25 SAVINGS NOTES

ISSUE YEARS	MARCH 1999		APRIL 1999		MAY 1999		JUNE 1999		JULY 1999		AUGUST 1999		ISSUE YEARS
	ISSUE MONTHS	$25	ISSUE MONTHS	$25	ISSUE MONTHS	$25	ISSUE MONTHS	$25	ISSUE MONTHS	$25	ISSUE MONTHS	$25	
1970	Oct.	128.14	June-Oct.	130.70	June-Oct.	130.70	July-Oct.	130.70	Aug.-Oct.	130.70	Sep.-Oct.	130.70	**1970**
	June-Sep.	130.70	May	130.08	May	132.68	June	133.31	June-July	133.31	June-Aug.	133.31	
	May	130.08	Jan.-Apr.	131.40	Jan.-Apr.	131.40	May	132.68	May	132.68	May	132.68	
	Apr.	128.82					Jan.-Apr.	131.40	Feb.-Apr.	131.40	Mar.-Apr.	131.40	
	Jan.-Mar.	131.40							Jan.	134.03	Jan.-Feb.	134.03	
1969	Dec.	131.39	Dec.	131.39	Dec.	131.39	Dec.	134.02	Dec.	134.02	Dec.	134.02	**1969**
	Nov.	130.79	Nov.	130.79	Nov.	133.41	Nov.	133.41	Nov.	133.41	Nov.	133.41	
	Oct.	129.54	June-Oct.	132.13	June-Oct.	132.13	July-Oct.	132.13	Aug.-Oct.	132.13	Sep.-Oct.	132.13	
	June-Sep.	132.13	May	131.47	May*	134.37	June*	135.00	June-July*	135.00	June-Aug.*	135.00	
	May	131.47	Jan.-Apr.*	135.70	Jan.-Apr.	135.70	May	134.37	May	134.37	May	134.37	
	Apr.	132.62					Jan.-Apr.	135.70	Jan.-Apr.	135.70	Jan.-Apr.	135.70	
	Jan.-Mar.*	135.70											
1968	Dec.	135.70	Dec.	135.70	Dec.	135.70	Dec.	135.70	Dec.	135.70	Dec.	135.70	**1968**
	Nov.	134.97	Nov.	134.97	Nov.	134.97	Nov.	134.97	Nov.	134.97	Nov.	134.97	
	Sep.-Oct.	136.18	Sep.-Oct.	136.18	Sep.-Oct.	136.18	Sep.-Oct.	136.18	Sep.-Oct.	136.18	Sep.-Oct.	136.18	
	June-Aug.	145.68	June-Aug.	145.68	June-Aug.	145.68	June-Aug.	145.68	June-Aug.	145.68	June-Aug.	145.68	
	May	143.37	May	143.37	May	143.37	May	143.37	May	143.37	May	143.37	
	Jan.-Apr.	156.29	Jan.-Apr.	156.29	Jan.-Apr.	156.29	Jan.-Apr.	156.29	Jan.-Apr.	156.29	Jan.-Apr.	156.29	
1967	Dec.	156.28	Dec.	156.28	Dec.	156.28	Dec.	156.28	Dec.	156.28	Dec.	156.28	**1967**
	Nov.	155.52	Nov.	155.52	Nov.	155.52	Nov.	155.52	Nov.	155.52	Nov.	155.52	
	July-Oct.	154.05	July-Oct.	154.05	July-Oct.	154.05	July-Oct.	154.05	July-Oct.	154.05	July-Oct.	154.05	
	June	154.04	June	154.04	June	154.04	June	154.04	June	154.04	June	154.04	
	May	153.33	May	153.33	May	153.33	May	153.33	May	153.33	May	153.33	

* SAVINGS NOTES WITH THIS AND PRIOR ISSUE DATES HAVE REACHED FINAL MATURITY AND WILL EARN NO ADDITIONAL INTEREST.

INSTRUCTIONS

VALUE: Locate the redemption month at the top of the appropriate table; follow the column down to the year and month of issue. During August 1999, a $50 Series I bond issue dated December 1998 has a value of $51.04, a $50 Series EE bond issue dated December 1998 has a value of $25.48, a $25 Series E bond issue dated June 1980 has a value of $72.28 and a $25 Savings Note issue dated October 1970 has a value of $130.70. The values of higher denomination securities are multiples of the amounts shown in the tables. For a $75 Series I or EE bond, multiply the value in the table by 1.5; for a $50 Series E bond or Savings Note, multiply the value in the table by 2.

INTEREST EARNED: To determine the interest earned to date, subtract the issue price from the value at redemption. The issue price of a Series I is 100% the amount shown on the face of the security, a Series EE bond 50%, a Series E bond 75% and a Savings Note 81%. For the issue and redemption dates and denominations shown above, the Series I bond earned $1.04, the Series EE bond earned $0.48, the Series E bond earned $53.53 and the Savings Note earned $110.45.

FINAL MATURITIES FOR SERIES E/EE/I BONDS AND SAVINGS NOTES

SAVINGS BONDS AND NOTES WILL CONTINUE TO EARN INTEREST ACCORDING TO THE FOLLOWING SCHEDULE

Series	Date of Issue	Date of Maturity	Term of Bond
Series E*	May 1941-Nov 1965	May 1981-Nov 2005	40 Years
Series E*	Dec 1965-Jun 1980	Dec 1995-Jun 2010	30 Years
Series EE	Jan 1980 and after	Jan 2010 and after	30 Years
Series I	Sep 1998 and after	Sep 2028 and after	30 Years
Savings Notes	May 1967-Oct 1970	May 1997-Oct 2000	30 Years

* All Series E bonds do not increase in value on the same basis. Maturity and yield have been revised several times; thus, older bonds may have less redemption value than more current bonds.

* SERIES A-D Bonds. All bonds of Series A, B, C, and D have matured and the redemption value of each bond of these series is the face amount printed on the bond.

NOTE:

Series E/EE Savings Bonds and Notes are eligible for exchange to Series HH Bonds for one year from the month in which they reach final maturity. For example, a Series E Savings Bond issued in March 1959 or March 1969 is eligible for exchange through March 2000. Series I Bonds are **NOT** eligible for exchange to Series HH.

*U.S. Government Printing Office: 1998 — 455-215/97919

Glossary

Accrual method (or basis) of income reporting: Income is reported when earned or when the taxpayer has an unrestricted right to the income. The timing of the actual receipt of the income does not matter under this reporting method.

Amended returns: An income tax return filed after the original tax return has been filed to correct or change items filed on the original return. Amended returns can be filed within three years of filing the original return to claim refunds.

Automatic default: The result that will take place if no specific steps are taken to choose another alternative.

Average market-based rate: The rate produced by totaling all the individual market-based rates published during the life of a bond and then dividing that total by the number of rates. *See* Market rates. The individual market rates used for this average are always based on 85% of the five-year Treasury yields.

Basis Points: A small measurement used to describe the change in a bond's yield and/or interest rate. For example: An interest rate that changes from 5.25% to 5.15% would represent a drop of 10 basis points or one-tenth of one percent. One basis point equals one-one hundredth of one percent. One hundred basis points equal one percent.

Beneficiary: The person designated as a POD (Pay on Death) on a savings bond. This person is entitled to the bond only upon the death of the first-named party on the bond.

Bureau of the Public Debt (BPD): Government office that acts under the direction of the Department of Treasury. It has two main functions pertaining to the bond program: The U.S. Savings Bond Marketing Office promotes the sale and retention of bonds; the U.S. Savings Bond Operations Office oversees all operational issues related to the bond program.

Cash method (or basis) of income reporting: Income is reported only when it is actually received, not when it was earned.

CPI-U: The CPI-U represents the Consumers Price Index for Urban Consumers. This measures the cost of a "basket" of goods. A change in the CPI-U used to measure inflation would take the cost of the basket of goods at two different time periods and then compute that change into an annualized percentage. For instance: Suppose that the basket of goods cost $160 on January 1st and $162 dollars on July 1st. This represents a change of $2. The change ($2) divided by the cost of the first time period measured ($160) equals 1.25%. Since this is a six-month period, we multiply the percentage change by two to get an annual representation (1.25% times two equals 2.5%). Thus we would say that inflation was growing at a 2.5% annual rate over the first six months.

Current income bonds: Bonds that produce an interest payment to the bond owner. H and HH bonds are examples of current income securities because they pay an interest payment to the bond owner every six months.

Date of purchase: *See* Issue date.

Decedent: The person named on a bond who is now deceased.

Deferral: Postponing the reporting of the income in a legal manner.

Denomination: *See* Face value.

Disposition: To transfer or part with by gift or sale.

Extended maturity: The term(s) of life-bearing interest granted to a bond after the bond reaches original maturity. It is normally ten years, except for the final extension, which may be less than ten years.

Exchange for HH bonds: The process of exchanging Series E or EE bonds, Savings Notes, or eligible H bonds for Series HH bonds.

Face value: The dollar amount printed on the front of the bond.

Federal Reserve Bank (FRB): "As fiscal agents of the United States, Federal Reserve Banks and Branches (FRB) perform a number of activities in support of the Savings Bond program, including issuing, redeeming, and reissuing Savings Bonds and Notes." (Department of Treasury, BPD, Part 353, 3-80, 6th Amendment, 3-4-94).

Final maturity: The date on which a bond stops earning interest.

Fixed rate: A rate that does not fluctuate for a designated period of time.

FRB: *See* Federal Reserve Bank.

Freedom Share: *See* Savings Notes.

GATT: General Agreement on Trades and Tariffs. Legislation passed by the United States Congress in December 1994.

Guaranteed interest rate: A fixed rate of interest that applies to a bond in an original maturity period or an extended maturity period. This rate is not tied to any specific market condition and is set at the discretion of the Department of Treasury.

HH direct deposit: For all new issues of HH bonds, the interest must be directly deposited to an account of the bond holder's choosing. This means that a check is not issued; the money is sent to the designated account on the day the interest is to be paid to the bond holder.

Interest accrual security: A bond in which the interest is added to the value of the bond; thus, the bond increases in value over time.

Interest income: The difference between the purchase price and the redemption value of Series E and EE bonds and SNs is interest income. For H and HH bonds, the amount received every six months via check (for older bonds) or direct deposit is considered interest income in the year in which it is received.

Issue date: The specific date assigned to a bond. This appears in the top right-hand corner of each bond. It will always involve a month and year. This date determines the set of interest rates, values, and timing issues that will apply to a given bond.

Market rate: Three market rates are published every May and November.

—For Series E, EE, and Savings Notes purchased prior to May 1995, the market rate is based on 85% of the five-year Treasury yields for the six months immediately preceding the month of publication. This rate will apply to bonds purchased May 1995 to April 1997 after they are five years old.

—For Series EE bonds purchased May 1995 to April 1997, the market rate is based on 85% of the six-month Treasury bill yields for the three months immediately preceding the month of publication. This rate will only affect these bonds for a given six-month period. Once the bond is five years old, it will receive the market rate described above.

—For Series EE bonds purchased May 1997 and after, the market rate is based on 90% of the five-year Treasury yields for the six months immediately preceding the month of publication.

Maturity periods: Bonds have an original maturity period, extended maturity period, and a final maturity period. Because each bond is unique, the maturity periods differ for each bond.

New guaranteed rate: The guaranteed rate most recently assigned to purchases of Series EE bonds from March 1, 1993 to April 30, 1995, and to Series HH bonds obtained after February 28, 1993. As of March 1, 1993, the guaranteed rate is 4%. This rate does not affect Series EE bonds purchased after April 30, 1995.

Nominee: A co-owner of a bond who redeems the bond, but is not legally liable for the tax on the interest received because the principal owner is living and the principal owner's funds were used to purchase the bond.

Original maturity: The time period that it will take a bond to reach face value at the guaranteed interest rate in effect at the time of purchase, or a set period of seventeen years for Series EE bonds purchased after April 30, 1995.

Payroll Savings Plan: A program that many companies offer that allows employees the option to have a regular amount deducted from each paycheck to apply to the purchase of U.S. Savings Bonds. Also known as payroll deduction and systematic purchase.

PD Forms: Forms issued by the BPD to collect the appropriate information to authorize specific bond transactions. *See* Chapter 19 for a listing.

Purchase application: The form a person completes to purchase a Series EE savings bond.

Rating: *See* The Savings Bond Informer Rating System[SM].

Redemption: The act of presenting bonds for payment.

Redemption value: The value of a bond at a given point in time.

Regional distribution site: A FRB that has been chosen as one of five sites to service bond transactions.

Registered security: A bond that is inscribed with the name or names of persons entitled to the bond.

Registration: The form of inscription upon a bond.

Reissue: The act of changing a registration upon a bond. This can only be done by a FRB or the BPD. A bond owner can never make marks on a bond to change the registration of that bond.

Residuary beneficiaries: The person(s) entitled to assets of an estate after all expenses have been paid by the estate and all assets that were designated to specific individuals have been distributed.

Savings Notes (SN): A bond also known as the "Freedom Share," it was issued during the Vietnam War era, from May 1967 to October 1970. It is similar to Series E and EE bonds in that it is an interest accrual bond. The major difference is that this bond was purchased for 81% of face value. These bonds will earn interest for thirty years.

Schedule B: Internal Revenue Service tax form to list itemized deductions.

Selective redemption: The process of specifically choosing one bond over another to redeem, based on the bond owner's evaluation of interest rates, timing issues, and maturity dates.

Series E: Commonly referred to as the old "War Bonds," because they were issued to help finance World War II. The first bonds in this series were issued in May 1941 and the last in June 1980. The purchase price was 75% of face value (these bonds are all worth more than their face value). Bonds issued before December 1965 earn interest for forty years. Bonds issued in December 1965 and after earn interest for thirty years.

Series EE: Issued since January 1980 until the present. An interest accrual bond, the value of the bond grows over time. It is always purchased for one-half of face value. The time period to original maturity varies from eight to eighteen years, depending on the date of purchase. This series will earn interest for thirty years from date of purchase.

Series H: A current income bond with an interest-producing life of thirty years. It was issued from June 1952 through December 1979.

Series HH: A current income bond that can be obtained only by exchanging Series E and EE bonds and Savings Notes, or through the reinvestment of eligible H bonds. This bond produces an interest payment to the bond owner every six months. It has been available since January 1980.

Series identification: The specific series that is printed on the face of the bond, indicating the type of bond. The most common bonds will be one of the following series: Series E, EE, H, HH, I, or Savings Notes (also known as Freedom Shares).

SN: *See* Savings Notes.

Stepped-up basis: When qualifying assets are inherited, the value of the asset at the original owner's death becomes the basis for determining the gain or loss if the new owner sells the asset. This is called "the basis" from the original cost of the asset to the fair market value in the decedent's estate. U.S. Savings Bonds do not qualify for "stepped-up basis" treatment.

Systematic Purchase: *See* Payroll Savings Plan.

1099-INT: The form a bond owner will receive from the redeeming institution when a bond transaction results in reporting interest income. A copy of the information on this form is also supplied to the Internal Revenue Service.

The Savings Bond Informer Rating System[SM]**:** This is a system developed by the author that provides a two- and five-year rating based on the bonds' future performance. Ratings are made based on rules and rates in effect at the time of rating. This provides bond owners with an opportunity to compare bonds within their portfolio or to other investment options.

Timing issues: Bonds are affected by time periods. Bonds purchased prior to March 1, 1993, will increase in value semi-annually. Timing a redemption or exchange to coincide with the increase pattern will result in the bond owner receiving a greater return on the bond investment. Another timing concern is the date that a bond enters an extended maturity period and is assigned a different guaranteed interest rate. Timing also is a factor when a bond reaches final maturity: The bond owner has only one year past final maturity to exchange bonds for Series HH bonds.

U.S. Savings Bonds report or statement: A detailed analysis of U.S. Saving Bonds. Bond owners can create this report themselves by following the instructions in Chapter 7 or they can order a report for a fee from The Savings Bond Informer, Inc. (see the last page of this book).

Bibliography

Bamford, Janet. "The Class of 2013." *Sesame Street Parents* (September 1994): 52-55.

Nadler, Paul S. "Uncle Sam Out of Line." *Banker's Monthly* 109 (November 1992): 8.

Research Institute of America. *The Complete Internal Revenue Code.* New York: Research Institute of America, 1997.

"Save-Bond." *Associated Press.* (24 August 1994) 2209PDT.

"Series EE Savings Bond pays interest at differing rates over life of bond." *Providence Journal-Bulletin,* 8 October 1996, sec. 6, p.1.

U.S. Department of the Treasury, Bureau of the Public Debt. *31 CFR Part 351,* "Public Debt Series No. 1-80; Final Rule." (March 1995).

U.S. Department of the Treasury, Bureau of the Public Debt. *Federal Register,* vol. 59, pt. 3, "Offering and Governing Regulations for United States Savings Bond; Final Rule." No. 43 (4 March 1994).

U.S. Department of the Treasury, Bureau of the Public Debt. *Federal Register,* vol. 59, "Offering of United States Savings Bonds Series HH." No. 43 (4 March 1994).

U.S. Department of the Treasury, Bureau of the Public Debt. *Federal Register,* vol. 58, pt. 4, "Offering of United States Savings Bonds and United States Savings Notes; Final Rule." No. 221 (18 November 1993).

U.S. Department of the Treasury, Bureau of the Public Debt. *Federal Register,* vol. 55, "Regulations Governing United States Savings Bonds, Series EE and HH." No. 4 (5 January 1990).

U.S. Department of the Treasury, Bureau of the Public Debt, U.S. Savings Bond Division. "A History of the United States Savings Bond Program." Washington, D.C.: Government Printing Office (1991).

U.S. Department of the Treasury, Bureau of the Public Debt, U.S. Savings Bond Division. "Buyer's Guide: 1993-1994." No. SBD-2085. Washington, D.C.: Government Printing Office (1993).

U.S. Department of the Treasury, Bureau of the Public Debt, U.S. Savings Bond Division. "The Savings Bond Question & Answer Book." Washington, D.C.: Government Printing Office (1994).

U.S. Department of the Treasury, Bureau of the Public Debt, U.S. Savings Bond Division. "U.S. Savings Bonds: Now Tax-Free for Education." No. SBD-2017.

U.S. Department of the Treasury, Bureau of the Public Debt, Savings Bond Marketing Division. "The Book on U.S. Savings Bonds." No. SBD-2080. Washington, D.C.: Government Printing Office (1994).

U.S. Department of the Treasury, Bureau of the Public Debt, Savings Bond Marketing Division. "Legal Aspects of United States Savings Bonds" No. SBD-2113. Washington, D.C.: Government Printing Office.

U.S. Department of the Treasury, Internal Revenue Service. "Investment Income and Expenses: For use in preparing 1993 Returns." Pubn. No. 550. Washington, D.C.: Government Printing Office (1994).

U.S. Department of the Treasury, Internal Revenue Service. "Your Federal Income Tax: For use in preparing 1993 Returns." Pubn. No. 17. Washington, D.C.: Government Printing Office (1994).

Index

U.S. Savings Bond Record Keeping Sheet

This form was designed to serve as a helpful document for you and/or your heirs. It can also be used to order a customized savings bond statement from The Savings Bond Informer, Inc. Record the issue date (month/year of purchase), face value (denomination), and series (E, EE, H, HH, I, SN, FS) for each bond to be analyzed.

Name(s) to appear on Bond Statement

To receive an analysis for each bond you own, attach your bond list to the TSBI order form and mail your payment to the address below. **Note:** You do not have to use this form to order a statement if a list including issue date, face value, and series already exists or if you have a photocopy of each bond.

The Savings Bond Informer, Inc.   Fax your order:
P.O. Box 9249   **OR**   (313) 843-1912
Detroit, MI 48209   VISA, MasterCard, AMEX, Discover

If you have any questions regarding how to order a bond statement or need additional order forms, call (800) 927-1901.

Quantity	Issue date (Top right-hand corner of bond)	Face value	Series E,EE,H,HH,I, SN,FS	Quantity	Issue date (Top right-hand corner of bond)	Face value	Series E,EE,H,HH, I,SN,FS

The cost of a statement is determined by the total number of bonds included.   30

Savings Bond Statement Order Form

1. Make a list of bonds to be analyzed including **issue date** (month/year of purchase), **face value** (denomination), and **series** (E, EE, H, HH, I, SN, FS) for each. You can use the form provided on the other side of this page, <u>or</u> make a photocopy of each bond, <u>or</u> photocopy any list that already has the necessary information.

2. Complete the following as it applies: ☐ I am a bond owner ☐ I am a financial professional

Name to appear on Bond Statement: _____

Company Name (if applicable): _____ **Phone:** _____ **Fax:** _____

Mail to Name: _____

Mail to Address: _____

City: _____ **State:** _____ **Zip:** _____ **E-Mail:** _____

3. The cost of a statement is determined by the total number of bonds. *Enter total number of bonds:*

NUMBER OF BONDS	TOTAL	ENTER COST
1 to 10 bonds	$ 15.00	
11 to 25 bonds	$ 24.00	
26 to 50 bonds	$ 34.00	
51 to 100 bonds	$ 49.00	
101 to 200 bonds	$ 59.00	
201 to 300 bonds	$ 69.00	
301 to 400 bonds	$ 79.00	
401 to 500 bonds	$ 89.00	
Over 500 bonds	Call for quote	
For multiple copies of the book *Savings Bonds: When to Hold...*	Call for quote	
	Total Cost:	

4. Please indicate your payment information below.
Checks should be payable to: The Savings Bond Informer, Inc., or TSBI
Please charge my credit card: ☐ VISA ☐ MASTERCARD ☐ AMERICAN EXPRESS ☐ DISCOVER

Card Number: _____ Exp. date _____ / _____

5. **Mail** this form with a list of your bonds and payment to: **The Savings Bond Informer, Inc.**
P.O. Box 9249 Detroit, MI 48209

Fax orders - Fax this order with credit card information to: **(313) 843-1912**
E-Mail - bondinform@aol.com

For questions about how to order, call 1-800-927-1901

Financial Professionals: Call 1-800-927-1901 to receive a <u>free</u> packet of information on how to work with savings bond owners.